Poker books from D&B

www.dandbpoker.com

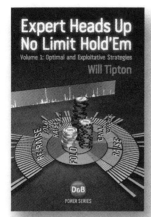

Expert Heads Up No Limit Hold'em
by Will Tipton
978-1-904468-94-3, 336pp, $29.95 / £19.99

Advanced Limit-Hold'em Strategy
by Barry Tanenbaum
978-1-904468-36-3, 256pp, $24.95 / £14.99

Secrets of Sit'n'gos
by Phil Shaw
978-1-904468-43-1, 224pp, $24.95 / £14.99

Secrets of Pro Tournament Poker, Vol. 1
by Jonathan Little
978-1-904468-94-3, 336pp, $29.95 / £19.99

Secrets of Pro Tournament Poker, Vol. 2
by Jonathan Little
978-1-904468-58-5, 272pp, $27.95 / £19.99

Secrets of Pro Tournament Poker, Vol. 3
by Jonathan Little
978-1-904468-95-0, 432pp, $29.95 / £19.99

Positive Poker
by Dr. Patricia Cardner with Jonathan Little
978-1-909457-07-2, 272pp, $29.95 / £19.99

Secrets of Professional Pot-Limit Omaha
by Rolf Slotboom
978-1-904468-30-6, 240pp, $25.95 / £15.99

The Education of a Modern Poker Player
by John Billingham, Emanuel Cinca & Thomas Tiroch,
978-1-909457-11-9, 272 pages, $29.95 / £19.99

Will Tipton began playing poker online in 2007. He steadily moved up in stakes in online HUNL tournaments to become a regular winner in the high stake games. He currently lives in Ithaca, NY, and is a PhD candidate at Cornell University.

Expert Heads Up
No Limit Hold'Em

Volume 1: Optimal and Exploitative Strategies

Will Tipton

POKER SERIES
www.dandbpoker.com

First published in 2012 by D & B Publishing

Copyright © 2012 Will Tipton

Reprinted 2014

British Library Cataloguing-in-Publication Data

A catalogue record for this book is available from the British Library.

ISBN: 978 1 90446 894 3

All sales enquiries should be directed to D&B Publishing:

e-mail: info@dandbpoker.com; website: www.dandbpoker.com

To Yuki

Cover design by Horatio Monteverde.

Printed and bound by Versa Press in the US.

Contents

Foreword

I've been publishing books for over twenty years and poker books for more than ten. In that time I have commissioned hundreds of books and also received a great many unsolicited manuscripts. As you will probably guess, these have been – shall we say politely – of varying quality. If you've ever watched the *X Factor* auditions, you'll probably get the idea.

I was therefore not unduly excited when a manuscript on heads up no limit hold'em was forwarded to me earlier this year. I have been a serious poker player for ten years but I had never heard of the author. However, he seemed to have already written the whole book – which is unusual in itself. Unsolicited contributions are normally just a few pages or, at most, a chapter. So, I started to read through it.

Within about ten minutes I had experienced what *X Factor* aficionados might call a "Susan Boyle moment". I was reading one of the very best poker books I had ever seen and I knew absolutely that we would definitely want to publish it. Furthermore I could see that – quite remarkably – the book was already very close to the finished product.

Heads Up No Limit is at the heart of the modern professional game. Will Tipton has taken this variant and stripped it down to the bare essentials – creating a mathematical framework to model all elements of play. It is a quite remarkable book.

Poker is a tough game. If you discern a few leaks in your game and want to fix them in five minutes, you'll have to look elsewhere. However, if you are prepared to take a good look at your game, and are willing to work hard to improve, then the information in this book is utterly invaluable.

I've been a solid winning player in the mid-stakes at the online tables for many years. I thought I played okay. Having read this book three times in the last six months I can see that I had huge gaps in my understanding and I am now improving rapidly. If you want to do the same – you should get this book.

Byron Jacobs,
October 2012

Preface

"Serious poker is no more about gambling than rock climbing is about taking risks." – Alfred Alvarez

Poker, especially the heads-up variety, is about figuring out what your opponents are doing and coming up with a plan to take advantage of it. In this book, we will develop a framework for visualizing an opponent's strategy and organizing our thought processes to develop exploitative responses. Unlike many other poker books, we will not tell you exactly how you should play particular hands in various situations. We will not give you a fixed strategy for playing heads-up no-limit. This book is designed to teach you to come up with your own strategies for dealing with new situations and opponents as profitably as possible – and to give you the tools to do so.

An approach based on identifying and exploiting opponents' mistakes is necessary for high-level success in heads-up play because of the nature of the game. With only one opponent to keep track of, you have the opportunity to make many observations about his style and to adjust to it. Your most profitable strategy can and will vary drastically from opponent to opponent. No fixed strategy will be best against all comers. Additionally, even good default strategies in various player pools can change quickly as popular moves and tendencies come and go. So in this book, we will focus on strategizing as opposed to playing a particular strategy. We will present the math behind adjusting to whatever the future holds.

This book is about both game theory optimal (GTO) and exploitative play, but we will tend to focus on the first of the two. If you are not quite sure what those words mean, don't worry! There is no reason you should, and by the end of Chapter 2, you will be very familiar with the terms. For now, however, GTO play is in some sense "correct". For example, in the game of rock-paper-scissors, the GTO strategy is to throw each choice randomly 1/3 of the time. Of course, it is hard for humans to be completely random, but insofar as you can, nobody will be able to beat you in RPS in the long term if you play this strategy. However, if you are ever playing a strategy that involves throwing any action with other than a 1/3 probability, your opponent can take advantage of you. In fact, he can do very well just by figuring out your most likely throw and using whatever counters it 100% of the time, at least until you notice and change your strategy.

This motivates the primary reason we will focus on GTO play. You have to have some idea of what it looks like before you can even start thinking about what your opponent is doing wrong and implementing a strategy to take advantage of it. You must know that the correct rock-throwing frequency is somewhere around 1/3, before you are able to come to the conclusion that an opponent who throws rock 40% is doing it "too much". Once you know what your opponent is doing and how that deviates from correct play, it is pretty easy to see how to exploit it. The same thing is often the case, to a degree, in poker. Once you know what "correct" play is and can compare it to an opponent's strategy, figuring out an appropriate response is usually not all that difficult. The difference between RPS and poker, however, is that poker is much more complicated. In fact, nobody really knows what this correct play is. As we will see, however, there is a lot that can be done to remedy this situation.

There is a lot of information available about exploitative play (and very little about GTO strategies). However, the notion of "correct" play that is used is generally just based on the author's experience, perhaps with some overly simplified mathematical rules thrown in. A lot of this information is pretty good, but a lot of it is not. Almost all of this advice could work out well in certain game conditions but be completely disastrous in others. Certainly, this sort of information tends to go out of date as the games change. Game theory optimal strategies, on which the current book is based, will never go out of date. Hopefully this will be a useful text for poker players for a long time.

Although parts of our discussion are moderately technical, we have always tried to keep accessibility in mind. The volume of algebra has been kept to a minimum, and we have used intuitive arguments where possible. Most importantly, applications to real play are always in the foreground. We do not spend any time on the traditional toy games presented in game theory texts – all of our discussion is in terms of genuinely useful heads-up no-limit hold 'em (HUNL) results. The academic prerequisites for understanding the book are fairly minimal: high school level math. Some familiarity with HUNL itself will, of course, also be helpful, although we make an effort to define terms, especially if they have ambiguous meanings in the poker literature.

Rarely in this book will you find examples or discussion which considers the play of a single holding. Doing so encourages and reinforces an incorrect approach to thinking about the game in terms of playing individual hands without reference to the other holdings you might play similarly. As we will see, correct poker strategy involves keeping in mind all of the hands with which you take any of your possible actions. At the beginning, this might be difficult. We have, however, tried to make it fun and to carefully explain more difficult concepts with examples. Read slowly and take time to reflect and apply new ideas to plays you see in your own games.

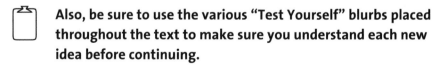 **Also, be sure to use the various "Test Yourself" blurbs placed throughout the text to make sure you understand each new idea before continuing.**

We begin in Chapter 1 with a discussion of what it means to talk about poker games and strategies for playing them, and we show how we can describe games and strategies precisely. In Chapter 2, we show how to play most profitably versus opponents whose strategies are known and consider how the situation changes when they are also trying to play well against us. In Chapter 3, we move right into the solution of preflop-only games. These are some of the simplest HUNL situations, but they apply directly to many real spots in short-stacked play. They will allow us to introduce many important concepts. In Chapter 4, we present the Indifference Principle which will help us to analyze many strategic situations. In Chapter 5, we make a quick discussion of hand and equity distributions which will be our primary tool for visualizing and describing the strengths of players' hand ranges. In Chapter 6, we discuss a general framework for playing hands postflop and establish a context for the rest of the book. In the next few chapters, the first of which is contained in this volume, we discuss GTO and exploitative HUNL play street by street. Future chapters will address the development and implementation of overall game-plans for exploiting opponents, the theory of recursive games which will let us consider the question of when it might be profitable to pass up small edges against weak opponents and "wait for a better spot", and other advanced topics.

I would like to acknowledge some people who have been very helpful to me in my poker career and in the writing of this book in particular. First, I have learned a ton from discussions over the years at the TwoPlusTwo HUSNG online forum and with people I met there. The regular posters there have had a very large influence on my thoughts about this game. I would like to acknowledge posters EvilSteve, AmyIsNo1, and plexiq for providing computational results against which I could check the correctness of my game theory software and for a number of enlightening technical discussions as well. I would also like to thank my students, and especially Yoni "Ph33roX" U., for a steady stream of thought-provoking hand histories and theoretical questions. *The Mathematics of Poker* by Bill Chen and Jerrod Ankenman has had a huge effect on the whole field of practical quantitative poker theory, and it's likely that this book would not have been possible had it not come before – many details of our treatment are derived from their approach. Byron Jacobs, Dan Addelman, Horacio Monteverde and everyone at D&B Publishing have been a pleasure to work with during the production of this book. Finally, my family has been very helpful and understanding during the writing and editing process, and I would like to especially thank Yuki and Michael for their suggestions and edits.

Chapter 1

Introduction to HUNL Strategy

Cards are war, in disguise of a sport. – Charles Lamb

1.1 Heads-up No-limit Hold 'em

No-limit hold 'em play has matured greatly over the past decade due to its increased popularity and acceptance in mainstream culture as well as convenient access to games in online cardrooms.

In traditional brick-and-mortar poker rooms, 9- and 10-handed play was the norm. At the beginning of the poker boom, 6-handed no-limit became many players' game of choice. In these short-handed games, fewer players at the table fought over the same amount of blinds, which meant that the average strength of the winning hand was weaker and that correct play was significantly more loose and aggressive. Players found themselves in more marginal, interesting situations with higher profit potential. This style of play was exciting to many people, and it also allowed skilled players to enjoy larger edges over their opponents.

The benefits of shorter-handed play led to the emergence of 2-handed or heads-up no-limit hold 'em as one of the most popular and profitable games available. HUNL games are spread in cash, single-table tournament, and multi-table shoot-out formats online and in many live cardrooms as well. The most profitable single-table tournament players online in recent years have been those who play heads-up single-table tournaments (HUSTTs), and many of the most celebrated cash game battles have been heads-up as well.

Since heads-up games pit players *mano-a-mano*, they offer lots of action. As we will see, it is correct to play many hands preflop (often all of them!), and there is no waiting time between hands since any time a player folds, another hand is immediately dealt. The play of so many marginal hands versus a single opponent gives heads-up players the greatest opportunity to observe their opponents' tendencies and to develop effective counter-strategies. In heads-up play more than in any other form of poker, it is important to observe and exploit the tendencies of other players. This is the topic of this book.

Despite the larger skill component present in heads-up games, they are also among the best for beginning players. HUSTTs in particular are well suited to players just starting to learn the game and build their bankrolls. The reason for this is that HUSTTs are spread at stakes as low as $1 at many popular online cardrooms. For this small buy-in, players receive enough tournament chips to fund dozens of hands of play. Because of the nature of heads-up play, many of these hands are played out postflop. The quick and constant exposure to a large variety of situations is especially valuable to new players.

Small-stakes HUSTTs are also good for building a bankroll since the level of play at the lowest stakes is generally very weak. If players ever do decide to switch to other forms of poker, they often find that the skills they learned heads-up give them a significant edge over other players. Additionally, many new players can be overwhelmed by the need to figure out the play of many opponents simultaneously and are only able to make shallow or cursory reads on their opponents when playing 9- or 6-handed. Heads-up play allows a player to think very deeply about what his opponent is doing, why he is doing it, and how his tendencies can be exploited. This is a very educational experience.

A solid understanding of heads-up play is also important for hold 'em players who never play explicitly heads-up formats. Standard multi-table tournament players are often weak at short-handed and heads-up play for lack of experience. However, the biggest pay increases in these tournaments are in short-handed play at the final table, and the largest is that between first and second place. Thus, it is important that tournament players work on their heads-up games outside of their normal sessions to maximize their expected results.

A short-handed or full-ring cash game player will often want the opportunity to start new tables. This is much easier to do if he is comfortable beginning play with a single opponent instead of a full line-up. Additionally, players' egos do flare at the poker table on occasion, and it is good to have the skills necessary to take advantage of an opportunity to have a weak player all to oneself.

Certain words will be used throughout the book to describe heads-up play. Much of this terminology will be well-known to readers, but we review it for the sake of completeness. Often in analyzing a situation, we will focus on optimizing the play of one player while referring to his opponent's tendencies or strategy. We will call the first player Hero and call his opponent Villain. Try to put yourself in Hero's shoes during these discussions.

Both players must put chips into the pot at the beginning of the hand without seeing any cards – one posts the small blind (SB) and the other posts the big blind (BB), which is exactly twice as much. The abbreviations *SB* and *BB* will be used to refer both to the amounts of chips they contain as well as to the players or positions of the players who post them. Additionally, since the size of these initial bets sets the scale of the action, we will always measure stack sizes in multiples of the BB. Being *on the button* is the same as being in the SB.

Suppose Hero is in the SB. After the blinds are posted, each player is dealt two cards which are known only to him. The SB acts first. He can fold, call, or raise. This first round of betting is known as the *preflop* round. If the preflop action ends with a call, a flop is dealt. The *flop* is three cards which are shared by both players, and we use the word flop to refer both to the cards themselves as well as the round of betting which occurs after they are dealt. In this second and all subsequent rounds of betting, the BB must act first. After the flop betting, a fourth shared card known as the *turn* is dealt and a third round of betting occurs. Finally, a fifth shared card, the *river*, is dealt and there is a final round of betting. If the river betting is completed without either player folding, the pot is awarded to the player with the best hand made of any five cards from his two private cards and the five public ones. The flop, turn and river are together known as *community cards*.

The smaller of the two players' stack sizes before a hand starts is known as the *effective stack size*. Since no more than this may go into the pot in any single hand, almost all strategic decisions are made with reference to the effective stack. Any additional chips that the larger stack contains are in most cases strategically irrelevant as they can not come into play.

A bet of the entire effective stack is known as an *all-in* bet, and allowable bet sizes in most cardrooms range from one BB to all-in. Allowable re-raise sizes must generally double the size of the previous raise. The smallest re-raise size is known as a minimum raise or a *minraise*.

Preflop, the first raise is called a raise, the first re-raise is called a 3-bet, the second re-raise is called a 4-bet, and so on. During any of the postflop rounds of betting, if a player bets and the other raises, then a subsequent re-raise is called a 3-bet, the next re-raise is a 4-bet, etc.

The final term we will define at this point refers to a very important concept. A *range* is a group of hands, and is often used to describe a player's strategy in a situational context. For example, we may refer to the range of hands which a player raises from the SB preflop. We will often specify ranges of hands using an abbreviated list. For example, the range of hands containing all pairs, all aces, and all suited kings may be written {22+,A2+,K2s+}.

Furthermore, it is possible that a range contains only some fraction of a particular hand. For example, suppose we are facing a raise preflop with A-A and our strategy involves re-raising it half the time and smooth calling the other half. Then, we would say that our re-raising range contains 50% of our A-A hands.

We will see that thinking about hands in terms of players' ranges is fundamental to strategic play. You have to think about your opponent's range to find your own best play. If your opponent is a sophisticated player, he is doing the same thing – he is thinking about your range. Thus, to reason about your opponent's ranges, you have to think about your own. So, for most situations in this book, we will consider the play of ranges versus ranges instead of individual hands.

At certain times in this book, we will refer briefly to the "top *X*% of hands." This is convenient for some examples where the details of the range are not especially important. It does imply some sort of ranking of the hands. There are many different conceivable ways of ranking hands, but for the purposes of these examples, unless otherwise noted, hands are ranked by their chance of winning when all-in preflop versus an opponent with a random hand, that is, an opponent who is equally likely to have any holding. Although hand rankings are sometimes hotly debated, the fact is that there is no single best or most correct method. The relative values of hands always depend on the situation being considered.

More technical terms will be defined as concepts are introduced.

1.2 Games and Strategies

It is often said that the game of heads-up no-limit hold 'em is too large and complicated to be solved with modern computers. However, it might not be clear precisely what is meant by this. What exactly is the entire game of HUNL? How would we write it down? What would it mean to solve it? If we had such a solution, how could we use it to play better poker, anyway? And what strategic progress might be made without the full solution?

We can describe the entire game of HUNL most elegantly by writing it down in the form of a *decision tree*. This tree is often drawn as a set of points connected by lines. Each point, called a *decision point*, represents a spot where one of the players must make a decision to take one or more actions. Each possible action is represented by a line coming off from the point. We may also refer to the set of actions available to a player as *choices, options,* or *strategic options*.

Figure 1.1 is an example of a section of a decision tree. The tree begins at a decision point known as the *root* which we will generally draw at the top. In HUNL games, the root decision point is controlled by the SB, and in this example, he has the option to fold or raise. If he chooses to raise, the play moves down the line labeled "raise" to a decision point controlled by the BB who then has several actions available to him. To fully specify the game, it is also necessary to give the players' stack sizes at the beginning of the hand.

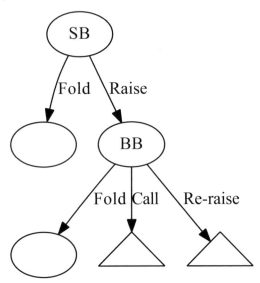

Figure 1.1: Example portion of a decision tree. Triangles are used to indicate that the whole tree continues but is not shown.

This tree segment can be thought of as the beginning of a HUNL hand. After the blinds are posted, the SB acts first, and unless he folds, the BB acts next. Of course, this is a simplified version of a game since, in the full game, the SB has more than two actions open to him at the beginning of the hand. In addition to folding, he may also call or raise to one of many different sizes. Each of these many choices would lead to a different BB decision point.

The BB, similarly, has many choices in the full game. The BB may choose to fold, in which case the hand is over. He may re-raise, and again each possible re-raise sizing leads to a distinct SB decision point. Additionally, the BB may choose to call. In this case, the game moves to a special type of decision point which is controlled by neither the SB nor the BB. It is generally said to be controlled by God or Nature, and the choice being made is that of which flop to deal. Nature will have similar decisions to make when it comes time to deal the turn and river cards.

Figure 1.2 shows an expanded decision tree which indicates that many raise sizes are possible and that Nature decides which cards to deal at the appropriate points. It also shows a few points which lead to no further action. For example, suppose the SB starts the hand by immediately folding. The hand is over, and we arrive at the point labeled "leaf" on the figure. Since this point is the end of a path through the tree and is furthest from the root, it is known as a *leaf*. (Clever, eh?) In general, these are the decision points reached by a fold, a call of an all-in bet, or a hand-ending action at the end of river play. Since leaves represent the end of a hand, they are where pay-offs happen.

A complete path from the root to a leaf may be called a *line*. This is essentially the same as the use of the word "line" in colloquial poker-speak. It refers to one complete set of actions that both players can take given particular community cards. Additionally, if you start at any particular decision point, call it A, then it, along with any decisions and actions which can be reached by moving down the tree are known as the *subtree* or *subgame* beginning at A. The two subtrees reached after the SB raises and the BB calls or re-raises are indicated by triangles in Figure 1.1. The *depth* of the tree is the greatest number of actions between the root and any of its leaves.

Now, we have still not shown the decision tree for the full game. Many raise/re-raise/re-raise possibilities have been neglected, not to mention all the possible flops, turns, and rivers. This is in the interest of space. Keep in mind that every possible combination of preflop actions leads to a whole different flop subtree and for each of these, many different flop plays are possible, each of which leads to distinct turn and river subtrees. We will turn to an approximation of the size of the full tree shortly, but first, we consider strategies for playing the games described by a tree.

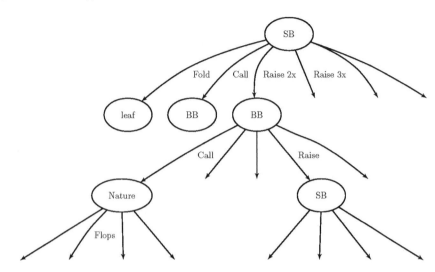

Figure 1.2: Extended decision tree portion.

Now that we know how to describe a game by organizing all of the different situations which may arise into a tree format, how do we describe strategies for playing that game?

Very simply, a player's *strategy* must describe what he will do in any situation he can face in the game. That is, it specifies how he will play each hand in his range at each of his decision points. In practice, this means that to describe a player's strategy, every action which he can take must have a range associated with it which specifies the hands with which he takes that action. Furthermore, at any particular decision point, all of the actions he can take must have ranges that "add up" to the range of hands with which he got to that decision point in the first place.

For example, consider again the simple decision tree segment we looked at in Figure 1.1. At the first decision point, the SB chooses to either raise or fold. Perhaps the range of hands associated with the raise action is any pair, ace, Broadway, or suited hand. The range associated with SB's folding choice must then be all other hands. The two ranges together must contain 100% of hands since the SB has 100% of hands to play at the beginning of the hand.

Now, how big would the full decision tree be if it were to describe all of no-limit? Really Really Big. To find an approximate answer to this question, we need to count the number of actions possible at each decision point. For example, let us consider again the SB's first action in a hand. He can either fold or call, and we need to specify more about the allowed bet sizes. While there are infinitely many numbers between 0 and any non-negative all-in bet size, in reality, players can not bet any amount. For practical purposes, online players must bet in increments of cents or tournament chips and live players must usually bet in increments of the small blind.

Still, at stack sizes of 100 BB, this only limits us to between several hundred and several thousand possible actions open to the SB at the very first decision point of every hand. That's a lot! For many of those actions, the BB will then have many different actions from which to choose a response. At that point, if there is action remaining after the preflop play, Nature can choose one of the 22,100 flops, and so on.

Keep in mind that each one of those decision points is essentially replicated under each of the similar actions which could lead to it. For example, suppose we had the (huge) subtree that described all the postflop action. That subtree would essentially have to be copied and placed under each one of the 22,100 flops. Then, that combined, gigantic subtree would have to be copied and placed under each of the lines representing all the possible preflop action. And so on. Thus, the size of the tree grows exponentially with the distance from root to leaf – HUNL is a huge game!

The exact size of the decision tree for any given stack size is not important to us, but a quick (under)estimate will help us appreciate the magnitude of the problem. Indeed, if we assume that each decision point gives a choice of 10 different actions, then we can see exactly how the size of the tree grows with its depth. While some decision points, such as those which are the result of a fold, lead to no actions, we have shown that most of them lead to many, many more than 10 actions, so this is a severe underestimation indeed.

A hand which went bet/raise/call on all streets would lead to a distance of about 12 between the root and leaf. Thus, 12 is a reasonable estimate for the average depth of the decision tree. Note that, if stacks are sufficiently deep, many parts of the decision tree will have greater than 12 actions between the root and leaves, and we are again making a rather severe underestimation of the size of the tree. Anyhow, a tree of depth 12 in which each decision point leads to 10 actions has a total of 10^{12} leaves.

Each of these leaves must be the destination of some action which is associated with some range. To specify a range, we must specify what fraction of each of the 1,326 hold 'em hands it contains. If each of these fractions is represented by a single-precision floating-point number, then a single range is about 5KB of data. Thus, a full strategy for HUNL then requires at least 5×10^{12}KB = 5,000TB just to store. That is something like the amount of information contained in five billion books of this size, and we have been careful to drastically underestimate the figure at a number of points. The real figure, which has been more carefully estimated elsewhere, is much, much larger. It is significantly more data than any modern computer can process. So, it is hard to say what you would even do if you had the strategy which was some sort of "full solution" to HUNL – it would be too much data to use!

Furthermore, it is obviously not something which could be learned exactly by a human for use at the tables. In this book, we will address these issues in a couple of ways to allow the practical use of game theoretic analysis to improve our play. We will study *approximate games*, those which do not include all of the possible situations in full HUNL. We will find strategies for playing these approximate games and try to extract general patterns and lessons for application to real play.

1.3 Approximate Games

Approximating the full game can make it more manageable from a computational perspective. It also allows us to focus on specific situations in order to distill general lessons from the results without having to take on too much complexity all at once. Therefore, we will often rely in this book on the study of approximate games.

They function as a great tool for analysis in that they allow us to clearly define the strategic options we want to consider and then, within those assumptions, to analyze the game completely. We will gain important insights by being able to solve realistic HUNL games. When done carefully, ignoring many strategic options does not hurt the analysis. For example, many HUNL players have a single standard raise size they use when first to act preflop on the button at most stack sizes. Even if they mix up this raise size somewhat, very few (winning) players regularly open raise to 5, 6, or 37 times the BB even though they have the option to do so. When we remove options such as these from consideration, the analysis does not lose much.

There are a variety of ways to remove elements from the full game of HUNL while retaining many of its nuances and its rich strategic structure. Some authors organize hands into groups which play similarly and solve for strategies for playing each group instead of each individual hand. For example, A6o-A8o play very similarly and may be considered a single "hand" for many purposes. However, this type of approximation can change proper strategy in subtle ways and make it difficult to connect the results of analysis back to real HUNL.

We will rely on three primary approximation methods:

1) Narrow players' strategic options

Many lines are always or almost always incorrect, such as putting a large majority of our stack in preflop and then folding. We can immediately exclude these actions from the game. However, we may also neglect lines which are merely uncommon. This is often justified from a strategic standpoint – many plays are just not in a player's arsenal, so they need not be considered when analyzing his strategy.

Additionally, we will generally consider only a small number of possible bet sizes for a player at any given decision point. If we choose a few sizes which span the range allowed in the full game, we can avoid drastically limiting the players' strategies. Also, this is similar to how many players actually play, and for good reason. Players regularly bet the same amounts in similar situations for information-hiding purposes.

2) Remove future card possibilities

There are 22,100 distinct flops in hold 'em. After the turn and river are dealt, there are over 2.5 million different boards. Preflop strategy in the full game may be very similar to that in an approximate game with many fewer different flops. Play on the flop may not change much if only a few select turn and river cards can actually come out.

The cards that can come later in a hand, however, do greatly affect play earlier in the hand, so it is important that a variety of different kinds of cards be possible. For example, to obtain preflop strategy results which mimic those in the full game, it is necessary that the approximate game contain about the right number of A-high flops, K-high flops, suited flops, etc. Postflop, it is important that the frequency with which draws come in be kept as close as possible to that in the full game.

In addition to limiting the number of future cards, we might also set up games such that the action is necessarily over on an early street, either by way of an all-in or fold. In this case, we do not really have to consider later cards at all.

3) Consider only part of a hand

Suppose we only want to analyze the river play in a hand. If we assume the stack sizes and ranges with which both players get to the river, we can evaluate river strategies without worrying about the play earlier in the hand. Similarly, we will often assume players' preflop ranges and begin the analysis of a hand after one particular flop.

We will study decision trees and approximate games throughout the book. Our plan will be to start with the simplest approximations and work our way to more complex ones. This will make it easier for us to gain familiarity with our various analytical tools. However, all of the approximate games we consider will be directly related to real HUNL situations. Our goal along the way will be to build intuition about what these solutions look like in order to improve our own play.

In addition to being easier to solve, approximate games are easier to write down and talk about. In fact, computers these days can handle quite large games – just writing out the decision tree and its solution for one large but computationally-feasible game might take many books. So, we will primarily work with small games and point out results from larger calculations when it is helpful.

There are a variety of ways to represent tree-structured data other than the classical node-link diagrams which we have shown. One format which is convenient for representing trees relatively compactly in print is known as an *outline view*. It is often used to display hierarchical information in computer user interfaces such as file managers. This representation of a tree is conveniently compact. Other presentations such as the *icicle tree* can make use of geometrical areas to clearly indicate how often each action is used. The cover of this book features a *sunburst tree*. The various methods all have their strengths and weaknesses but can be useful for visualizing strategies.

1.4 You Should Now...

- ♠ Know how the game of HUNL is played and why it is an important skill for players of all formats of NLHE

- ♠ Know the meaning of the word "range" and understand the use of the concept in strategic situations

- ♠ Understand how decision trees can be used to model the entire game of HUNL or more specific situations in a particular hand

- ♠ Understand exactly what we mean by a strategy for playing a game described by a decision tree

- ♠ Understand why the simple act of writing down a non-trivial strategy for the full HUNL decision tree would be impossible and have some idea about how we will proceed using approximate games

Chapter 2

Game-theoretic Strategies

If you think the math isn't important, you don't know the right math.

– Chris Ferguson

There is a natural way to divide the process of developing a strategy against most opponents into two tasks:

1. Identify his strategy – how he plays his hands. In other words, identify the ranges with which he takes each action at each decision point he controls.

2. Compute the most profitable response to this strategy.

These two skills are largely independent. The first is essentially information gathering and requires observation and experience drawing conclusions about what an opponent's play in some spots might say about his actions in others. Then, once you know his strategy, finding your most profitable response is just math, although experience and work away from the tables can go a long way towards making the correct adjustments quickly.

One might say that the first of the two is really the focus in HUNL tournaments while the second skill is more important in cash games. In cash games, you tend to play many hands in similar situations which makes it relatively easy to gather information about your opponent's strategy, and the challenge is then to make the most efficient use of that information. In tournaments, you generally play hands at a much wider range of effective stack sizes, and it can be quite difficult to figure out what your opponent is doing in the different situations.

In any case, both are important in any form of poker, and working on these two skills separately is important for developing a clear thought process. Good hand-reading can only help you so much if you make poor adjustments. On the other hand, making plays based on "feel" without explicitly identifying the reasons behind them will make you only as good as those tendencies which you have happened to come across through luck or trial-and-error. Only by explicitly identifying opponents' tendencies and then working out your best response to them can you improve surely and quickly as a player and maximize your profits in the game.

The need for strategy identification arises first in actual play since you must figure out Villain's ranges before you can exploit them. However, we will begin with a discussion of the second point. We will assume we know Villain's strategy, and we will see how to find our most profitable counter-strategy. This is, in some sense, an easier problem than discovering the unknown strategy in the first place, and we can do it exactly. Additionally, the discussion leads to many important strategic issues and concepts including that of the Nash equilibrium.

First, however, we have a few comments about expected value.

2.1 Expected Value

Our use of the term 'EV' is subtly different than that in many other poker texts. We feel that our convention is simpler and more intuitive, especially when studying complicated situations. However, the break from tradition raises the possibility of confusion. That said, the material in this section is extremely fundamental to the rest of the book.

We will often encounter and want to talk about numbers whose values are unknown. The *expected value* of some quantity which depends on random events is the average of all the possible values of that quantity weighted by the likelihood of each value. This is also known as the *expectation* of the quantity or its EV for short.

A simple example is found in the case of a single roll of a fair, six-sided die. The die can land with any number one through six face up. Each of these outcomes is equally likely and happens with probability 1/6. To find the average value of the outcome of a single roll, we sum the value of each possible result times the chance of that outcome. Thus, the expected value of the result of one roll is

$$1 \cdot \frac{1}{6} + 2 \cdot \frac{1}{6} + 3 \cdot \frac{1}{6} + 4 \cdot \frac{1}{6} + 5 \cdot \frac{1}{6} + 6 \cdot \frac{1}{6} = \frac{21}{6} = 3.5$$

Of course, in no single trial can you roll a 3.5. However, if you rolled the same die a very large number of times, then the average result would be about 3.5.

Now, technically we can talk about the expected value of many different quantities whose values are uncertain. However, in poker, our stack size is by far the most important quantity. So, we will use the term EV to refer specifically to the expectation of stack sizes. In particular, we will want to focus on expected stack sizes after we take a certain action. For example, we will refer simply to "the EV of calling" when what we mean is "the expectation value of the size of the player's chip stack at the end of the hand if the player makes the decision to call". When faced with a poker decision, we will generally seek to find the expected value of the size of our chip stack after taking each of the options available to us, averaging over things we can not control (the cards which will come) or we do not know (our opponent's holding). We can then make the most money on average by going with the choice which has the largest expectation.

A simple example will help to make this clear. Suppose Hero finds himself facing an all-in bet on the river in a hand where both players started with 75 BB. There are 50 BB in the pot, and Villain's river bet size is also 50 BB. Thus, Hero must risk 50 BB to call the bet and have a chance to win 100 BB. Hero knows that he has the best hand 40% of the time. What is the expected value of his stack size after calling and after folding, and which should he choose?

Firstly, if Hero folds, he knows exactly how many chips he will have at the end of the hand: 50 BB. If he calls, however, there are two possibilities. He will double up for a stack of 150 BB 40% of the time, and he will go broke 60% of the time. Thus, the expected size of his stack if he calls is

$$150BB \times 0.4 + 0BB \times 0.6 = 60BB.$$

Since 60>50, the correct play is for Hero to call. Calling is worth 10 BB more than folding, on average.

So what happened here? We considered a situation where Hero had two options, and then we found how many chips he would have at the end of the hand (on average) as a result of each choice. We chose the more profitable action. This is the basic idea behind the solutions to almost all of the strategic decisions we will face. We will choose between our options by calculating the EV of each one and picking the largest.

Now, the sophisticated reader may have noticed that the convention used here is actually different than that found in most poker literature. In this book, we will work in terms of expected stack sizes at the end of the hand. A more common choice is to deal with the expected change in stack size relative to the current stacks. Notice first that this is not a strategically-significant difference. The option which leads to the largest expected stack size at the end of the hand is the same as the one which maximizes expected change in stack size from the current decision point onward.

Let us take an example which relates to the discussion in the next section to see exactly how these different choices of convention can play out. Suppose both players have 10 BB stacks. It is the beginning of the hand, Hero is in the SB, and he is choosing between folding and raising. First, what is the EV of folding? Second, what is the EV of raising if we know that the BB will fold to our raise?

Using our convention, this is easy.

$$EV(\text{folding}) = 9.5 \text{ BB}$$

$$EV(\text{raising given that the BB folds}) = 11 \text{ BB}$$

If the SB folds, his total stack size at the end of the hand is 9.5 BB. If he raises and the BB folds, then he ends up with 11 BB.

Now, what if we are working in terms of the expected change in stack size relative to that at the point of Hero's decision? In this case, we have

$$\text{EV(folding)} = 0 \text{ BB}$$

$$\text{EV(raising given that the BB folds)} = 1.5 \text{ BB}$$

since if we fold, our stack size at the end of the hand is the same as at the decision point. That is, there is 0 change. If we raise and the BB folds, our stack size is 1.5 BB more than it was at Hero's decision point.

Thirdly, especially in the case of preflop decisions, you may sometimes see people work in terms of changes in stack size relative to the stacks at the beginning of the hand. What would our result be if we took this approach? We would have the following.

$$\text{EV(folding)} = -0.5 \text{ BB}$$

$$\text{EV(raising given that the BB folds)} = 1.0 \text{ BB}$$

By folding, we end up with 0.5 BB less than we started the hand with. By raising, we earn 1 BB more than we started the hand with, assuming the BB folds.

Now, since we are just interested in comparing our options, it is the *differences* between the values of our options that is actually important. Notice above that the difference between the two numbers is 1.5 BB in every case. Thus, we could use any of the approaches as long as we are consistent. However, we can not calculate the EV of folding one way and that of raising another way and then compare the values meaningfully.

We will see that the expected total stack size at the end of the hand is the easiest quantity to work with in practice for a number of reasons. First, with the other approaches, players frequently make mistakes in keeping their point of reference consistent throughout a problem. Perhaps they have learned that the EV of folding is always 0, but they calculate the EV of other actions as compared to their stack at the beginning of the hand or the beginning of the street or at some other point in the spot they are considering. With our approach, we need not constantly be stating our point of reference when writing down the EV of an action. For us, the point at which EV equals 0 is always the same – it is when we go broke.

We will find the advantages of working with total stack sizes even more clear when considering more complicated calculations where we are looking at the value of a holding over multiple actions or perhaps even different streets. Suppose we want to compare the value of holding a hand in a preflop spot to that of holding it in a particular turn situation. The comparison can be made easily by just figuring out how large our stack will be at the end of the hand starting in each of the situations. Performing multi-street calculations with the alternate methods is much more confusing and error-prone, at least for me!

There are many ways to make errors in EV calculations, but if we always work with the total stack sizes at the end of the hand, it is relatively easy to keep things straight even in complicated spots. For these reasons, *we will always work in terms of the expected value of players' total stack sizes at the end of the hand*. We will see plenty of applications of these ideas starting shortly. Occasionally we do find it useful to refer to the expected change in stack size over the course of a hand. In this case we will use the terms *average* or *expected profit*.

Now, the word *equity* refers to the share of the pot that a player expects to win on average if all betting is stopped and both players check to showdown. This share of the pot is an average over all the cards which can come off and all hands in Villains' range. It is not quite the chance of winning since the case that the pot is split must be taken into account. In particular, the equity is the chance of winning plus half the chance of splitting. This chance of winning if both players check down is, of course, the same as the chance of winning if both players are all-in.

In the first example in this section, Hero was facing an all-in bet on the river, and we assumed that he had the best hand 40% of the time. That is, assuming he was never splitting the pot, he had 40% equity. Sometimes we may also average over all of Hero's possible holdings to find the average equity of a hand from Hero's range. We then have the share of the pot expected to be won versus Villain's range on average over all hands in Hero's range. The equity of a hand or range is often used to give an indication of how strong it is in a particular situation.

We will mostly use "equity" to refer to a player's expected share of the pot in terms of a percentage or fraction, but we can also refer to his share of the pot in terms of the total chip amount represented. For example, expecting to win 150 BB 40% of the time is an equity of 60 BB. Accurately calculating hand-versus-range and range-versus-range equities is very important for hold 'em hand analysis. The free computer utility PokerStove is highly recommended for this purpose.

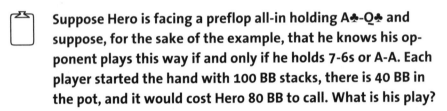 **Suppose Hero is facing a preflop all-in holding A♣-Q♣ and suppose, for the sake of the example, that he knows his opponent plays this way if and only if he holds 7-6s or A-A. Each player started the hand with 100 BB stacks, there is 40 BB in the pot, and it would cost Hero 80 BB to call. What is his play?**

First, the EV of folding is 80 BB – after a fold, Hero will have that much left. Villain holds 7♣-6♣, 7♥-6♥, 7♦-6♦, 7♠-6♠, A♥-A♦, A♥-A♠, and A♦-A♠ with equal probability, so if Hero calls, he will run into A-A 3/7 of the time and 7-6s 4/7 of the time. His equity versus A-A is 12.54%, and his equity versus 7-6s is 61.45%, so he wins

$$3/7 \times 12.54 + 4/7 \times 61.45 = 40.49\%$$

of the 200 BB pot when he calls for a total EV of 200 x 0.4049 = 80.97 BB. Since 80.97>80, Hero should call.

Note that we could have also said that Hero's equity versus the combined range {A-A,7-6s} is 40.49%. Also notice the importance of combination counting and card removal in this calculation. There are normally six ways Villain can hold A-A and four ways to hold 7-6s, but the fact that Hero's hand contains the A♣ changes these numbers.

2.2 Maximally Exploitative Strategies

A *maximally exploitative* strategy is what it sounds like – the most profitable response to some particular, fixed strategy of your opponent. This is also called a *best response strategy*. Colloquially, these strategies may be referred to as optimal, but in much game theory literature, the word optimal is reserved for a very specific and different meaning.

The *value* of a game with respect to a pair of strategies is the amount Hero expects to make on average by playing it once given those strategies. This is basically his expected profit when playing a single hand of poker, on average, considering all the hole card combinations which could be dealt and given a particular decision tree and player ranges. Consider the following quick example.

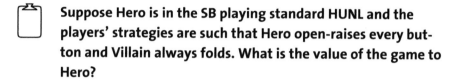 **Suppose Hero is in the SB playing standard HUNL and the players' strategies are such that Hero open-raises every button and Villain always folds. What is the value of the game to Hero?**

1 BB. We win 1 BB per hand with any two cards. Easy game. Furthermore, notice that when playing HUNL, the BB need never settle for a strategy which gives him an average profit of less than –1 BB per hand because a very simple strategy can guarantee that he does at least that well. Similarly, the SB should never need to adopt a strategy which yields a profit of less than –0.5 BB per hand.

Another way to say we are trying to find our best response strategy is to say that we are trying to choose our strategy so as to maximize the value of the game to us. In some sense this whole book is about finding maximally exploitative strategies and especially about doing so quickly at the table. We will not try to cover that all in this section. Here we describe the mechanical procedure of finding the exact best response to a fixed opponent strategy. Although this is a sufficiently computationally-intensive task that we will not often be doing it by hand in practice, understanding the process in principle is important for knowing what maximally exploitative strategies look like and learning how to reason about them.

To begin, assume we have a decision tree, and Villain's ranges at each of his decision points are known. We are trying to find our most profitable response. The first very important thing to notice is this: *our most profitable overall strategy is to play every individual combination of hole cards as profitably as possible.* The value of the game is just the average of our expected profit with any pair of hole cards. Clearly, for a fixed opponent strategy, we maximize this average by maximizing the individual expectations of all hands.

Notice also that this implies that a best response strategy involves making the same decision every time in a particular situation. That is, we play a particular hand the same way every time – we play it the most profitable way possible. The only possible exception to this is in the case that two choices are exactly equal in EV. Maximally exploitative ranges do not include plays which are made for the sake of "mixing up" one's play. They certainly do not include "loss leader" type plays where one hand is played less profitably than it might be for the sake of the whole strategy. This may be unintuitive or go against some players' notions of balance, etc. Many of those common notions are incorrect, and the rest only arise when supposing that Villain's strategy might change to adapt to our own.

2.2.1 The Most Profitable way to Play a Hand

Given the above discussion, we can find a maximally exploitative strategy by just finding the most profitable way to play each particular pair of hole cards individually. To see how this works, we can just consider one arbitrary hole card combination, call it H, and find how to play it most profitably given a decision tree and Villain's ranges. Here we will address both how to play H to maximize our EV as well as how to find exactly what that EV is.

The first thing to notice is that we can actually talk about the expected value of holding H at any decision point P in the tree. Let us call this value $EV_{H,P}$. As a quick example, suppose Hero is in the BB with 8♣-3♥, a hand he will fold if the SB raises. At the point after the SB raises, Hero's EV is $S-1$ where S is his stack size at the beginning of the hand. That is, his total stack size at the end of the hand will be $S-1$, because he is just about to fold and surrender his blind. Hero should have a higher expectation at the point after SB limps. When the SB limps, we should be able to end up with more than $S-1$ on average, even if our strategy is to only put any money into the pot when we happen to flop very well. If we call the decision point which is arrived at after Villain makes a raise *A* and that after he limps *B*, then in our notation, we have

$$EV_{8\clubsuit 3\heartsuit,B} > EV_{8\clubsuit 3\heartsuit,A} = S - 1$$

A few other points should be made about hand values. First, notice that the value of Hero's hand *H* depends strongly on Villain's strategy. Also, recall that the EV of a hand at a decision point is different than its equity. Equity describes the fraction of the pot a hand would be entitled to on average if all betting stopped and hands were checked down. $EV_{H,P}$ refers to the expected total stack size at the end of the hand including future betting, folding, etc. Finally, notice that the EV of playing the whole hand with holding *H* is just the EV at the root decision point which we might write as $EV_{H,root}$.

Let us start by considering the shove/fold game for an example. Shove/fold is the simplest approximate HUNL game. Its decision tree is shown in Figure 2.1. The SB can either fold or shove all-in, and if he shoves, the BB can either call or fold. It is fairly common for players in the SB to restrict themselves to a shove-or-fold strategy preflop at sufficiently short stack sizes. Suppose Hero is in the SB, and both players start with 10 BB.

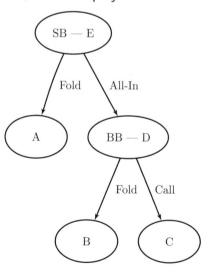

Figure 2.1: Decision tree for the shove/fold game.

There are three different kinds of decision points in a decision tree.

1. Points which Hero controls

2. Points which someone else (either Villain or Nature) controls

3. Leaves which indicate that the hand is over and there is no choice to be made

Let us first look at how to find the EV of having a hand at a leaf since this is the simplest case. There are no decisions to be made here, and the payoffs actually happen at the leaves, so it is very easy to find the EVs. There are two kinds of leaves.

1. Ones which follow a fold

2. Ones which indicate a showdown – either after the river or earlier if we have an all-in

There are two leaves following a fold in the shove/fold game. First, Hero can open-fold his button. This brings the state of the game to the point labeled *A* in the figure. Hero's EV is 9.5 BB at this point. That is, his average total stack size at the end of the hand is 9.5 BB after folding. In fact, the averaging is unnecessary in this case – his stack size at the end of the hand is exactly 9.5 BB no matter what hand he folded.

Now, if Villain folds to Hero's shove, the game reaches the leaf labeled *B*. The value, $EV_{H,B}$, of any of the SB's holdings here is 11 BB since he wins Villain's BB without a showdown – he ends the hand with 11 BB regardless of his holding.

The game arrives at the final leaf, point *C*, if Hero shoves and Villain calls. Here, Hero's expectation depends on his hand *H*. In particular, since both players are all-in, Hero's EV is the frequency with which he wins the hand (and half the times they chop) times the size of the pot: $20BB \times EQ_H$ where EQ_H is the equity of *H* versus the BB's calling range. This is Hero's total expected stack size at the end of the hand. This expression comes straight from the definition of equity. 20 BB is the total size of the pot after the players get all-in, and EQ_H is the fraction of the pot Hero wins on average when the players show down without any additional action.

That does it for the leaves. Now, what about those decision points which somebody else controls? Assuming that Hero is in the SB, there is only one of these in the shove/fold game – the point where Villain in the BB has the decision to call or fold. This is labeled D on the figure. What is Hero's expectation with H at that point? Well, it depends on how often the BB folds to the shove and how often he calls. Suppose for example that BB always folded. It would be just as if his choice to call did not exist. The play would always move to point B, and so Hero's EV with H at point D would be the same as that at point B: 11 BB. On the other hand, if Villain always called, then $EV_{H,D}$ would just be that at point C: 20BB x EQ_H.

However, point D is Villain's decision point, and in general he will take both actions some of the time. Thus, to find Hero's expectation at the point, we have to average over both probabilities according to Villain's strategy. Suppose Villain calls C_H of the time and folds F_H of the time. Then, Hero's EV of having hand H at point D is C_H times his EV when Villain calls, plus F_H times his EV when Villain folds. That is,

$$\begin{aligned} EV_{H,D} &= F_H \cdot EV_{H,B} + C_H \cdot EV_{H,C} \\ &= F_H \cdot 11 \text{ BB } + C_H \cdot (20 \text{ BB } \cdot EQ_H) \end{aligned}$$

Notice, by the way, that C_H and F_H must sum to one. Also, they do depend slightly on H due to card removal effects. For example, if H contains an ace, it is slightly less likely that Villain holds an ace, and thus, assuming he plays a reasonable strategy, it is slightly less likely that he will call the shove.

Now, there are no decision points in this game which are controlled by Nature, i.e. where new cards are dealt. If there was such a point, then the value of having H there would just be the average of the values of having it after each specific new card comes. That is, we would find our expectation at that point by averaging over all the possible actions in Nature's "strategy" just as we did for a decision point controlled by our opponent. This average must be weighted by the probability of each card's being dealt. The likelihoods of any cards being dealt that are not already on board or contained in H are usually approximately equal. However, they are not exactly so because they do depend slightly on Villain's range. If his range is such that he is particularly likely to hold a certain card, then it is less likely that that card will be dealt. On the other hand, if his range does not include a certain card, it is more likely that that card will be dealt. We will treat subtle effects like this correctly in our calculations in this book but will not dwell on them except in the rare cases they actually turn out to be significant.

Finally, there are the decision points we have control over. Point E, where Hero decides to shove or fold, is the only of these in the shove/fold game. What is his expected total stack size at the end of the hand given that he makes it to point E with a holding H? Well, this is a point we have control over, so the value depends on our choice of how to play H. Our choice will either take us to point A or to point D. So, the value of having the hand at point E will be that of having it at point A if we decide to fold, and it will be the value of having it at point D if we decide to shove. Since it is our decision point, we get to choose which it will be. In practice, we are of course looking for the most profitable way to play each hand, so we just go with the bigger of those two. Thus, the value of a hand H at point E is

$$\mathrm{EV}_{H,E} = \max(\mathrm{EV}_{H,A}, \mathrm{EV}_{H,D})$$

where the *max* function gives whichever of its two arguments is bigger.

Now we know how to find the value of a hand H for the Hero at any decision point in terms of the values of the points below it. Remember that the value of H for the whole hand is its value at the root. If we figure out our most profitable plays with each of the 1,326 hold 'em hand combinations, we have found our maximally exploitative strategy. Finally, the value of the whole game is just the average over all hand combinations of the EVs of the individual hands.

Since these are such important ideas, we will go over a couple quick examples. In the first, we will continue looking at the shove/fold game, but we will focus on the case when Hero is in the BB. In the second example, we will consider a slightly more complicated game and try to guide you to work through it yourself.

So, what is the EV of a hand in the shove/fold game when Hero is in the BB? That is, what is the value of a hand H at point E, $EV_{H,E}$? Since the BB does not control point E, it is just

$$EV_{H,E} = F_H \cdot EV_{H,A} + S_H \cdot EV_{H,D}$$

where F_H and S_H are the proportion of times SB folds and shoves, respectively. Now, we need to proceed recursively to find the unknown EVs referenced on the right-hand side of this equation. At point A, our total stack size is $EV_{H,A}$ = 10.5 BB with any hand. The action at point D is our choice, so our EV there is

$$EV_{H,D} = \max(9 \text{ BB}, 20 \text{ BB} \cdot EQ_H)$$

where EQ_H is the equity of H versus the SB's shoving range. Hero's two choices are to fold and end up with 9 BB or to call and end up with 20BB x EQ_H, and he chooses the greater of those for any particular hand H. Thus, all in all, the BB's total EV at the beginning of the hand is

$$\begin{aligned} EV_{H,E} &= F_H \cdot EV_{H,A} + S_H \cdot EV_{H,D} \\ &\doteq F_H \cdot 10.5 \text{ BB} + S_H \cdot \max(9 \text{ BB}, 20 \text{ BB} \cdot EQ_H) \end{aligned}$$

Now we look at a slightly more complicated game. The decision tree for the raise/shove game is shown in Figure 2.2. The SB starts out by either folding or raising. When he raises, the BB can fold or go all-in, and when BB goes all-in, the SB can call or fold.

Suppose that Hero is in the SB, his initial raise is a minraise (i.e. to 2 BB total) and both players again start with 10 BB. We have labeled all the decision points. We know the ranges with which Villain in the BB shoves or folds when facing a raise. Now, follow the series of questions to find how Hero should play each of his hands and his EVs when he does so. Try to answer them yourself before reading the solutions.

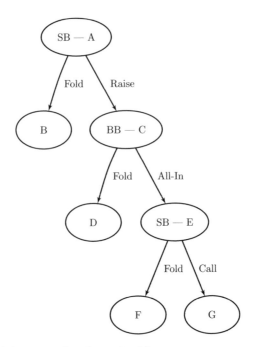

Figure 2.2: Decision tree for the raise/shove game.

Which point is the root of the tree?

Point *A*, where play starts.

At which points do payoffs occur?

At the leaves: *B*, *D*, *F*, and *G*.

Which of the leaves are led to by folds and what is Hero's total expected stack size at the end of the hand if he has a hand *H* there?

♠ Point *B*. Hero folded his SB so *H* has an EV of 9.5 BB for any *H*.

♠ Point *D*. Hero raised and Villain surrendered his BB so *H* has an EV of 11 BB for any *H*.

♠ Point *F*. Hero raised and folded to Villain's shove so *H* has an EV of 8 BB for any *H*.

Which of the leaves involves a showdown and what is the value to Hero of having H there?

Point G. Here we saw a raise, shove, and call. The total pot size is 20 BB, and Hero's EV is simply his equity share, 20BB x EQ_H.

What is the value to Hero of holding H at the root decision point A?

We have control over this decision, so we choose the maximum of the two options available to us: folding, which takes us to point B and a guaranteed EV of 9.5 BB, and raising, and thus going to point C.

(2.1) $$EV_{H,A} = \max(9.5 \text{ BB}, EV_{H,C})$$

This leads to the question:

What is our value at point C?

Villain controls this point, so Hero's EV is just a weighted average of the two possibilities.

$$EV_{H,C} = 11 \text{ BB} \cdot F_H + EV_{H,E} \cdot S_H$$

where F_H and S_H are Villain's folding and shoving probabilities.

This leads to the next question:

What is the value at point E?

Hero has control over this decision, so he just chooses the best of the two options given his particular hand:

$$EV_{H,E} = \max(8 \text{ BB}, 20 \text{ BB} \cdot EQ_H)$$

where EQ_H is the equity of hand H versus the BB's shoving range.

So, what is the total EV for the SB of playing hand H? Now that we know the values at all the other points, we can just plug in the values for the other points into our earlier result, Equation 2.1.

$$\text{EV}_{H,A} = \max(9.5 \text{ BB}, \text{EV}_{H,C})$$
$$= \max(9.5 \text{ BB}, [F_H \cdot 11 \text{ BB} + S_H \cdot \text{EV}_{H,E}])$$
$$= \max(9.5 \text{ BB}, [F_H \cdot 11 \text{ BB} + S_H \cdot \max(8 \text{ BB}, 20 \text{ BB} \cdot \text{EQ}_H)])$$

We have found the total EV of playing any hand in the shove/fold and raise/shove games against arbitrary opponent ranges, implicitly finding the best line for Hero with each hand as well. Let us take an example so as not to get too bogged down in the math.

Suppose we are playing the raise/shove game where both players start the hand with 10 BB. Hero is in the SB with 7-4o. Villain's strategy facing a raise involves shoving with the range

$$33+, \text{A2s}+, \text{K2s}+, \text{Q5s}+, \text{J8s}+, \text{T8s}+, \text{A2o}+, \text{K4o}+, \text{Q8o}+, \text{J9o}+$$

and folding all other hands. What is Hero's EV and maximally exploitative play with 7♥-4♣? We find this by plugging into the above equation. Given Hero's hand and Villain's strategy, we have Villain's folding frequency F_H = 0.5812, Villain's shoving frequency S_H = 0.4188, and the equity of Hero's holding versus Villain's shoving range EQ_H = 0.3267. Thus, we have

$$\text{EV}_{H,A} = \max(9.5 \text{ BB}, [F_H \cdot 11 \text{ BB} + S_H \cdot \max(8 \text{ BB}, 20 \text{ BB} \cdot \text{EQ}_H)])$$
$$= \max(9.5 \text{ BB}, [0.5812 \cdot 11 \text{ BB} + 0.4188 \cdot \max(8 \text{ BB}, 20 \text{ BB} \cdot 0.3267)])$$
$$= \max(9.5 \text{ BB}, [0.5812 \cdot 11 \text{ BB} + 0.4188 \cdot \max(8 \text{ BB}, 6.53 \text{ BB})])$$
$$= \max(9.5 \text{ BB}, [0.5812 \cdot 11 \text{ BB} + 0.4188 \cdot 8 \text{ BB}])$$
$$= \max(9.5 \text{ BB}, 9.744 \text{ BB}])$$
$$= 9.744 \text{ BB}$$

So, if Hero plays maximally exploitatively, he ends the hand with 9.744 BB on average. How exactly does he play his 7♥-4♣? Each of the spots where we evaluated one of the *max* functions in the above represents a spot where Hero chose to make one play over another. In particular, on the third line in the sequence of equations, we found that 8BB>6.53BB so that folding is better than calling if we get jammed on after we raise. Then, on the fifth line, we found 9.5BB<9.744BB so that raising initially is better than folding. So, Hero's best line here is to raise and fold if Villain shoves.

Finding maximally exploitative strategies is one of the most important skills in poker. Remember that these strategies contain no loss-leader type plays – multiple lines are taken with the same hand only if the EVs of both choices are exactly the same. Since this is important, consider working through a few examples of your own for particular hands H or different decision trees.

2.2.2 The Equilibration Exercise

Once we have gained some facility in thinking about maximally exploitative ranges, we can put it to use to gain strategic insights. There is an exercise to help in doing this which we have dubbed the equilibration exercise for reasons which will become clear shortly. It is a particularly effective way to practice developing exploitative strategies and to think about how this material might be used to improve your own play. The exercise goes as follows.

1) Consider a situation

It is helpful to visualize your situation explicitly as a tree. Draw it out. It can be either a full decision tree, or you can focus on one subtree. That is, it may start in a particular preflop or postflop spot and consider only the play for the rest of the hand. If this is unclear, our examples should help.

2) Specify a strategy for one of the players, Player 1

Specify ranges for all decisions in the tree for one of the players. These ranges might represent your default play in the spot, or how you expect a specific opponent to play, or what you think most players might consider "standard". Your choice will depend on what you want to learn.

3) Find Player 2's best response

The next thing to do is to find the most profitable way for the other player to respond, and to find the expectation of his new strategy.

Suppose that you started by assigning Player 1 your own default play in the situation. Then, here you will find what opponents should be doing to best exploit you. Consider the following questions.

♠ Is Villain's best response making a lot of money versus you? (That is, is your default strategy very exploitable?)

♠ What might you notice in terms of Villain's statistics, frequencies, hands shown down, etc., if Villain was exploiting you in this way? These are things you should look out for at the table.

♠ It is important to realize how your default play is exploitable and be wary of being exploited. Do you often see players in your games making these adjustments?

Thinking about the *incorrect* adjustments which Player 2 could make is very helpful too, but not our primary focus presently.

Suppose now that you started out (in 2.2.2) by considering an opponent's play in the spot. You can ask yourself questions similar to those above to similar advantage. You may also simply start out with the plays of standard player stereotypes. Additionally, it is often helpful to work out strategies for combating standard plays that are popular with players in your regular games. Is check-raise bluffing paired flops a common trick in your player pool? How should you adjust and counter-adjust?

4) Find Player 1's best counter-adjustment to Player 2's adjustment, etc.

Now, go back and find the original player's best response to his opponent's adjustment. Then repeat. It is often enlightening to go back and forth a few times, looking at the players' strategies and answering the same questions.

It is important to keep in mind, however, that the worse your opponents are, the less relevance these later iterations will have to a particular gameplay situation. Suppose you start out by identifying Villain's play in some spot and make an exploitative adjustment. How should Villain respond? The adjustment found by the equilibration exercise is his best choice only if he believes that you made your first adjustment correctly. Afterwards, how should you re-adjust? You can only rationally trust the second adjustment found by the equilibration exercise to be your best response if you know that Villain knows that you correctly made your first adjustment and you believe that your opponent correctly found the best response to that. And so on. In fact, the terms *perceived ranges* and *perceived strategy* refer to what Villain thinks your strategy is. In practice, if you are trying to stay one level ahead in this adjustment process, it is Villain's response to your perceived strategy that is most important.

When choosing spots to analyze in this way, do not focus merely on special or uncommon situations. Every single situation which arises or decision you have to make can be approached in this manner, and the more common the spot, the more money you will make in the long run by playing it correctly. Finally, the way games play in certain card rooms is always changing. It is good to go through this exercise whenever you notice that some move or tendency is becoming more or less popular in your player pool.

The strategies themselves are the most valuable part of this exercise, but we saw earlier that the process of finding them is nontrivial. However, in many cases, the simple process of setting up the problem can lead to important insights. Hero's best response to his opponent's strategy will often be clear after simply specifying the decision tree and the opponent's strategy. This is because almost all players' strategies have large leaks which become apparent when they are written down and looked at closely. In practice, these players are saved primarily by the hidden information aspect of poker.

For example, suppose that Hero is raising his SB with a wide range of hands, and Villain is 3-betting from the BB fairly frequently. In one particular pot, Hero calls a 3-bet, and the flop comes A♠-9♥-3♣. Suppose that Villain's strategy at this point is to bet the flop 100% of the time, and then, if called, to check and fold to a turn bet whenever he does not have an ace or better. This probably describes, with good accuracy, the strategies of many mediocre tight-aggressive players and is likely to work well for them against many opponents, at least until their tendency is found out. Once you have it, however, Hero's maximally exploitative postflop play becomes obvious for a wide range of stack and bet sizes. He should call the flop bet 100% of the time and then bet his bluffs on the turn when checked to.

Finally, calculating exact best response strategies manually can be tedious, especially when considering decision trees which include many strategic options, cards to come off, etc. A computer program is thus very useful for solving these situations. All of the game theoretic calculations in this book were performed using custom software. However, there exists publicly-available software which is capable of doing exactly what we are discussing in this section: defining an approximate decision tree, defining one player's strategy, and finding his opponent's best response. Using a software package to find the exact answers is also helpful for testing one's intuition. We can first try to "solve" a situation using our best guess, and then calculate the exact strategies to see how close we were.

2.2.3 The Equilibration Exercise Applied

An example will aid in understanding this exercise and seeing why it can be so useful. We will analyze the river action in the following hand.

Effective stacks: 75 BB
Preflop:
Villain raises to 2.5 BB, Hero calls 1.5 BB
Flop: J♠ 6♥ 3♠ (Pot: 5 BB)
Hero checks, Villain bets 3 BB, Hero raises to 9 BB, Villain calls
Turn: J♦ (Pot: 23 BB)
Hero bets 15 BB, Villain calls
River: 2♦ (Pot: 53 BB)

There are 48.5 BB behind on the river.

Since we are only looking at one subtree, not a whole hand, we have to assume some ranges for both players at the beginning of the river play. That is, we have to make some assumptions about the players' ranges for getting to the river in this way. Our focus in this example is on the river, but in order to choose these starting ranges and to get a feel for the hand in general, we give some thoughts on the early-street play. Keep in mind that the results of our river analysis will depend strongly on the choice of these ranges. Later we will take more holistic approaches to hands.

We will narrow down the players' ranges starting with the preflop play. Suppose that both players are competent, thinking, and aggressive. Hero is in the BB, and Villain is opening a wide range on the button, say 80% of hands. Hero is continuing versus a raise with something like 40% of hands but tends to 3-bet with the strongest of those. His flat-calling range is largely composed of strong but not premium preflop holdings.

The flop comes J-6-3 with a flush draw. Villain is likely going to continue betting with most of his hands on this flop: with only one high card, it is relatively unlikely to have hit Hero's calling range, so it is a reasonable spot to try to bet and take it down. Hero is likely to check-raise the flop for value with good jacks, 3-3, 6-6, J-6 if he happens to defend it preflop, and the occasional slow-played over-pair. He may also check-raise semi-bluff with spades or straight draws.

Additionally, because of Villain's perceived high bluff frequency on this flop, Hero is also likely to check-raise bluff with even weaker hands with some frequency. The presence of the flush draw is important to Hero's check-raise bluffing strategy. Firstly, Villain will have to be less prone to 3-betting the flop as a re-bluff since the flush draw's presence gives Hero a lot more hand combinations with which he can go all-in. On the other hand, Hero might be more prone to check-raise bluffing this flop if his hand contains a single spade since he can often continue his bluff profitably on spade turns.

So Hero raises the flop and Villain calls. Villain can likely call with any pair, although he could fold some weaker ones, and he can also have either draw. He may also choose to slow-play some strong value hands. Notice the difference between the two players' ranges at this point. Both can likely have most of the draws, and both can hold very strong hands (although this is relatively rare as strong hands are hard to make). Villain, however, has a lot of weak-to-mid strength made hands but few-to-no pure bluffs. Hero, on the other hand, figures to have more medium-to-strong hands such as good jacks judging by his tighter preflop range, aggressive play, and tendency to not check-raise middle pairs, but he also likely has more pure bluffs as well.

The turn pairs the jack. This card is generally very good for all hands that were made on the flop but bad for any drawing hands. Villain's middle pair holdings become significantly stronger since there are less ways Hero can have a jack. For this reason, this turn presents a fairly poor spot for Hero to continue with a bluff. Of course, since both players know that it is a bad spot to bluff, a bluff may get a lot of credit. Also, Hero may plan to go all-in on a lot of rivers to exert maximum pressure on Villain's weaker made hands. Hero's turn bet sizing is also interesting as it would put him in an unfortunate spot with good draws if he were to get jammed on. Thus, the turn bet may exclude some of these from his range.

Finally, the 2♦ river is, like the turn, largely good for made hands and bad for draws, as it improves only some (relatively unlikely) straight draws. As a result, Hero's range on the river contains a sizeable amount of hands with no showdown value as well as many strong-to-nut hands. Villain may have somewhat less air as he would have sometimes played strong draws more aggressively or folded weak draws on earlier streets. He still has many more weak-showdown type hands than Hero such as threes, sixes, and pocket pairs.

For concreteness, we will assume that Hero's range at the beginning of the river play is A♣-J♣, K♣-J♣, Q♣-J♣, J♣-10♣, 5♣-4♣, K♣-J♥, Q♣-J♥, K♦-J♣, Q♦-J♣, 5♦-4♦, K♦-J♥, Q♦-J♥, K♥-J♣, Q♥-J♣, A♥-2♥, A♥-5♥, A♥-8♥, A♥-J♥, K♥-J♥, Q♥-J♥, J♥-10♥, A♠-10♣, K♠-J♣, Q♠-J♣, A♠-10♦, A♠-10♥, K♠-J♥, Q♠-J♥, Q♠-6♠ - Q♠-10♠, 10♠-7♠, 9♠-7♠, 8♠-7♠, 3♦-3♣, 3♥-3♣, 3♥-3♦, 6♠-6♣, 6♦-6♣, 6♦-6♠, A♠-A♣, A♦-A♣, A♥-A♣ excluding those hands which conflict with the board. This is 45 hand combinations. This includes half of the combinations of hands such as A-A and A-Js which could have been 3-bet preflop, all 6-6, 3-3, many good jacks, some pure bluffs, and some draws.

We will assume that Villain's range at the beginning of the river play is 44-55, 77-JJ, A3s, A6s, K6s, KJs, Q6s, QJs, J2s+, 62s-64s, A6o, K6o, Q6o, J4o+, T6o, 96o, 86o, 76o, 65o, 10♠-4♠+, 9♠-4♠+, 8♠-4♠+, 7♠-6♠, 6♠-5♠, 3♦-3♣, 6♦-6♣, Q♠-Q♣, Q♦-Q♣, Q♥-Q♣, K♠-K♣, K♦-K♣, K♥-K♣, A♠-A♣, A♦-A♣, A♥-A♣ excluding those hands which conflict with the board. This is 218 hand combinations. Here we have discounted both strong hands and big draws which might have played more aggressively on earlier streets.

We are now ready to specify the strategic options available to both players. To simplify the analysis, we will keep this very bare-bones. Since there is less than a pot-sized bet left, we assume any bets are all-in. This is a reasonable approach for Hero anyway since his range is so much nuts or air. For the same reason, Hero is unlikely to have any weak showdown hands he might want to check-call with, so if he checks, it is always to check-fold. Thus, Hero can shove the river in which case Villain can call or fold, or he can check and give up the hand. This decision tree is shown in Figure 2.3.

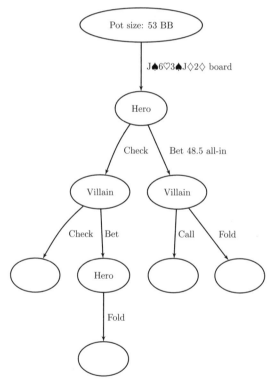

Figure 2.3: Decision tree for the river situation for which we demonstrate the equilibration exercise.

We now need to choose one of the players' strategies. Notice that there is really only one range in question here in each of the players' strategy. Hero needs to decide only on his shoving range since he check-folds everything else. Villain only needs to decide on his calling range when Hero shoves, since he folds everything else. Also, Villain should always go all-in when checked to on the river since Hero is always check-folding.

Let us start by guessing at Villain's strategy. We mentioned earlier that Hero might be prone to continue with all his bluffs on the river. Given this, Villain might think that it makes little sense to call on the turn and fold on such a harmless river with hands that can beat bluffs. Thus, let us assume to begin that Villain calls with all hands that can beat a bluff, i.e. A-high or better.

We will now go back and forth, finding the maximally exploitative strategies for each player in turn. You should, however, think about what you expect the answers to be before reading on. We will also list the expected total stack sizes at the end of the hand for each player with each strategy pair. As a point of reference, if both players were forced to check down on the river with the ranges we assigned, then Hero would win 82.5 BB on average and Villain 67.5 BB. Clearly, Hero has more showdown value here. We will see if Villain's positional advantage during the river betting round can help to even things out.

Iteration 1

Assuming Villain is calling with all hands with showdown value, his calling range is 44-55, 77-JJ, A3s, A6s, K6s, KJs, Q6s, QJs, J2s+, 62s-64s, A6o, K6o, Q6o, J4o+, T6o, 96o, 86o, 76o, 65o, 10♠-6♠, 9♠-6♠, 8♠-6♠, 7♠-6♠, 6♠-5♠, 3♦-3♣, 6♦-6♣, Q♠-Q♣, Q♦-Q♣, Q♥-Q♣, K♠-K♣, K♦-K♣, K♥-K♣, A♠-A♣, A♦-A♣, A♥-A♣ (excluding combinations which conflict with the board, of course). This is 206 hand combinations. Then, we find that Hero's best response is to shove with 33, 66, AJs, KJs, QJs, J-10s, KJo, QJo, 5♣-4♣, 5♦-4♦, Q♠-6♠, A♠-A♣, A♦-A♣, A♥-A♣ and to check-fold all of his other holdings. This is 32 hand combinations. In this case, Hero's EV is 106.8 BB. Hero has gained greatly by an exploitative betting strategy on the river.

Iteration 2

Now assume Hero is shoving with the range we found in Iteration 1. Villain's best calling range is then JJ, KJs, J2s-J3s, J6s, J6o, 3♦-3♣, 6♦-6♣. This is only 15 hand combinations. Villain folds his other 203 hands – the vast majority of his range. The EV of this is 81.9 BB for Hero.

Notice that Villain's strategy is in some sense the complete opposite of his previous one. Intuitively, in Iteration 1, Villain was never folding any hands which could beat a bluff, and so Hero was never bluffing. In reaction to Hero's no-bluffing strategy, Villain began folding all but his strong value hands. Indeed, Villain is folding hands as strong as Q-J(!), and this is his most profitable strategy if Hero is not bluffing on the river.

Iteration 3

Now assume Villain is calling with the tight value range we found in Iteration 2. Then Hero's best response is to jam with 33, 66, AJs, KJs, QJs, J-10s, KJo, QJo, 5♣-4♣, 5♦-4♦, A♥-2♥, A♥-5♥, A♥-8♥, A♠-10♣, A♠-10♦, A♠-10♥, Q♠-6♠-Q♠-10♠, 10♠-7♠, 9♠-7♠, 8♠-7♠, A♠-A♣, A♦-A♣, A♥-A♣. The EV of this play is 95.9 BB for Hero. This is 45 hand combinations. That is, Hero is shoving with the whole range of hands with which he gets to the river. Hero has begun bluffing every chance he gets in response to his opponent's tight calling range. Let us continue for a few more iterations to see how this is going to end up in the long run.

Iteration 4

Hero shoves all 45 hands with which he gets to the river. Villain can best exploit this by calling with JJ, K6s, KJs, QJs, J2s+, K6o, J4o+, A♣-3♣, A♣-6♣, Q♣-6♣, A♣-6♦, Q♣-6♦, A♣-6♠, Q♣-6♠, A♦-6♣, Q♦-6♣, A♦-6♦, Q♦-6♦, Q♦-6♠, Q♥-6♣, Q♥-6♦, Q♥-6♠, 3♦-3♣, 6♦-6♣, Q♦-Q♣, Q♥-Q♣, K♠-K♣, K♦-K♣, K♥-K♣, A♦-A♣ or 98 hands total. The EV of this spot is then 90.8 BB for Hero.

Iteration 5

If Villain calls with the 98 holdings we found in Iteration 4, then Hero's maximally exploitative strategy, it turns out, is to continue shoving with all the hands with which he gets to the river. So, the EV of this play is still 90.8 BB for Hero.

Iteration 6

If Hero shoves with the range we found in Iteration 5 (all of his 45 possible holdings), then the question of Villain's best response is a question we already answered in Iteration 4. His best response is again to call with the 98 hand combinations listed previously. The EV of this play is again 90.8 BB for Hero.

There are a couple of things to notice here. First, the differences in strategies between the first few adjacent iterations are large. We start out with Villain calling with 206 hands. Against this, Hero value-bets 32 hands. But against this, Villain begins folding the vast majority of his range and only calls with 15 hands. In response, Hero bets 45 hands (all of those with which he gets to the river), and subsequently, Villain adopts a more moderate calling range. Coming up with these exploitative strategies, at least approximately, is easy once you know your opponent's strategy. If Hero is not bluffing, Villain should not call much, etc. Additionally, the player who is playing exploitatively in these situations was able to improve his expectation greatly.

After the fourth iteration, however, the nature of the play changes significantly. This iteration starts with Hero shoving all of the hands with which he gets to the river. Villain's best response is to call with 98 hands. Then in the fifth iteration, we find that Hero's best response is to keep shoving all hands. In the next iteration, since Hero's strategy did not change, Villain's best response is to keep calling with 98 hands. You can convince yourself that both players' strategies would stay constant as many times as we went back and forth since neither has any incentive to deviate. They are simultaneously both playing as profitably as possible given the other's strategy. This rather special situation is the topic of the next section.

Before we get to that, however, let us take a closer look at these strategies and see why they are both playing maximally exploitatively versus each other, at the same time. First, consider Hero's strategy. His options are to fold and give up the pot or to go all-in, and he finds it better to go all-in with all of his hands. Why is this? Well, consider Hero's weakest bluffing hands. If he checks and gives up he ends up with 48.5 BB. If he bets, Villain calls with 98 of his 218 holdings, or about 45% of the time. So, if Hero jams with pure bluffs, he ends up with his stack plus the pot = 48.5+53 = 101.5 BB 55% of the time, and he goes broke the other 45% of the time, for an average EV of about 0.55 x 101.5 = 55.8 BB. Since this is bigger than 48.5 BB, Hero's best option is to shove, even with hands that never win when called. With actual value hands which do have the possibility of getting called by worse, the advantage that jamming has over check-folding becomes even greater.

Now consider Villain's play. He has some strong value hands, some missed draws, and plenty of holdings in-between. How can he best play each of them when facing a shove? Well, if he folds, he also ends up with 48.5 BB. If he calls, he ends up with 150 x EQ_H where EQ_H is the equity of his hand H versus the BB's shoving range. He should call with any hand such that 48.5<150 EQ_H, that is, any hand which has at least 48.5/150=32.3% equity versus the BB's range. The set of such hands is the 98 holdings given above. So, nothing magical is going on here – Villain's best response strategy is simply to call when he is given the right odds to do so.

At the beginning of the previous hand example, we found the share of the pot that each player would win if both players just checked down their entire ranges without any betting. We asked if the SB's positional advantage would let him do better than this, on average. Did it? Why or why not? We will come to understand this sort of situation very well when we discuss river play.

When we introduced the equilibration exercise, we listed a series of questions which are useful to ask oneself at each step. Consider each of them in the context of this hand for the first few iterations where exploitative play is possible.

2.3 Nash Equilibria

At the end of the previous example, we found a situation where each player, upon trying to find his best response to his opponent's strategy, could not improve upon the strategy he was already playing. When Hero was shoving the river with all of his hands, Villain's best response was to call with a certain 98 hands. When Villain was calling with those 98 hands, Hero's best response was to shove all of his holdings.

Together, this pair of strategies constitutes what is called a *Nash equilibrium* for our approximate game. There are two equivalent ways of looking at and defining a Nash equilibrium strategy pair, both of which we saw above. They are two strategies such that:

♠ Both strategies are maximally exploiting the other, simultaneously.

♠ Neither player can change his strategy to improve his own expectation.

In particular, the expectation for Hero at the equilibrium was approximately 90.8 BB. This is known as the equilibrium value of the game. Neglecting the rake, HUNL is a zero-sum game. That is, all value to one player comes directly from the other. The players' combined profit must sum to zero. Thus, Villain's expectation at the equilibrium is 150–90.8 BB = 59.2 BB. When they were playing at the equilibrium, neither player could change his strategy to improve his EV.

Now, this is a pretty special set of circumstances, and it is not obvious that such a pair of strategies should always exist, especially in more complicated games. But, they do. John von Neumann is the game theorist who first proved the existence of these equilibrium strategy pairs in games such as HUNL. John Nash extended the result to a variety of different types of games.

The Nash equilibrium turns out to be an extraordinarily useful concept in analyzing the types of games in which we are interested. The reason is that two sufficiently intelligent players will always adopt equilibrium strategies when facing one another. By "sufficiently intelligent," we mean that they are both capable of determining maximally exploitative and equilibrium strategies (and that they are both aware of each other's capabilities).

To see why this is the case, suppose that two players, *A* and *B*, are playing non-equilibrium strategies. From the definition, this means that at least one of them, say player *A*, will be able to change his strategy to improve his expectation. He will do this because he likes money. His new exploitative strategy will give him an expectation greater than (or equal to) his equilibrium one. If it did not, then it would not be a maximally exploitative strategy since he can achieve at least his equilibrium value by playing his equilibrium strategy.

At this point, unless they are now playing at the equilibrium, player *B* has an expectation less than his equilibrium value. Because he is smart and likes money, he can and will adjust his own strategy. And so on. At any point during the game, one player will have an incentive to change his strategy unless they are both playing with equilibrium ranges. More specifically, unless the values of the game to both players are their equilibrium values, one of the players will necessarily be able to improve his EV by switching to his equilibrium strategy. At this point, from the definition of equilibrium, the other player will maximize his EV by playing his equilibrium strategy as well.

Because both players tend to play equilibrium strategies and have no incentive to deviate from them, the Nash equilibrium is known as a *solution concept* for this type of game. For other types of games (those with 3 or more players, in particular), other concepts might make more sense to refer to as solutions. However, we will always use the word *solving* a HUNL game to refer to finding a pair of Nash equilibrium strategies.

At this point, we can see why the equilibration exercise was given its name. As in the example of Section 2.2.3, we start with some reasonable strategies and then go back and forth finding each player's best response. Eventually, we arrive at some "happy medium" where neither player can do anything else to improve his expectation – the equilibrium. This is what happened in the example and is the best way to visualize the process in most cases.

Things do not always quite work out so nicely, however. Sometimes the players' strategies just alternate back and forth and never settle down to the equilibrium. In this case, the "happy medium" still exists, and we can find it by making a slight change in the way we have the players adjust.

Instead of switching all the way to his best response at each iteration, each player can just adjust his strategy a little bit in that direction. For example, suppose Hero's strategy involves checking a particular hand in a particular spot at one step in the process. Suppose we calculate Villain's new strategy and then Hero's new best response, and we find that the hand is now best played with a bet. Rather than switching Hero's play all the way to a bet in this spot, we update Hero's strategy to involve betting the hand 10% of the time while continuing to check the remaining 90%. Essentially, this helps the process settle down more smoothly. In this case, we can actually arrive at equilibrium strategies which involve playing a particular hand in more than one way with non-zero probability, a possibility we will discuss in more detail in Section 2.3.1. This simple equilibrium-finding method forms the basis of the algorithm known as *fictitious play*.

The Nash equilibrium also has much value from a strategic standpoint. Notice from the previous discussion that, if Hero is playing a non-equilibrium strategy, then it is possible that Villain is taking advantage of this such that Hero's EV is lower than his equilibrium value. That is, playing a non-equilibrium strategy leaves you open to being exploited. Playing the equilibrium strategy, however, guarantees Hero to gain at least his equilibrium value. For this reason, we call non-equilibrium strategies *exploitable* and equilibrium strategies *unexploitable*.

We will use the adjectives 'equilibrium', 'game theory optimal' (GTO), and 'unexploitable' interchangeably to describe and indicate Nash equilibrium strategies. Although they have slightly different connotations, these words all mean exactly the same thing for us: Nash equilibrium. The word "optimal" itself is a bit problematic. Some game theory literature uses it to mean maximally exploitative. Other game theory books use the same word to refer to equilibrium strategies. This leads to confusion since the terms mean similar things in some contexts but very different things in others. In some sense, the first way seems best since it matches up with colloquial usage of the word. However, the authors of *The Mathematics of Poker* chose the second way, helping it to gain a solid foothold in the poker community. Your present author sympathizes with the second choice, and this is reflected in this book's subtitle. That said, in order to avoid confusion, we will generally avoid unqualified use of the word 'optimal'.

A fourth term, *minimax strategy*, is also sometimes used to refer to unexploitable play since our GTO strategy is the one which *mini*mizes our *max*imum expected loss. Why is this? We arrived at unexploitable play by assuming Villain is always playing his best response to our strategy. That is, he is playing so that we lose the maximum amount given our strategy, and in this case, playing unexploitably ourselves minimizes that loss. Since HUNL is a zero-sum game, the reverse is also true – we can think of GTO play as maximizing our minimum expected win.

Now, what is the equilibrium value of the game? Notice first that players do not necessarily expect to break even when playing unexploitable strategies. In the Nash equilibrium we found for the approximate game we used to model the river situation on J♠-6♥-3♠-J♦-2♦, Hero expected to make quite a profit on the hand. Now, this was largely because we assumed he started on the river with a significantly stronger range than his opponent. However, even in the full game of HUNL, the SB will win money at the equilibrium, at least at most stack sizes. The difference can not be too large, though – we argued earlier that regardless of stack sizes, the BB's expected profit must be at least -1 BB, and the SB's expected profit must be at least -0.5 BB.

All that said, if two GTO players face each other, a player's losses in the BB will be made up for by his winnings in the SB because of the symmetry of the game, and both players will expect to break even, not accounting for the rake. That is, Hero can play his equilibrium strategy and be guaranteed to at least break even on average. He would likely even make money with his GTO strategy if Villain were playing exploitably.

Thus, it is reasonable that in actual play, Hero adopt his equilibrium strategy against an unknown opponent. We can think of this as a somewhat defensive posture from which Hero can not be exploited and from which he can observe his opponent's play. It might seem that this is unnecessarily pessimistic in that it gives an opponent a lot of credit for playing well. We will see in the next section, however, that GTO play is a good approach not only against mind-reading super-computers, but also against weaker players whose tendencies are simply unknown to us. Of course, playing a perfectly GTO strategy is currently impossible, and we will refer to our attempts to do so as *near-equilibrium* or *pseudo-equilibrium*. If and when Hero identifies an exploitable tendency in his opponent, he can change his own strategy to take advantage of it. This is known as *adjusting* or *making an adjustment*.

Thus, this is the conceptual approach we will take to match play: we will try to play unexploitably against unknown opponents and make exploitative adjustments once we make some reads. Notice, by the way, that once we deviate from GTO play to take advantage of an opponent's mistakes, we are now playing exploitably ourselves. However, this is only a problem in practice if Villain takes advantage of it. That is why, when you make an exploitative adjustment, you should always keep in mind how Villain could adjust to exploit you, and what sort of indicators you might see in his play if he were to do so.

However, it is true that in reality no opponent is a complete unknown. In live play, we will be able to make guesses as to a player's age and sex. Online, we have his location and screen name. In both venues, we know our opponent's buy-in and are also likely to know something about the general tendencies of the player pool from which he comes. Thus, we can often start making educated guesses about an opponent's play right from the start of a match and immediately adopt an exploitative strategy. Maxwell Fritz, a very successful hyper turbo HUNL player, coined the term *population tendencies* to refer to the strategy of an average opponent in a specific player pool. Explicitly studying the population tendencies in your games and adjusting to them before you ever sit down at a table is an important skill in HUNL, especially in formats such as the hyper turbo single-table tournament where you are likely to play only a few hands versus a particular opponent.

Conceptually, this approach to match play is the same as the original one. We started out by considering GTO play, we made some assumptions about how Villain was likely to deviate from it, and we began exploiting those deviations. It is just that we did so by considering the average tendencies of the players in our games rather than those of our particular opponent. We will usually talk about starting matches playing a pseudo-equilibrium strategy in order to observe and adjust from there, but this is just for convenience of discussion. In reality, we will often do some amount of learning and adjusting before a match actually starts. Of course, it is important to re-adjust as quickly as possible when our initial assumptions turn out to be inaccurate.

2.3.1 Balance

A strategy describes how you will make every decision you can be faced with in a game. A *pure strategy* is one in which the same play is always made in the same situation. In rock-paper-scissors, there are three pure strategies available: always throw rock, always throw paper, and always throw scissors. A *mixed strategy* is one which involves playing more than one pure strategy with some probability. For example, if you sometimes 3-bet and sometimes just call with aces when facing an open-raise in the BB, you are playing a mixed strategy. Playing a mixed strategy is crucial to long-term success in some games (such as rock-paper-scissors), but it is not immediately obvious that this is the case in HUNL.

Equilibrium strategies are maximally exploitative when played versus an unexploitable opponent, so in this case, they share all the properties of best response strategies that we saw earlier. In particular, GTO play never involves playing a hand less profitably than it might otherwise be for the sake of "balancing" or "protecting one's ranges". Again, it is easy to see why this is the case. Suppose there was such a play in Hero's equilibrium strategy. Then, he could unilaterally increase his EV by removing it. This contradicts the definition of the Nash equilibrium, and so there are no such loss-leader type moves in unexploitable strategies. Thus, the only way a hand can be played in more than one way at the equilibrium is if multiple strategic choices have exactly the same EV.

This reality appears to conflict with common but incorrect notions about game theory optimal play – that it involves the ability to "show up with any hand at any time" or that it teaches us to make losing plays with bluffs in order to gain more with our value hands. That said, if Villain is playing poorly, these wrong ideas about GTO play could work out to be true in some sense. It could turn out that playing Hero's equilibrium strategy involves playing some hands less profitably than they could be otherwise against Villain's exploitable strategy. And if this is true, it must be the case that Hero's winnings with other hands more than make up for it, on average. For example, GTO play certainly involves making bluffs. When a GTO strategy involves using a hand to bluff, it is because bluffing is at least as profitable as any other action we could take with that hand, at least when facing an unexploitable opponent. However, if we continue playing this strategy versus a particularly loose opponent, it may be that we begin to lose money with our bluffs since Villain is not folding enough. In this case, the profit we gain from our value hands more than makes up for it.

However, this is not the fundamental reason for why GTO strategies are the way they are. They are certainly not "designed" to lose with some hands in order to gain more with others. Equilibrium strategies arise from the attempt to play every hand as profitably as possible when Villain is trying to do the same. In general, since we like money, we should usually try to play all our hands as profitably as possible at all times, regardless of whether or not Villain is playing exploitably. Certainly, it is not the recommendation of game theory that we give up potential profits for the sake of balance. The proper conception of balance and its use in real play are often misunderstood and deserve a bit more elaboration.

Balance refers to a couple related properties of strategies. First, balanced strategies generally involve playing multiple different hands the same way. This is obviously very often correct for information-hiding reasons. It also refers to playing a single hand multiple different ways, something which may seem less reasonable given the proceeding discussion. However, it turns out that many situations do arise in GTO play where multiple actions have exactly the same EV and where hands should be played in more than one way. We can think of this as arising naturally out of the equilibration exercise. Let us take an example.

Consider the case of play with pocket pairs 22-55 facing an open-raise in the BB with effective stacks of 35 BB. We will address preflop play more systematically later, but for now, notice that 3-betting all-in with such hands at this stack size can make a lot of sense. Since these small pocket pairs are a small favorite over most hands with two overcards, it is difficult for an opponent who is open-raising a large fraction of his SBs to take advantage of this play even if he knows the BB's hand. He will rarely have a good enough hand to be happy to call. So, going all-in will be superior to folding these hands for the BB. Furthermore, it is likely that shoving is better than calling or making a smaller 3-bet since small pocket pairs are often weak and hard to play profitably postflop.

Suppose, then, that Villain is in the SB and is raising a lot of hands to 2 BB, and Hero is going all-in preflop with 22-55 but is playing all other hands differently since he figures that all of his other hands can be played more profitably otherwise. Now, what is Villain's best response? He will happily call the shove with all pairs 44+. Also, although Villain must fold most of his overcard hands to the all-in, he can actually profitably call with more unpaired hands than you might think. The exact range is not important here, but it is about 38% of all hands and includes holdings as weak as 8-5s and 8-6o. Hands such as J-10s are actually significant favorites preflop versus small pocket pairs.

So, suppose Villain starts calling all-in with all of these hands. At this point, it is no longer the case that all of Hero's non-small pair hands are best played in a way other than shoving. Because Villain is calling the shove with such a wide range of hands, shoving has become a very profitable option for Hero with hands like A-K or even those such as A-A or K-J. In fact, shoving with a lot of these strong holdings will likely then be much more profitable than playing them any other way. Thus, Hero's counter-adjustment involves beginning to shove all-in preflop with a variety of high-card and premium holdings.

But now, how will Villain re-adjust? He will stop calling the shoves "light," and Hero's play will lose much of its value. However, Villain also adjusts to the fact that Hero's non-shoving preflop ranges include no premium hands such as A-K. He will become more willing to put in a lot more money with weaker aces and kings both postflop and in preflop situations after Hero has 3-bet not-all-in. In this case, playing A-K his original way (perhaps with a non-all-in 3-bet) becomes much more valuable for Hero, and maybe he switches back...at which point the process starts over. In the end, there is some happy medium between 0% and 100% for Hero's frequency of shoving preflop with various strong hands. If he never shoves with big high cards but only with small pairs, Villain's adjustments make it very profitable for him to do so. If he always shoves with his high cards, however, the play loses value, and Villain's counter-adjustment incentivizes him to switch back. In particular, whenever the EV of one line is greater than that of the other, Hero plays it the first way a little more often, but then Villain's counter-adjustment devalues that choice just a little. Thus, the only time when Hero is not incentivized to change his strategy is at the equilibrium where the EVs of both choices must be equal.

Of course, it is probably not the case that the BB's true equilibrium strategy at 35 BB includes some chance of 3-bet shoving preflop with all of his strong holdings. Hands like A-A are probably going to be more profitably played with a smaller 3-bet or even a call. That said, 3-bet shoving small pocket pairs is probably a significant part of the the BB's GTO strategy in this situation for the reasons given above, and clearly shoving with *some* big card hands will be necessary for balance reasons. By "balance reasons," we do not mean that it is necessary to "protect" the small-pair part of our shoving range but simply that shoving these big card hands is our most profitable option versus an opponent who is capable of calling it off light after observing our strategy. Holdings such as A-K are probably good choices for this purpose.

Since balance is an important concept, we will consider a couple of post-flop examples as well. Suppose Hero defends a raise out of position 150 BB deep and the flop comes Q♥-9♥-4♠. How are his flush draws played at the equilibrium? It should be fairly intuitive now that, at the equilibrium, flush draws are sometimes played with a check-call and sometimes a check-raise (and sometimes perhaps other ways as well, but we will consider just the two options for simplicity).

Let us suppose Hero always check-raises flush draws on this flop. Then, when he does check-call the flop and the third heart hits (a fairly frequent occurrence), he can not have a flush. Villain, in this case, would be very prone to putting in a lot of money with flushes but also with weaker value hands since he need not worry that Hero has a flush. Furthermore, as we will show later, the fact that he has so many value betting hands allows him to get away with having a very wide bluffing range as well. All in all, Villain will be able to play very profitably knowing that Hero can not have a flush, and his play will involve putting in a lot of money with many non-flush hands. Of course, the thing to notice here is that, at this point, it has become very profitable for Hero to check-call the flop with his flush draws because Villain is so prone to putting in money when the flush comes in. And so, when Hero always check-raises with flush draws, Villain's counter-strategy incentivizes him to begin check-calling them.

On the other hand, if Hero always check-calls with his flopped flush draws and Villain adjusts, the situation changes for Hero's flush draw hands such that check-calling loses most of its value and check-raising becomes very profitable. The reason for this is analogous to the one described previously. If Hero can not have a flush after he check-raises and the third heart comes, Villain can take advantage of the situation by playing very aggressively, and this incentivizes Hero to check-raise some flush draws.

Thus, at the equilibrium, Hero will sometimes check-call and sometimes check-raise with his flush draws. If Hero is playing near the equilibrium but has deviated such that the EV of a check-raise is greater than that of a check-call, then he can move towards the equilibrium and increase his EV by check-raising a little more and check-calling a little less, and vice versa.

Now, we are glossing over a few details here. For example, depending on the board and the situation, it may be the case that Hero's equilibrium strategy involves check-raising with 8♥-7♥ 100% of the time, check-calling with A♥-4♥ 100% of the time, and playing each of his other flush draw holdings exactly one way or the other. In this case, he is not really playing a mixed strategy despite the fact that he is sometimes raising and sometimes calling with flush draws. However, I think the big ideas are clear.

In general, it will often be the case that Hero will want to play a type of hand a variety of different ways. Not doing so will lead to Villain playing an exploitative strategy which takes advantage of the knowledge that Hero can not have certain hands in a certain spot. At this point, it usually becomes the case that showing up with those unexpected hands becomes very profitable for Hero. On the other hand, it is not the case that Hero should be able to have "any hand in any spot." It is sometimes not worth it to protect oneself from contingencies which happen rarely, especially in shorter-stacked situations.

Now, it may seem at this point that GTO play and balanced ranges as we have described them are mostly just useful for defensive purposes when playing against an opponent who magically knows our ranges and is also very skilled at computing counter-strategies. However, it is also very reasonable to try to play pseudo-equilibrium versus a new opponent who you do not know much about, even if you expect him to be a relatively weak player. Consider the following turn spot where Hero is in the BB. Villain is largely unknown to Hero and may or may not be a good player.

Effective stacks: 30 BB
Preflop:
Villain raises to 2.5 BB, Hero calls
Flop: K♣ 7♥ 3♦ (5BB)
Hero checks, Villain checks
Turn: K♦ (5BB)

What is Hero's play on the turn with each part of his range? Of course, it depends on the SB's range for checking back on the flop. The first standard thought here is that the SB probably does not have an especially strong hand since he did not bet the flop. On the other hand, he likely has a little something or else he would have taken the opportunity to bluff on this board. That is, something like A-high or bottom pair make up a lot of many players' ranges in the SB's position here. So, a value-bet is usually in order for Hero with any hand that can beat bottom pair, but what about the weaker hands that make up most of Hero's range on this board?

Villain's weak made hands are ahead of most of these, but they may not be able to stand too much heat. So, one approach is to go for a semi-bluff play. We bet, expecting the SB to fold many hands which are actually ahead of us. If he calls, we still have a good chance of making a hand to value bet on the river, since most rivered pairs will be sufficient to value-bet. So, we have two ways to make money with the semi-bluff: Villain can fold outright, and if he does not, we can still improve to win the hand. Additionally, building the pot on the turn lets us put in a bigger bet and get more value if we do improve on the river, and it also gives us the opportunity to make a bigger and scarier bluff there as well if we decide to try to take him off a weak hand that he checked back on the flop.

This thought process makes some sense with most of our weak hands here when they are considered by themselves, but what would our entire strategy look like if we took this approach? We would be betting with almost our entire range. Is that a problem? Well, it depends on Villain's strategy. Certainly, we are in danger of simply getting called down a lot by high-card hands. Indeed, some opponents know that they have weak ranges after checking back the flop but do not believe that we often have much either and frequently decide to call down on a lot of turn and river cards with weak hands that can only beat bluffs. Against this type of player, our plan to bet the turn and river a lot with bluffs is terrible! Even with a "real" draw such as diamonds, we probably do not make our hand often enough to make the semi-bluff profitable versus this opponent. Our best plan in this case is likely to only bet when we can do so for value.

On the other hand, some players are not so suspicious and are prone to just give up any unpaired holding when facing a turn lead. Versus an opponent with this strategy, we should probably bet the turn with our bluffs but give up on the river if we are called since Villain must have had something decent to call on the turn. A bet on the river would just be giving money away. Other guys will call one street with high-card-type holdings but then give them up on the river. Versus these, bluffing one street and then giving up is our worst choice, bluffing twice is probably best, and not betting at all is somewhere in-between.

The point is that we can not confidently make any exploitative play unless we have some reads on Villain's tendencies that we can exploit. If Villain is folding all of his unpaired hands to turn leads and all low pairs to a river bet, then betting twice with a ton of our hands is great. If he is calling down with high cards frequently, then that strategy is terrible. Versus some players, betting just the turn but giving up if called is our best line, and versus others, it is the worst.

 What Villain tendencies might make over-bet leading, under-bet leading, check-raising the turn, or checking the turn but bluffing the river each be best?

So, without reads, playing a pseudo-equilibrium strategy is probably best. GTO play tends to be a happy-medium sort of approach, and we will see that it tends to do well on average versus a wide variety of opponents. In this situation, GTO play will almost certainly involve leading just the turn with some (semi-)bluffs, leading the turn and river with others, and check-calling and check-folding other hands, etc. The details are material for later chapters. Anyhow, playing unexploitably versus unknown opponents is generally the best approach. Even if we assume our opponent is a poor player and is probably not capable of exploiting us on purpose, any "exploitative" approach that we take without a good reason is just about as likely to hurt as to help us, simply because we do not know how Villain is playing. Once we make some reads, we can adjust exploitatively.

2.3.2 Inducing and Encouraging Mistakes

Now, one thing which can be confusing about the use of balance at the tables is this: most opponents we encounter are not immediately adjusting to our initial strategy nor to our adjustments, nor are they playing unexploitably themselves even when we are. If they were, then to continue with the second example in the previous section, Hero would be maximizing his EV by playing a mixed strategy with his flush draws on the flop. However, versus an opponent who is not at the equilibrium and is not necessarily adjusting quickly or well to our play, one line is probably more profitable than the other, and it is likely to stay that way for many hands if not forever. In this case, our maximally exploitative response is to take the more profitable line 100% of the time, and we probably should do so.

This is a common property of many different HUNL situations. Hero's equilibrium strategy is mixed. However, as soon as Villain deviates slightly from the equilibrium, one option becomes strictly better than the other, and Hero's maximally exploitative response is to take the single most profitable action 100% of the time. That is, there is no gradual transition from the equilibrium frequency to the exploitative one.

This discussion raises some new questions about how we should approach matches against unknown opponents. We have already argued that we should start a match playing as close to the equilibrium as possible, but how should we adjust when we spot a weakness in Villain's play? Should we change our frequencies to take the most profitable line 100% of the time? We might then run the risk of Villain noticing what we are doing and changing his strategy to make fewer mistakes.

The worse a player Villain is, the less likely he is to notice if Hero turns his exploitative frequencies all the way up. Also, Villain is more likely to notice your tendencies in spots that come up often as opposed to those which come up rarely. For example, most preflop spots come up often, and most river spots come up rarely. Ultimately, Hero has to decide whether it is best to maximally exploit Villain's mistakes or whether more value will be gained in the long run by holding back a bit so Villain does not catch on. You should always, however, try to consider your strategic adjustments in these terms. Do not indiscriminately take weird or wacky lines in the name of balance.

There are, of course, many different ways to try to induce changes in Villain's strategy or otherwise encourage him to make mistakes so that you can take advantage of them. You can try to make Villain make irrational or emotional plays by needling, etc. You can try to make Villain make rational but incorrect plays by giving misleading information about your strategy. Here we are not focusing on the various ways to induce mistakes, however, but on the proper way to approach the use of any of them in a game theoretic framework. Thus, we we will just consider a single example and use it to motivate the discussion.

Suppose Hero has been playing Villain for several hundred hands, and Villain seems fairly solid and not especially prone to getting out of line. Villain is particularly tight when facing 3-bets. This fits with Villain's overall conservative tendencies. It seems as if Villain feels most comfortable avoiding play in 3-bet pots unless he has a strong holding. He raises most of his buttons but only continues in the hand when facing a 3-bet about 14% of the time. (This 3-bet defending frequency may or may not seem excessively tight to you – it certainly does to me – but it was actually pulled directly from the recommendations of an article written by a moderately successful cash game player).

Often, we see players in Hero's spot who want Villain to loosen up versus 3-bets. Perhaps these players are frustrated at not being able to build large pots preflop with their strong hands. Perhaps they are not satisfied playing so many small pots in general, they are frustrated when they fail to get action with big hands, or they think there is automatically something to be gained by taking Villain out of his comfort zone by making him take a wider range to the flop in 3-bet pots. Whatever the reasoning, Hero decides to start 3-betting especially lightly and shows his bluffs when Villain folds. He hopes this will induce Villain to widen his defending range. Take a minute to think about it before reading on – is this a good game plan for Hero? Why or why not?

To evaluate this play, we have to think about where our money is coming from in this match. In general, our money comes from taking advantage of whatever it is Villain is doing wrong. From the discussion in the previous couple of sections, we can approach this more concretely.

When Villain is playing near the equilibrium, it is hard to make money – he is not very exploitable. Of course, there is no clearly defined "distance" from the equilibrium, but in some sense, the "further" away he is from equilibrium the more exploitable he is and the more money we can make from him. Although it is not a perfect measure, we can often think about an opponent's distance from equilibrium play in terms of the difference between his frequencies and the corresponding frequencies in GTO play. This is one reason why it is helpful to have a good sense of unexploitable play in a variety of spots – to be able to identify opportunities to exploit your opponents.

What might be Villain's GTO frequency for continuing versus 3-bets? It depends on stack sizes and Hero's 3-bet size, but Villain's equilibrium 3-bet defense frequency will almost always be larger than his current 14%. Suppose that Hero has decided that Villain's unexploitable continuing frequency would be about 35%, a reasonable enough number in many cases. Is it clear now whether his attempt to induce a change in Villain's strategy was a good idea?

What if the plan works as expected? Villain will loosen up his 3-bet calling frequency which will then grow upwards, closer to 35%, the unexploitable frequency. That is, Villain will be playing closer to the equilibrium and so less exploitably, and thus Hero will be able to make less money from him. This is the primary reason why Hero's plan was a bad one – it is making Villain play less exploitably, a generally unprofitable move.

Also consider for a moment how the plan might fail to work as expected. In particular, short-term gameflow issues could significantly affect the play. The very next time Hero 3-bets after showing the bluff, might Villain not expect him to be strong? If Hero just showed a 3-bet bluff, would he really 3-bet bluff again immediately afterwards? Maybe, taking this line of thought, Villain actually decides to tighten up a bit or continue his conservative play, for a while at least, after Hero shows his bluff. This is a potentially good result for Hero, but only if he expects it. If he expects the opposite, as is likely given his initial plan, it can lead to poor strategy decisions. This is a secondary reason that Hero's play is no good – at least without some further reads, it is not clear what effect showing a 3-bet bluff could have, and this uncertainty leads to less effective exploitation of Villain.

Finally, it is worth considering the argument that perhaps inducing Villain to play "better" preflop might be made up for by profitable spots postflop where Villain is out of his comfort zone. Maybe Villain is prone to play back at perceived 3-bet bluffs by calling more preflop but he still folds to flop bets with a high frequency. This is possible. However, the immediate preflop edge described here is a big one, and it is very rarely correct to give up an immediate edge for an uncertain one in the future. It is often better to milk guaranteed edges for whatever they are worth for as long as possible. At the same time, you can keep an eye out for the preflop-loosening-up adjustment he is likely to make eventually if you exploit him by 3-betting a high frequency. When it comes, you can then take advantage of his postflop tendency to fold to continuation bets, if this tendency does happen to materialize. In some sense, there are often only so many iterations in the equilibration game before it reaches equilibrium – take advantage of each edge for as long as possible.

We can summarize the important points to keep in mind when considering making plays to induce exploitable changes in an opponent's strategy.

♠ Determine specifically which tendency you are trying to affect, such as Villain's continuing frequency versus 3-bets.

♠ Estimate Villain's equilibrium strategy in this situation, such as continuing with some 35% of hands.

♠ Compare the unexploitable strategy to Villain's current play.

♠ Consider only making moves to make him play worse (that is, further from equilibrium).

♠ Make sure your moves will have the desired effect. This requires some amount of experience or psychology. However, if you show a bluff and then find yourself uncertain about Villain's response, you are likely to be less profitable against him, not more profitable. Inducing Villain to change his strategy in an unpredictable fashion is usually worse than not making him change at all.

♠ Do not forget to consider other tendencies your play might affect. For example, if showing a 3-bet bluff makes you look bluffier in general, it could increase his frequency of playing back at you in spots other than 3-bet defense.

Taking this discussion into account, we can reconsider the play against our tight opponent. If anything, we would like to try to induce Villain to play even tighter versus 3-bets and thus be more exploitable. Perhaps Hero could accomplish this by just showing premium hands after 3-betting. It is possible that this would make Villain feel good about whatever tight fold he just made and encourage him to make more folds in the future. However, this plan is fairly prone to backfiring as well. Villain is likely to at least ask himself why his opponent is showing some strong hands especially when he has been 3-bet so frequently, and his assumption is likely to be that Hero must have bluffs the times he does not show. And so Villain will start thinking about whether he is being exploited by those 3-bet bluffs and will probably come away from it playing a bit better. In general, in spots where Villain is playing so poorly as he is in this section's example, it is generally best not to draw his attention to the issue in any way if possible so that he keeps making the same mistake simply for lack of giving it enough thought.

Thus, the situation described here is perhaps one of the rare ones where trying to play maximally exploitatively might not be appropriate. What would maximally exploitative play actually entail?

Choose a reasonable stack size, 3-bet size, and Villain SB opening frequency corresponding to the games you play and the opponent described in this section. Suppose that Villain only continues versus a 3-bet 14% of the time. When facing a preflop open raise in the BB, what is Hero's EV of folding a hand? What is his EV of 3-betting if we assume that he just gives up and loses the pot whenever he is called?

In the above problem, you probably found that 3-betting was better than folding, even in the worst-case scenario that Hero gives up the pot whenever he is called. In reality, Hero should certainly be able to do even better than this with the 3-bet, even with a simple strategy which only involves putting more money in the pot when he flops a particularly strong hand. So, what consequences does this have for our strategy versus this opponent? Basically, our maximally exploitative strategy will never involve folding to a preflop raise. With a weak hand that we might fold versus most opponents, it turns out that we do better to just 3-bet instead.

However, if we *never* fold out of position to a raise preflop, and instead 3-bet most of the time, even the dullest of opponents is likely to notice and then start to play better. So, in this case, it might be best to hold back and not play maximally exploitatively in order to preserve the very profitable situation we have here. Instead, perhaps we could 3-bet bluff with a high frequency but continue to fold often as well. Additionally, we should probably just flat call with all of our strong and premium hands. First, these play fine postflop and are indeed likely played more profitably by taking a flop since Villain will just fold so often if we 3-bet. Second, we are trying to limit our total 3-betting frequency, and flatting these helps to keep our overall 3-betting frequency low which lets us save our 3-bets for bluffing hands which actually do gain a lot of EV by being 3-bet.

All that said, situations where you know a play is maximally exploitative but you should do something else instead really are few and far between. You would likely do fine to just assume they never happen and always take the most profitable line when you know it. Doing otherwise can be used to maximize long-term profit, but there is also a big risk of using these ideas to rationalize bad play. In particular, you really should not give most opponents too much credit for being able to realize what you are doing and counter it effectively. Only in spots like the one described in this section which come up almost every other hand are your extreme frequencies bound to be recognized and correctly adjusted to by most players. In spots which occur less often (such as those which come up on later streets), you should almost always just make the most profitable play whenever you can. Besides, you usually do not know how many hands you will get to play against a particular opponent, so you might as well make the most money while you can.

2.4 Conclusions

We began this chapter by dividing strategic play into two parts: (1) find Villain's strategy, and (2) find Hero's best response. For simplicity, we approached (2) first. We developed the ideas necessary to solve exactly for Hero's maximally exploitative response to any of Villain's possible strategies. This discussion led naturally to the concept of unexploitable or Nash equilibrium play. With these tools, we laid out a broad strategic framework for approaching a HUNL match versus a new opponent: start out playing near-equilibrium, make reads, and then adjust appropriately. Discussions of balance and inducing mistakes provided occasion to elaborate a bit on the nature of GTO play and to introduce some of the considerations which might arise when implementing adjustments.

Our task for the rest of this book will be to expand on these ideas. In particular, we want to:

- ♠ Explore what GTO strategies look like in HUNL and develop some general principles for estimating them on the fly.

- ♠ Develop intuition and methodology for identifying Villain's strategy.

- ♠ Explore what maximally exploitative strategies look like and develop some principles for estimating them during play.

We will start with the simpler cases in order to develop some intuition and a few more technical tools. We turn first to simple preflop-only games. Our analysis will make use of and help us to better understand the ideas we have developed in this chapter.

2.5 You Should Now...

♠ Be comfortable with our (somewhat non-standard) use of the term EV, and understand the difference between expected value, expected profit, and equity

♠ Understand the method underlying our approach to almost every strategic situation – evaluate the EV of each of our options and go with the largest

♠ Know what a best response strategy is, be familiar with some of its properties, and know how to find it given a decision tree and Villain's strategy

♠ Know how to find the value of playing such a maximally exploitative strategy

♠ Understand the equilibration exercise and have used it to work through some strategies and counter-strategies in a couple situations of interest to you

♠ Know what we mean by a Nash equilibrium strategy, have an intuitive sense for how we might find such a pair of strategies, and understand why it makes sense to refer to them as the solution to a game

♠ Understand the connection between best response strategies and equilibrium strategies

♠ Properly understand the concept of balance

♠ Be familiar with our general approach to play versus a new opponent

Chapter 3

Preflop-only Games

The deal is of no special value, and anybody may begin – Robert Schenck, 1872

Before diving into the meat of multi-street play, we will consider preflop-only games – approximate games which include only preflop betting. Preflop play is relatively simple since the ranges the players start with are well known and have a simple structure, and preflop-only games are even simpler since there are no future cards to worry about.

On the other hand, we will see that these games are actually quite relevant, especially in short-stacked play where getting it all-in preflop is very common. In deep-stacked play, a postflop component will usually be important, but the discussion will still directly apply to certain deep-stack situations. Studying these games will also give us a chance to get a better feel for the theory we have talked about so far. Additionally and most importantly, many critical HUNL concepts and themes will come out of our analysis of these relatively simple situations.

We will start with the simplest preflop-only games and gradually introduce complexity. In practice, this will also mean that we start by considering the shortest-stacked situations and move deeper so that we can focus on regimes where the games might approximate real play.

3.1 Shove/fold

The very simplest HUNL game is preflop shove/fold. Its tree is shown in Figure 3.1, and we have labelled the SB's payoffs at each leaf. First, the SB can either fold or shove, and, if he shoves, the BB can either call or fold. Since each player has just one decision point with two options, only two ranges are needed to fully specify the players' strategies: the SB's shoving range and the BB's calling range. Most of our discussion of this game will focus on very short-stacked situations since that is where it might best approximate real play.

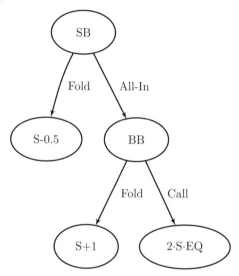

Figure 3.1: Decision tree of the shove/fold game. The total expected SB stack size is written on each leaf where S is the players' starting stack size and EQ refers to the SB's equity versus the BB's range.

We will neglect a detailed explanation of the process of finding solutions for this game and most others in this book. However, working through some of the calculations yourself can be helpful since an understanding of the process is important for developing intuition about game-theoretic play. Review Chapter 2 if it has gotten fuzzy.

GTO ranges for the shove/fold game depend on the effective stack size.

There is a compact way to show ranges at all stack sizes. We use a table which is labelled A-2 horizontally and vertically so that each square represents a hand. For example, the top left square represents A-A. You might notice that each non-pair hand is represented twice in this construction. For example, AK is both to the left of and directly below A-A. We use this doubling of non-pair hands to indicate suitedness: hands listed above the diagonal (that is, those on the upper-right portion of the table) are suited, and those below the diagonal are unsuited. In the square corresponding to each hand, we indicate the stack sizes for which the hand is contained in the range. Thus, we can represent the range at all stack sizes in a single chart.

This representation has a couple of disadvantages. We can not distinguish between hands which differ only by suits (e.g. Q♣-J♣ and Q♠-J♠), but this is unimportant preflop. We also can not express situations where a hand is only fractionally in a range, i.e. where a hand is played sometimes one way and sometimes another. These are the prices we pay for having a compact way to express the information.

In this way, we show the GTO SB shoving ranges in the shove/fold game for stack sizes up to 100 BB in Figure 3.2. Similarly, BB calling ranges are shown in Figure 3.3. The numbers in the squares indicate those stack sizes for which a given hand is in the range. Single numbers in the table indicate that the corresponding hand is contained in the range at all stack sizes up to that number. These tables were generated by solving the game at stacks from 1 to 100 BB in intervals of 1/10BB. To deal with cases where hands are fractionally contained in the ranges, we indicate that a hand is in the range if it is with frequency greater than 50 percent.

There are also a number of cases where a hand's occupancy in a range does not go quickly and smoothly from 1 to 0 at any particular threshold stack size. It fluctuates up and down, passing the 50% mark several times. This is illustrated in Figure 3.4 where we show the fractions of a particular hand in the equilibrium SB shove range with respect to stack size. In these cases, we pick a representative value for the sake of the chart or, when no such single value can be chosen, indicate several ranges of values. Much more care has been taken to maintain the details of the solutions at low stack sizes where they are likely to be used in real play.

SB shoving ranges

	A	K	Q	J	T	9	8	7	6	5	4	3	2
A	100+	100+	100+	100+	100+	90.5	71.9	56.5	51.2	100+	*	*	47.5
K	100+	100+	100+	100+	100+	77.4	55.4	49.0	36.2	32.2	25.1	19.9	19.3
Q	100+	79.4	100+	100+	100+	70.3	50.5	30.2	29.4	24.4	16.3	13.5	12.7
J	100+	79.2	53.9	100+	97.3	71.4	49.8	32.3	18.6	14.7	13.5	10.6	8.5
T	57.9	66.5	42.6	46.0	100+	72.0	53.5	35.5	24.7	11.9	10.5	7.7	6.5
9	44.8	24.1	24.3	28.3	31.8	100+	53.8	36.1	26.8	14.4	6.9	4.9	3.7
8	42.6	18.0	13.0	13.3	17.5	20.3	100+	43.3	30.9	18.8	10.0	2.7	2.5
7	39.7	16.1	10.3	8.5	9.0	10.8	14.7	88.3	35.7	23.8	13.9;	2.5	2.1
6	34.6	15.1	9.6	6.5	5.7	5.2;	7.0	10.7	100+	29.3	16.3	*	2.0
5	36.9	14.2	8.9	6.0	4.1	3.5	3.0	2.6	2.4	88.2	23.4	*	2.0
4	33.8	13.1	7.9;8.3	5.4	3.8	2.7	2.3	2.1	2.0	2.1	82.1	*	1.8
3	30.0	12.2	7.5	5.0	3.4	2.5	1.9	1.8	1.7	1.8	1.6	70.8	1.7
2	28.6	11.6	7.0	4.6	2.9	2.2	1.8	1.6	1.5	1.5	1.4	1.4	59.7

A-3s 54.2;69.6-70.2;94.0+
A-4s 57.1;66.3-72.0;82.2+
6-3s 2.3;5.1-7.1
5-3s 2.4;3.8-12.9
4-3s 2.2;4.9-7.8;8.6-10.0

Figure 3.2: Table representation of SB's shoving range in the GTO solution of the shove/fold game at different stack sizes.

BB calling ranges

	A	K	Q	J	T	9	8	7	6	5	4	3	2
A	100+	100+	100+	76.1	62.3	46.7	40.2	35.2	30.5	30.0	25.4	24.6	23.2
K	100+	100+	55.3	44.7	31.4	22.2	17.6	15.2	14.3	13.2	12.1	11.4	10.8
Q	90.2	41.5	100+	27.8	23.4	16.1	13.0	10.5	9.9	8.9	8.4	7.8	7.2
J	63.0	26.4	19.5	100+	18.0	13.4	10.6	8.8	7.0	6.9	6.1	5.8	5.6
T	50.5	23.4	15.3	12.7	100+	11.5	9.3	7.4	6.3	5.2	5.2	4.8	4.5
9	38.2	17.1	11.7	9.5	8.4	96.1	8.2	7.0	5.8	5.0	4.3	4.1	3.9
8	33.4	13.8	9.7	7.6	6.6	6.0	79.4	6.5	5.6	4.8	4.1	3.6	3.5
7	28.5	12.4	8.0	6.4	5.5	5.0	4.7	66.5	5.4	4.8	4.1	3.6	3.3
6	21.4	11.0	7.3	5.4	4.6	4.2	4.1	4.0	55.6	4.9	4.3	3.8	3.3
5	20.5	10.2	6.8	5.1	4.0	3.7	3.6	3.6	3.7	42.2	4.6	4.0	3.6
4	18.3	9.1	6.2	4.7	3.8	3.3	3.2	3.2	3.3	3.5	31.2	3.8	3.4
3	16.6	8.7	5.9	4.5	3.6	3.1	2.9	2.9	2.9	3.1	3.0	22.3	3.3
2	15.8	8.1	5.6	4.2	3.5	3.0	2.8	2.6	2.7	2.8	2.7	2.6	15.0

Figure 3.3: Table representation of BB's calling range in the GTO solution of the shove/fold game at different stack sizes.

Fraction of 43s in SB shoving range in GTO shove/fold

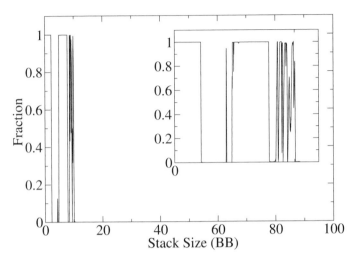

Figure 3.4: Occupancy of 4-3s in the equilibrium SB shoving range for the shove/fold game with respect to effective stack size.

Remember the meaning of these GTO solutions. Each player is playing most profitably given the strategy of his opponent. Neither player can unilaterally change his play to improve his expectation. In practical terms, this means that if the SB shoves with a particular hand at a certain stack size, then that is because shoving it is at least as profitable as folding it when facing an opponent playing unexploitably. If this were not the case, then the SB could unilaterally improve his expectation by folding that hand instead of shoving it. Similarly, the BB is playing all of his hands in the way which is most profitable versus the SB's GTO shoving range. This is a point of frequent confusion about Nash equilibrium strategies. Although it is true that if Villain deviates from equilibrium play, these unexploitable ranges are no longer maximally exploitative, it is still the case that Villain could only have lowered his expectation by deviating.

The general thrust of the solutions should be intuitive. Both players are faced with the decision: to get it in or not to get it in, and of course they get it in with some of the best hands and fold the rest. Something which stands out to many people is the fact that suited hands are in many cases shoved by the SB at much greater stack depths than their unsuited counterparts. Consider 6-5s which is in the SB's shoving range up to 29 BB as compared to 6-5o which is only in the range up to 2.4 BB. The fundamental reason for this is that shoving at these stack sizes is more profitable than folding with the suited hands but not with the unsuited hands. For example, when 20 BB deep, the total EVs of shoving 6-5s and 6-5o are approximately 19.6 BB and 19.3 BB, respectively, at the equilibrium. Since his other option, open-folding, has a total EV of exactly 19.5 BB, we see that one of the hands is indeed a profitable shove and one is not.

However, we can give a little more intuition as to why this turns out to be the case. First, remember that there are 12 combinations of 6-5o and only 4 of 6-5s. Also notice that, since they make more flushes, the suited hands do have at least as much equity versus any range. So, if the SB was only going to shove a few 6-5 hand combinations, it would make sense to add the suited ones to the shoving range first, since they are strictly better. Now, notice that the BB's calling range at 20 BB includes A-5 and A-6 but no other 5's or 6's. So, if the SB shoves 6-5 and gets called, he almost always has two live cards. The fact that 6-5 is very rarely dominated adds greatly to its value in the SB's shoving range. The reason why it is very rarely dominated is that it would be unprofitable for BB to start calling shoves with many fives and sixes besides A-5 and A-6 – they are too weak and would fare poorly versus most of the SB's shoving range. However, if the SB started shoving with too many 6-5 hands (or other low fives and sixes), then the BB's exploitative calling range would start to include K-5, Q-5, etc, and soon enough, even 6-5s would be unprofitable to shove. Therefore, it best that the SB only shove a few combinations of 6-5, and the best of those to choose are the suited ones.

Similar considerations can be used to explain the "broken" strategies of certain hands. For example, 6-3s is included in the SB's shoving range at stack sizes under 2.3 BB and from 5.1-7.1 BB, but not in between. Why is this? The SB can jam 6-3s profitably below 2.3 BB simply because stacks are so short and there is enough money in the pot from the blinds. From 2.4-5.0 BB deep, stacks are short enough that the BB is calling all-in with many threes and sixes that have 6-3s dominated. However, at slightly deeper stacks, there are less dominating hands in the BB's calling range, and shoving 6-3s becomes profitable once again.

It is interesting to quantify some card removal effects in the context of this game. At 10 BB deep, the BB's calling range contains about 496 hand combinations (37.4 percent of all hands). However, the particular holding of the SB can eliminate some of the BB's folding range and his calling ranges. How do the BB's frequencies change depending on the SB's hand? We show how some particular SB blockers change the size of the BB's ranges in Figure 3.5.

Effect of the SB's holding on the BB's frequencies

SB hand	Calling range size	Folding range size	Calling frequency
A♡A♣	394.6	830.4	0.322
K♡K♣	412.6	812.4	0.336
Q♡Q♣	445.8	779.2	0.363
J♡J♣	454.6	770.4	0.371
T♡T♣	456.6	768.4	0.372
9♡9♣	462.6	762.4	0.377
8♡8♣	470.6	754.4	0.384
7♡7♣	472.6	752.4	0.385
6♡6♣	473.8	751.2	0.386
5♡5♣	474.6	750.4	0.387
4♡4♣	480.6	744.4	0.392
3♡3♣	480.6	744.4	0.392
2♡2♣	480.6	744.4	0.392
A♡2♣	437.6	787.4	0.357
K♡2♣	445.6	779.4	0.363
Q♡2♣	462.2	762.8	0.377
J♡2♣	466.6	758.4	0.380
T♡2♣	467.6	757.4	0.381
9♡2♣	470.6	754.4	0.384
8♡2♣	474.6	750.4	0.387
7♡2♣	475.6	749.4	0.388
6♡2♣	476.2	748.8	0.388
5♡2♣	476.6	748.4	0.389
4♡2♣	479.6	745.4	0.391
3♡2♣	479.6	745.4	0.391
2♡2♣	480.6	744.4	0.392

Figure 3.5: The number of hands in the BB's GTO shove/fold ranges and his calling frequency at 10 BB deep depends on the SB's holding in a significant way.

Despite the fact that the BB has wide ranges, we see that the SB holding high-card hands actually blocks a significant amount of the BB's calling range. Similarly, if the SB holds low cards, it significantly increases the BB's calling frequency. We will see that these so-called *card removal effects* can have a significant impact on strategy, especially in spots where players' ranges are tighter.

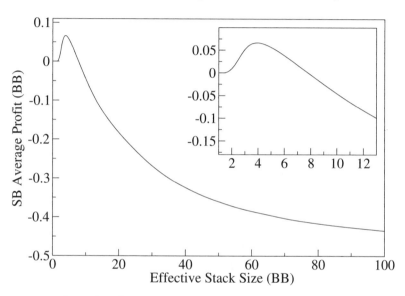

Value of the shove/fold game for the SB at equilibrium

Figure 3.6: The SB's advantage in the shove/fold game is that his blind is smaller. As stacks get deeper, this is overwhelmed by the disadvantage that comes from having to act first. At equilibrium, the SB's average profit peaks at around 4.0 BB and is non-negative until around 7.8 BB.

Now, what is the value to each player of playing these equilibrium strategies? We can plot the EV averaged over all possible holdings with respect to stack size. In Figure 3.6 we show the value of the game for the SB. Since this is a zero-sum game, the value to the BB is just the opposite. The first thing to notice is that at large stack sizes, the value of the game nearly approaches –0.5 BB for the SB. This is because at large stacks, the SB can not shove very often. He almost always just surrenders his blind.

With intermediate stacks, playing this game is still a losing proposition for the SB. Intuitively, the rules of the game are stacked against the SB. He is put to a decision for all his chips in every hand, and, at most stack sizes, with a very poor risk/reward ratio. He is forced to jam with some frequency in order to avoid giving up his blind so often, but he must risk a lot to do it. It is then relatively easy for the BB to choose a good spot to pick him off. On the other hand, at very short stacks, the game does have positive value for the SB. This is simply because of the larger size of the big blind.

Finally, to build a little more intuition about what edges look like in these situations, we consider the players' expectations with some particular holdings. We want to look at the hands' expectation at all of the decision points in the hand. First, of course, the EVs of all hands are the same if the SB chooses to fold – the SB loses a SB and the BB gains a SB. Similarly, the EVs of all hands are the same for both players after the SB shoves and the BB folds (BB loses a BB and SB gains a BB). So, we are really just interested in the EVs before any action, after SB shoves, and after BB calls. In Figure 3.7, we show the EVs for each player at each of those 3 decision points with hands A-A, A-5o, Q-Js, J-4o, 8-7o, and 5-4s, for the case of 12 BB effective stacks.

SB EVs

SB hand	Before action	After SB shove	After BB call
AA	15.09	15.09	20.59
A5o	12.40	12.40	11.05
QJs	12.31	12.31	10.90
J4o	11.5	11.22	7.67
87o	11.53	11.53	8.67
54s	11.64	11.64	9.05

BB EVs

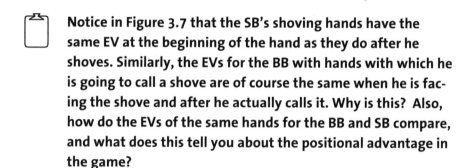

BB hand	Before action	After SB shove	After BB call
AA	16.37	20.31	20.31
A5o	12.42	12.35	12.35
QJs	12.51	12.52	12.52
J4o	11.69	11	8.80
87o	11.70	11	9.10
54s	11.68	11	9.22

Figure 3.7: The EV for each player of holding select hands at several decision points in the 12 BB shove/fold game at equilibrium.

Notice in Figure 3.7 that the SB's shoving hands have the same EV at the beginning of the hand as they do after he shoves. Similarly, the EVs for the BB with hands with which he is going to call a shove are of course the same when he is facing the shove and after he actually calls it. Why is this? Also, how do the EVs of the same hands for the BB and SB compare, and what does this tell you about the positional advantage in the game?

Now we will address exploitative strategies in the shove/fold game. That is, we want to describe how we can adjust most profitably when Villain is not playing the equilibrium strategies described above. The way we find these adjustments is just an application of the methodology described in Section 2.2. Actually, since this is such a simple game with only one decision point for each player, solving for a player's best response just amounts to a simple EV calculation for each holding. We neglect to repeat the math here, but it is important to understand, so review Section 2.2 if necessary.

There are, of course, an infinite number of Villain strategies we could consider playing against, and so it would be hard (and likely not especially profitable) to consider play against all of them individually. However, we can reasonably assume some things about the form of most players' nonequilibrium strategies. When forced to shove or fold from the SB, a reasonable SB will choose to shove some amount of the "best" hands (i.e., it does not make sense to fold with a hand *A* and call with a hand *B* if hand *A* is better than hand *B*), and the BB will construct his calling range similarly. Now, different players may have differing opinions as to which hands are better than others, but for simplicity here we will just consider hands as ranked by their preflop all-in equity versus a random hand. These ranges can then be designated simply by their size, i.e., the percent of hands they include.

SB exploitative shove/fold jamming frequencies

BB Call %	Effective stack size (BB)														
	2	3	4	5	6	7	8	9	10	12	15	18	25	50	100
5	1.00	1.00	1.00	1.00	1.00	1.00	1.00	1.00	1.00	1.00	1.00	1.00	1.00	0.79	0.09
10	1.00	1.00	1.00	1.00	1.00	1.00	1.00	1.00	1.00	1.00	1.00	1.00	1.00	0.14	0.07
15	1.00	1.00	1.00	1.00	1.00	1.00	1.00	1.00	1.00	1.00	1.00	1.00	0.49	0.13	0.09
20	1.00	1.00	1.00	1.00	1.00	1.00	1.00	1.00	1.00	1.00	0.88	0.58	0.28	0.15	0.10
25	1.00	1.00	1.00	1.00	1.00	1.00	1.00	1.00	1.00	0.89	0.57	0.36	0.26	0.18	0.13
30	1.00	1.00	1.00	1.00	1.00	1.00	1.00	0.99	0.87	0.62	0.40	0.31	0.26	0.18	0.15
35	1.00	1.00	1.00	1.00	1.00	1.00	0.94	0.79	0.66	0.46	0.35	0.30	0.27	0.21	0.17
40	1.00	1.00	1.00	1.00	1.00	0.90	0.76	0.61	0.51	0.40	0.35	0.30	0.27	0.23	0.21
45	1.00	1.00	1.00	1.00	0.91	0.75	0.60	0.51	0.46	0.39	0.35	0.32	0.30	0.26	0.22
50	1.00	1.00	1.00	0.95	0.78	0.63	0.54	0.47	0.44	0.40	0.36	0.33	0.30	0.27	0.26
55	1.00	1.00	1.00	0.84	0.66	0.57	0.50	0.47	0.44	0.40	0.38	0.35	0.32	0.29	0.27
60	1.00	1.00	0.92	0.74	0.60	0.54	0.49	0.48	0.44	0.42	0.39	0.37	0.34	0.31	0.30
65	1.00	1.00	0.84	0.67	0.59	0.54	0.49	0.48	0.47	0.44	0.41	0.39	0.37	0.33	0.31
70	1.00	0.95	0.76	0.64	0.58	0.54	0.51	0.49	0.48	0.44	0.42	0.41	0.38	0.35	0.35
75	1.00	0.90	0.71	0.63	0.59	0.54	0.52	0.50	0.49	0.48	0.44	0.43	0.41	0.38	0.36
80	1.00	0.83	0.70	0.64	0.60	0.54	0.53	0.52	0.50	0.49	0.47	0.45	0.43	0.41	0.39
85	0.99	0.79	0.70	0.63	0.60	0.58	0.54	0.53	0.52	0.50	0.49	0.47	0.45	0.41	0.40
90	0.95	0.79	0.70	0.64	0.60	0.59	0.56	0.53	0.53	0.52	0.50	0.49	0.48	0.45	0.43
95	0.91	0.76	0.70	0.65	0.60	0.60	0.57	0.57	0.54	0.53	0.53	0.51	0.50	0.48	0.47
100	0.89	0.77	0.70	0.66	0.63	0.60	0.60	0.59	0.57	0.56	0.53	0.53	0.53	0.51	0.50

Figure 3.8: SB's maximally exploitative shoving frequency with respect to stack size when BB is calling with some percentage of the top hands.

BB exploitative shove/fold calling frequencies

SB Jam %	Effective stack size (BB)														
	2	3	4	5	6	7	8	9	10	12	15	18	25	50	100
5	0.56	0.10	0.06	0.04	0.04	0.03	0.03	0.03	0.03	0.03	0.03	0.02	0.02	0.02	0.02
10	0.98	0.21	0.10	0.08	0.07	0.07	0.06	0.06	0.06	0.06	0.06	0.05	0.05	0.05	0.04
15	1.00	0.38	0.19	0.14	0.12	0.10	0.10	0.09	0.09	0.08	0.08	0.08	0.08	0.07	0.07
20	1.00	0.48	0.27	0.20	0.18	0.16	0.14	0.13	0.12	0.11	0.10	0.10	0.10	0.09	0.08
25	1.00	0.61	0.32	0.26	0.22	0.19	0.19	0.18	0.16	0.14	0.14	0.13	0.11	0.11	0.11
30	1.00	0.66	0.36	0.28	0.26	0.25	0.23	0.22	0.20	0.18	0.17	0.15	0.15	0.14	0.13
35	1.00	0.71	0.40	0.31	0.28	0.27	0.26	0.25	0.25	0.23	0.21	0.20	0.18	0.17	0.14
40	1.00	0.76	0.47	0.36	0.32	0.30	0.28	0.27	0.27	0.26	0.24	0.22	0.21	0.20	0.18
45	1.00	0.78	0.49	0.39	0.36	0.32	0.32	0.30	0.30	0.27	0.27	0.26	0.25	0.22	0.21
50	1.00	0.83	0.55	0.44	0.39	0.37	0.35	0.33	0.32	0.30	0.30	0.29	0.27	0.26	0.25
55	1.00	0.85	0.58	0.49	0.43	0.40	0.38	0.37	0.35	0.34	0.32	0.31	0.30	0.27	0.27
60	1.00	0.86	0.61	0.51	0.48	0.44	0.42	0.40	0.39	0.37	0.35	0.34	0.32	0.30	0.29
65	1.00	0.87	0.65	0.56	0.49	0.48	0.44	0.44	0.42	0.40	0.38	0.37	0.35	0.32	0.31
70	1.00	0.90	0.69	0.60	0.54	0.51	0.49	0.48	0.45	0.44	0.41	0.39	0.38	0.35	0.35
75	1.00	0.91	0.73	0.63	0.59	0.54	0.52	0.50	0.49	0.48	0.44	0.42	0.41	0.38	0.36
80	1.00	0.93	0.76	0.68	0.62	0.59	0.55	0.54	0.52	0.50	0.48	0.47	0.43	0.41	0.39
85	1.00	0.95	0.79	0.70	0.65	0.61	0.60	0.59	0.54	0.53	0.51	0.49	0.47	0.43	0.40
90	1.00	0.95	0.83	0.76	0.70	0.65	0.63	0.60	0.60	0.54	0.53	0.52	0.50	0.46	0.45
95	1.00	0.97	0.86	0.79	0.73	0.70	0.66	0.64	0.63	0.60	0.57	0.54	0.53	0.50	0.48
100	1.00	0.98	0.89	0.82	0.77	0.73	0.70	0.68	0.66	0.63	0.60	0.59	0.55	0.53	0.51

Figure 3.9: BB's maximally exploitative calling frequency with respect to stack size when SB is shoving with some percentage of the top hands.

Now, suppose that Hero is in the SB wondering what hands to shove. The SB's best response strategies for each Villain calling frequency and effective stack size are shown in Figure 3.8. Here we give Hero's shoving frequency for a variety of effective stack sizes and BB calling frequencies. This does not give Hero's exact exploitative shoving range, but the frequencies give a good idea of the range.

So, what is going on here? For example, suppose you are playing with 12 BB effective stacks. From the GTO shove/fold charts (Figures 3.2 and 3.3), we see that the equilibrium frequencies are: SB shoves 53.2% and BB calls 33%. Now, if the BB plays too tight by calling, say, 30 or 25 percent of the time, Hero's maximally exploitative strategy is to start shoving more since he gains value by stealing blinds. The tighter the BB is, the more hands we can profitably shove.

However, Hero's maximally exploitative adjustments are not always so straightforward. If the BB is calling slightly looser than GTO, Hero should jam a slightly tighter range in order to get the money in with stronger holdings versus his opponent's wide range. However, if we expand the BB's calling range even more, the trend reverses. When the BB gets to be calling all-in very loosely, the SB's exploitative shoving range starts to loosen up as well to take advantage of weakness of the BB's get-it-in range. The point here is that there is no easy exploitative method such as, "if he loosens, we should tighten, and vice-versa." There are trade-offs involved which must be weighed given the details of the situation.

Now, suppose that Hero is in the BB. The BB's maximally exploitative calling ranges with respect to stack size and SB shoving frequency are shown in Figure 3.9. Suppose that the effective stack size is still 12 BB. Then, the BB's unexploitable calling frequency is again 33%. As the SBs' shoving range gets tighter, BB calls less and less, and as the SB's shoving range gets looser, the BB calls more and more. This is simple and intuitive, and there are no trade-offs in this case.

Why is it that there is no simple trend for the SB's exploitative strategies whereas there is for the BB's? Recall the game's decision tree. The SB's decision happens first, and he is deciding between the more profitable of his two options: shove or fold. Folding always has the same EV, but the EV of shoving depends on the BB's strategy. Now, there are two reasons why shoving can be more profitable than it is at the equilibrium (i.e. there are two reasons that the SB should do it more): either the BB is folding too much or not folding enough. Either extreme is something the SB can profit from. This is a simple (overly simplistic in some ways) example of a principle of exploitative play which should be intuitive: Hero profits by giving his opponent a chance to make a mistake. In other words, he wants to make decisions that lead to part of the game tree where Villain will play badly. The SB's EV of open-folding his button is known, but the worse the BB plays facing a shove, the more value there is in taking a line that leads to that part of the decision tree.

The situation for the BB in this game is different. After the BB's decision, the hand is essentially over. So, the BB has no opportunity to make plays that lead to parts of the game tree where the SB might make a mistake. The BB must simply calculate his EVs given the events which have already occured. (In particular, the SB has already made his decision, and it was to shove.) Whereas, when SB is making his decision, it is uncertain whether or not BB will be getting it in, the reverse is not uncertain at the BB's decision point. So, the BB is just comparing the EV of folding to that of calling. The EV of folding is constant, and the EV of calling strictly decreases as the SB's shoving range gets stronger.

Now, having found each player's best response to a variety of opposing strategies, we find another way to visualize and understand what is happening at equilibrium play. The axes of Figure 3.10 indicate SB shoving frequency and BB calling frequency, that is, the single number that (approximately) represents each player's strategy. The curve labeled "SB best responses" shows just that – for any particular BB strategy, that curve gives the maximally exploitative SB strategy at 12 BB stacks. If the SB and BB are playing with frequencies that lie on that line, then the SB is maximally exploiting the BB. Similarly, the "BB best responses" curve shows BB's maximally exploitative calling frequency at that stack size. All points on that curve correspond to ranges such that the BB is maximally exploiting the SB. Recall the condition for equilibrium play – it occurs when both players are maximally exploiting each other, simultaneously. Can you see the one pair of frequencies for which this is the case? Of course – it is the point where the two curves intersect.

Finally, when and how should shove-fold strategies be used in real play? In the BB, it is easy – you are playing the shove/fold game whenever the SB wants to play it. If the SB is playing by either folding or shoving each button, then the strategies discussed in this section are directly applicable. If the SB is sometimes taking other actions, then they are not.

Many opponents have some stack size under which they switch to playing strictly shove-or-fold from the SB. For most players, this transition occurs somewhere between 6 and 13 BB deep. In order to effectively apply exploitative adjustments, it is very important to try to identify the stack size at which this happens as well as how an opponent's preflop ranges change in general with varying stack sizes.

12 BB shove/fold game best response curves

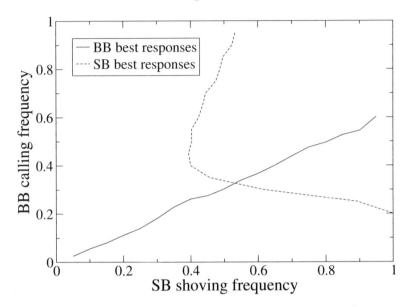

Figure 3.10: At every point on the SB Best Responses curve, the corresponding SB shoving frequency is maximally exploiting the corresponding BB calling frequency, and vice versa for the BB Best Responses curve.

What about playing shove-or-fold in the SB? Although we have thoroughly covered the decision between shoving and folding, the SB can make other plays. Evaluating these completely would be getting ahead of ourselves, but we can make a couple comments here in anticipation of later results. Consider the SB's option to make a non-all-in raise. Clearly the SB will use this option when stacks are relatively deep. To see how short the effective stack must become before this is no longer an option, we might ask the question: at which stack sizes can we raise and then fold to a shove? For, if the SB must call a shove with all of his button opening range, he may as well just open shove himself. Not doing so just gives the BB more strategic options without giving himself any, something which can only help the BB. In the next section, we will find evidence that the stack size at which the SB no longer folds to a shove after raising at the equilibrium happens at around 7 BB deep. For this reason, we suggest not playing strictly shove-or-fold above this stack size unless there is a compelling exploitative reason to do so – the option to raise-fold is valuable.

An evaluation of the SB's last option, limping, must necessarily take post-flop play into account and so must be left for later. We will see, however, that the SB's GTO strategy likely incorporates a significant amount of limping even below 7 BB deep. However, the difference in value between playing shove-or-fold and playing the full equilibrium is quite small at these short stack sizes. On the other hand, playing shove-or-fold on the button greatly simplifies the game, and the equilibrium strategies described here are fairly widely known these days. So, stronger players may find more opportunities to make exploitative plays if they do not restrict their options.

Lastly, we consider a common case where SB is only deviating slightly from a shove/fold strategy. In particular, a common tendency of weak players is to play shove/fold in the SB at sufficiently short stacks with all holdings except for premium starting hands, say JJ+. Perhaps they think that just going all-in is tantamount to wasting these strong holdings, and they want to be sneakier. How should we evaluate this strategy? Let us again take 12 BB effective stacks for example and see how the BB's strategy changes due to this SB tendency.

At this stack size, the equilibrium BB calling range is

$$\{22+, A2s+, K4s+, Q8s+, J9s+, A2o+, K7o+, QTo+, JTo\}$$

but if we remove JJ+ from the SB opening range, the BB's exploitative calling range widens to also include K-3s, 10-9s, K-6o, and Q-9o. Then, for the SB, some hands which were marginally profitable shoves might become marginally unprofitable. For example, shoving 5-3s had an EV of 11.51 BB previously but an EV of 11.41 now. However, some shoving hands become more profitable versus this wider calling range. K-Qo has an EV of 12.74 BB now, up from 12.66 BB. Overall, BB's adjustment to SB's new strategy does not much change the EVs of the hands SB is shoving.

What is much more significant is the loss of EV by the hands that are no longer being shoved. A-A, K-K, Q-Q, and J-J have expected profits of 3.1, 2.6, 2.3, and 2.1 BB, respectively, when shoved into an equilibrium calling range. So, if the BB is responding to the SB's exploitable strategy in any sort of exploitative manner, these hands will lose much of their value. The BB's exploitative response might be to play quite tight after facing a SB limp or non-all-in raise in order to avoid losing more than his BB unless he flops well. The point here is that not having premium hands in the shoving range does not largely effect the EV of the SB's other holdings too much, but it kills the EV of those premium hands versus an observant and correctly-adjusting opponent.

There are a couple other approaches to shove-or-fold play that should be mentioned. Neither of these is particularly useful. However, they are often advocated in articles describing shove-or-fold play, and it is important to clear up any confusion that this might have caused.

The SAGE system gives shove-or-fold ranges in short-stack scenarios. It was created by first assigning a numerical score to each pair of hole cards – the higher the score, the better the hand, in general. Then, the authors of the system restricted themselves to strategies which could be described by a single number, that is, strategies of the form: the SB jams all hands with a score of at least X, and the BB calls with all hands with score at least Y. Within these artificial constraints, the authors solved for the equilibrium strategies. However, there is no way to assign a score to a hand which accurately describes its value in all situations, and the SAGE system's approach, which relies heavily on the ranks of the individual cards, does an especially poor job describing play with hands such as 5♦-4♦. The system's only redeeming quality is that it is fairly easy to memorize. If you are playing in a situation where you can use a chart, then you may as well reference the true equilibrium for strategic purposes.

Chubukov numbers are the answer to the following question: suppose Hero is in the SB with a particular hand. He turns it over and shows it to his opponent. At what stack sizes is shoving still better than folding for Hero, assuming Villain plays correctly? For example, if Hero has aces, jamming is better than folding no matter how deep the stack sizes are. It does not matter that Villain knows his hand. If Hero holds K♠-Q♠ and shoves, then, at most stack sizes where shove/fold is played, Villain will call with any pair, any ace, and K-Q. However, Villain usually does not have one of these hands, and when he does, Hero still wins sometimes. It turns out that shoving is better than folding up until we are a bit over 43 BB deep. With 5♦-4♦, however, we can only shove at stacks below about 2.4 BB. This contrasts with the equilibrium shove-or-fold strategies wherein the SB shoves that hand until stacks are about 23 BB deep. The reason for the difference, of course, is that when Villain knows we hold 5♦-4♦, he can call with all kinds of hands like 7♦-2♠ that he would fold otherwise. The bottom line is that the question which is answered by the Chubukov numbers is not particularly relevant in actual play. In order to play any particular holding, we have to consider how Villain plays his whole range. And in real poker, Villain decides on his strategy by considering our ranges, not our exact hand.

3.2 Raise/shove

The second simplest HUNL game is the raise/shove game. Its decision tree is shown in Figure 3.11. First, the SB makes a non-all-in raise. Then, the BB can either shove or fold. If he shoves, the SB can call or fold. In a complete decision tree, the SB's initial bet size would also be specified, but we left it off the figure. The proper choice of SB bet size will be a matter of discussion in this section.

This is another game which can often approximate real play at certain stack sizes – stacks which are just slightly deeper than those at which the shove/fold strategies apply. First, it is quite common for the SB to raise any time he enters the pot. Then, the BB might want to play raise or fold versus this raise since flatting the raise and seeing a flop out of position is often undesirable. In deep stacks, this is a poor strategy since 3-betting all-in has a poor risk-reward ratio, but this is less of a problem for sufficiently short stack sizes.

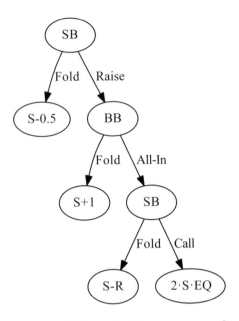

Figure 3.11: Decision tree of the raise/shove game. The total expected SB stack size is written on each leaf where S is the players' starting stack size, R is the SB's open raise size, and EQ refers to the SB's equity versus the BB's range.

First of all, the GTO solutions to this game with respect to stack size are shown in Figure 3.12 for the case of button minraising. We will argue that minraising is the SB's best choice of raise sizing in this game and that the SB should generally choose to be minraising his button in the real situations to which it applies. In the discussion below, we will be referring to the minraising version of the game until otherwise noted. (Larger, color versions of the following three charts can be found at www.dandbpoker.com).

SB opening ranges

	A	K	Q	J	T	9	8	7	6	5	4	3	2
A	ALL	ALL	ALL	ALL	ALL	ALL	ALL	ALL	ALL	ALL	ALL	ALL	ALL
K	ALL	ALL	ALL	ALL	ALL	ALL	ALL	ALL	ALL	ALL	ALL	ALL	ALL
Q	ALL	ALL	ALL	ALL	ALL	ALL	ALL	ALL	ALL	ALL	11.9,12.5+	10.8,14.6+	*
J	ALL	ALL	ALL	ALL	ALL	ALL	ALL	ALL	ALL	ALL	ALL	ALL	ALL
T	ALL	ALL	ALL	ALL	ALL	ALL	ALL	ALL	ALL	7.6,9.1+	7.4,12.3+	7.0,15.4+	6.5,18.0+
9	ALL	ALL	ALL	ALL	ALL	ALL	ALL	ALL	ALL	7.7,9.1+	6.5,10.8+	4.9,13.5+	3.7,14.2+
8	ALL	ALL	ALL	ALL	ALL	ALL	ALL	11.2,15.1+	9.4,12.5+	8.0,15.9+	7.0,16.7+	2.7,19.0+	2.5,21.2+
7	ALL	ALL	ALL	ALL	ALL	ALL	9.3,10.3+	ALL	10.0,18.4+	8.5,20.2+	7.4,20.6+	2.5,22.5+	2.1,24.1+
6	ALL	ALL	ALL	6.5,6.9+	5.7,7.1+	5.2,7.8+	6.8,10.5+	7.1,16.1+	ALL	9.0,19.3+	7.7,22.3+	*	2.0,25.1+
5	ALL	ALL	ALL	6.0,7.1+	4.1,9.1+	3.5,9.1+	3.0,15.1+	2.6,19.3+	2.4,17.9+	ALL	8.3,24.5+	*	2.0,25.8+
4	ALL	ALL	ALL	5.4,8.2+	3.8,12.3+	2.7,10.8+	2.3,16.7+	2.1,20.6+	2.0,22.1+	2.1,22.8+	ALL	*	1.8,27.7+
3	ALL	ALL	ALL	*	3.4,15.4+	2.5,13.5+	1.9,19.0+	1.8,22.5+	1.7,24.7+	1.8,25.6+	1.6,27.7+	ALL	1.7,28.4+
2	ALL	ALL	ALL	*	2.9,18.0+	2.2,14.2+	1.8,21.2+	1.6,24.1+	1.5,25.1+	1.5,25.8+	1.4,27.7+	1.4,28.4+	ALL

J-3o 5.0,8.0-9.0,9.7-10.8,14.6+ **63s** 2.3,6.1-6.8,24.7+
J-2o 4.6,8.0-9.0,9.7-10.8,19.1+ **53s** 2.4,3.8-7.3,25.7+
J-2s 9.0,9.7-10.8,19.1+ **43s** 2.2,4.9-7.0,27.7+

BB shoving ranges

	A	K	Q	J	T	9	8	7	6	5	4	3	2
A	100+	100+	100+	100+	100+	100+	100+	100+	100+	100+	100+	100+	95.0
K	100+	100+	100+	100+	100+	100+	100+		72.5	64.5	50.1	39.8	38.6
Q	100+	100+	100+	100+	100+	100+	100+	51.2,57.3-60.4	54.8,56.9-58.8	40.0,41.3-48.8	32.6	24.5	*
J	100+	100+	100+	100+	100+	100+	99.5	64.7	37.3		6.1	5.8	5.6
T	100+	*	85.2	92.0	100+	100+	100+	69.5,70.6-71.3	*		5.2	4.8	4.5
9	89.6	48.3	41.8,47.7-48.7	*	62.0	100+	100+	72.2	5.8,8.7-53.6	5.0,22.5-28.9	4.3	4.1	3.9
8	85.3	36.0	14.0,16.5-20.6	9.7	*	*	100+	6.5,7.3-86.6	5.6,8.4-61.8	4.8,10.1-37.7	4.1	3.6	3.5
7	79.5	32.2	9.2	6.4	5.5	5.0	*	100+	5.4,7.8-71.4	4.8,9.4-47.6	4.1	3.6	3.3
6	69.2	30.2	8.4	5.4	4.6	4.2	4.1	4.0	100+	*	4.3,12.0-32.7	3.8	3.3
5	73.8	27.1	6.8	5.1	4.0	3.7	3.6	3.6	3.7	100+	4.6,9.2-46.8	4.0	3.6
4	67.8	22.2	6.2	4.7	3.8	3.3	3.2	3.2	3.3	3.5	100+	3.8	3.4
3	60.1	17.6	5.9	4.5	3.6	3.1	2.9	2.9	2.9	3.1	3.0	100+	3.3
2	57.2	16.1	5.6	4.2	3.5	3.0	2.8	2.6	2.7	2.8	2.7	2.6	100+

J-9o 50.4,54.0-55.0,55.6-56.7
T-6s 6.3,9.0-41.4,45.2-49.5
10-8o 6.6,18.3-20.2,21.2-35.0
J-5s 7.6,9.7-12.0,13.7-29.5
K-To 73.8,84.8-92.4
Q-2s 11.9,16.3-18.4,20.1-21.4
8-7o 4.7,20.4-29.4
6-5s 4.9,8.5-55.5,56.8-58.7
9-8o 6.0,13.4-40.6

SB calling ranges

	A	K	Q	J	T	9	8	7	6	5	4	3	2
A	100+	100+	100+	100+	100+	93.6	80.6	70.4	61.1	60.0	50.9	49.2	46.5
K	100+	100+	100+	89.4	62.8	44.5	35.3	30.4	28.6	23.6	19.8	17.7	15.3
Q	100+	83.2	100+	55.6	46.6	32.3	21.4	13.9	12.9	11.7	10.7	10.1	9.5
J	100+	52.9	39.0	100+	36.0	24.5	15.0	11.5	9.5	8.9	8.1	7.7	7.4
T	100+	46.7	30.7	22.9	100+	18.1	13.3	10.7	9.1	7.6	7.0	7.0	6.5
9	76.5	34.3	16.7	11.8	10.8	100+	12.8	10.7	9.1	7.7	5.7,6.1-6.5	4.9	3.7
8	67.0	26.7	11.3	9.0	8.2	8.3	100+	11.2	9.4	8.0	7.0	2.7	2.5
7	57.1	20.2	9.2	7.4	7.2	7.3	7.6	100+	10.0	8.5	7.4	2.5	2.1
6	42.9	16.3	8.6	6.5	5.7	4.9,5.2-5.2	6.8	7.1	100+	9.0	7.7	2.3,6.1-6.8	2.0
5	41.1	13.6	7.9	6.0	4.1	3.5	3.0	2.6	2.4	84.3	8.3	2.4,3.8-7.3	2.0
4	36.7	12.0	7.5	5.4	3.8	2.7	2.3	2.1	2.0	2.1	62.5	2.2,4.9-7.0	1.8
3	33.3	11.0	7.1	5.0	3.4	2.5	1.9	1.8	1.7	1.8	1.6	44.7	1.7
2	31.7	10.3	6.8	4.6	2.9	2.2	1.8	1.6	1.5	1.5	1.4	1.4	30.1

Figure 3.12: GTO ranges with respect to stack size for the minraise/shove game. Numerical ranges give the stack sizes for which the corresponding hand is in the range. A single number means that the hand is in the range up to that size. The notation 100+ means that the numerical threshold is above 100 BB, if it exists.

To understand this game, we can work backwards from the bottom to the top of the game tree. The bottom-most decision is SB's: he is facing a BB shove and can call or fold. This decision is very similar to that of the BB in the shove/fold game. The decision requires a simple EV calculation for the SB with each hand against the BB's shoving range. Moving up the tree brings us to the BB shove-or-fold decision which is much the same as the SB's shove-or-fold decision in the shove/fold game. The only difference is that the opponent's range which he is shoving into is not 100% of hands but is the SB opening range. At this point, you might get the feeling that we made the raise/shove game from the shove/fold game by just adding another decision point on the top of the tree.

This brings us to the SB opening decision point, in some sense the "new" decision in this game. On the surface, the SB is deciding between two actions with each hand in his range: raise or fold. However, it is helpful for analyzing his strategy to think of him as actually partitioning his range into three sub-ranges: open-folding hands, raise-folding hands, and raise-calling hands. That is, the SB is weighing the EVs of his two options: raising and folding, but those hands which will not have the odds to call facing a shove can be thought of as raise-folding hands and those that can profitably call are raise-calling hands. In other words, the SB is comparing the EV of raising versus that of folding each particular hand, but the EV of raising a raise-folding hand is the EV of raise-folding, and the EV of raising a raise-calling hand is the EV of raise-calling.

What then are the EVs of each of these actions? Finding that of folding is easy. His total EV is one SB less than what he started with, i.e., he profits -0.5 BB. Raise-folding is also easy. The SB profits a BB when the BB folds and loses 2 BB when the BB shoves. Now, before we consider the EV of raise-calling, it is interesting to compare just the first two options. They both have the property that, when SB takes either of those actions, his holding matters little, since the hand never goes to showdown. In particular, the EV of folding is constant, and the EV of raise-folding depends on only one thing: how often the BB shoves. If the BB is shoving very rarely, raise-folding is a lot better than open-folding, but the more often BB shoves, the less attractive the raise-folding option becomes. This leads to the question: how frequently does the BB have to be shoving so that raise-folding is better than open-folding? We can state this as an inequality. If X_H is BB's shoving frequency when the SB holds hand H, then raise-folding is better than open-folding when

$$\text{EV}_{\text{SB}}(\text{raise } H) > \text{EV}_{\text{SB}}(\text{fold } H)$$
$$X_H \cdot (S - 2\text{BB}) + (1 - X_H) \cdot (S + 1\text{BB}) > S - 0.5\text{BB}$$

which is satisfied for X_H<0.5.

In English, what we have found is this: regardless of the hand the SB holds, if he is going to get shoved on less than half the time, minraise-folding is better than open-folding, and if he going to get shoved on more than half the time, open-folding is preferable to minraise-folding. In other words, to play most profitably, if the BB is shoving less than 50%, the SB should *never* open-fold – he should raise the button 100%. Conversely, if the BB is shoving more than 50%, then open-folding is always better than raise-folding. In this case, the SB should *never* raise-fold. He should raise only holdings with which he is calling a shove and open-fold everything else.

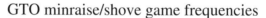 **How does this critical frequency change for different SB opening raise sizes?**

GTO minraise/shove game frequencies

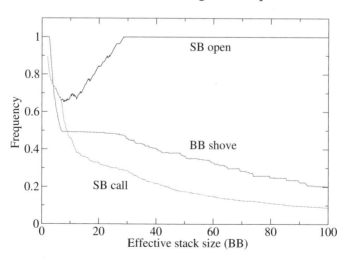

Figure 3.13: GTO frequencies in the minraise/shove game.

If we plot the frequencies with which players make their actions at the equilibrium, we can see this trend very clearly. Figure 3.13 shows the GTO SB opening, BB shoving, and SB calling frequencies at various stack sizes. (Folding frequencies, etc. can be found by the appropriate subtraction.) We can see that when the BB is shoving over 50% of hands, the SB's frequency of opening is the same as that of calling, i.e. he is never raise-folding, and when the BB is shoving less than half the time, the SB opens his button with 100% of hands.

There is one small caveat to this rule to keep in mind which has to do with card removal effects. Suppose that the BB's shoving range is exactly 50% of all hands. Then, if SB holds 2-3o, he actually blocks some of the BB's folding range, and if he raises, the BB will shove more than 50% of the time. On the other hand, if the SB holds A-A, he blocks some of the BB's shoving range, and after raising, he will get shoved on less than 50% of the time. So the relative profitability of open-folding versus raise-folding is not completely independent of the SB's holding. It matters a little bit because of how it affects his opponent's ranges through card removal.

This effect does directly affect the players' GTO ranges. For example, 20 BB deep, the SB raise-folds 10-9o but open-folds 4-3s. The hands' actual value does not matter since neither ever gets to showdown. However, holding the higher-card hand makes it slightly less likely that the BB will shove. If it were not for card removal effects, the actual hands which made up the raise-folding range would not matter at all. That said, the edge gained by blocking the BB's shoving range is relatively slight. In related real play situations, a SB's raise-folding range might be better constructed by considering which hands play best postflop in case the BB does just call the raise.

An additional important issue to notice from Figure 3.13 is that the SB's opening and calling ranges coincide up to about 6.8 BB deep. That is, the SB is never raise-folding below this stack depth. This is because he is getting odds with his entire raising range to call the BB's shove. Thus, at these low stack sizes, the button minraise is essentially the same as an open shove, and the BB's getting-it-in range here is the same as his getting-it-in range versus the open shove in the shove/fold game. You can verify this by looking at the two games' solutions. This observation that the SB can not raise-fold (without an exploitative reason to do so) forms the basis of our suggestion that the SB should play shove-or-fold under 6.8 BB deep rather than opening for smaller raises.

We now turn to the BB's frequencies, also shown in the figure. At very short stacks, the BB is getting it in quite frequently since the blinds are large relative to stacks. At the other extreme in deep stacks, the SB is opening 100% to steal the blinds, and the BB's play basically revolves around a trade-off between losing money by getting it in too light and losing money from having his blinds stolen. However, at an intermediate range of stack sizes from about 7 to 28 BB, there is a plateau in the BB shoving frequency at right around 50%. This plateau ends at exactly the same stack depth where the SB reaches a 100% opening range. What is going on here?

Recall that the SB is automatically profiting more by raise-folding than by open-folding when the BB is playing back less than 50% of the time. In deep stacks, the SB is making a large profit by stealing blinds because the BB can not go all-in 50% of the time. Doing so would lose him more than it saved as he would just be putting too much money in too loosely. As effective stacks become shorter, the BB is adding hands to his shoving range as fast as is profitable to try to keep the SB's raise-folding range from automatically profiting. At around 28 BB deep, he finally reaches a shoving range near 50%.

Now, at this point, there is no reason for the BB to push his shoving frequency any higher than 50%. If he does, the SB will just stop raise-folding any hands. He will only raise with the intention of calling a shove, and the BB will only lose money by getting it in too lightly while gaining none from stealing the SB's minraises. So, the BB stops expanding his jamming range right at the frequency at which raise-folding becomes no longer profitable for the SB relative to folding. That is, the SB is *indifferent* to open-folding versus raise-folding – both options have the same EV. (We are neglecting some small card removal effects to make the concept more clear.) This is the situation down until the 6.8 BB threshold where raise-folding disappears from the SB's strategy.

This is a particular case of a common and interesting phenomenon. The equilibrium here occurs when the BB has made the SB indifferent to pursuing two of his options. Between about 7 and 28 BB deep, the BB was able to jam just enough to keep the SB from having a clearly exploitative play with the hands he is unwilling to get all-in. If the BB is shoving too much, then the SB's exploitative strategy involves only open-folding or raise-calling but no raise-folding. Similarly, if the BB is shoving too little, then the SB should never open-fold. The equilibrium occurs right in the middle when the BB is shoving just enough so that the SB has no preference between raise-folding and open-folding – the EVs of those two options are equal, at least before card removal effects. Similar patterns show up very frequently in equilibrium play, and we will return to consider these issues in detail in Chapter 4.

We now consider exploitative strategies for the minraise/fold game. The SB's exploitative strategies are easy. First, his opening range: we have already shown that the SB will be opening either 100% of hands or just his raise-calling range depending on whether the BB is shoving less than or more than half the time. Next, consider the SB's calling range facing a shove. This is just a pot odds problem, similar to that decision facing the BB in the shove/fold game. In particular, since there are 3 BB in the pot in this game when SB is facing a shove, whereas there were 1.5 BB in the pot in shove/fold when BB was facing a shove, the SB's shove-calling range at stack size S in the minraise/shove game is exactly the same as the BB's shove-calling range in the shove/fold game at stack size $S/2$. So, we can just refer back to Figure 3.9 with this in mind to get the SB's exploitative shove/calling frequencies for a given BB shoving frequency.

Next up are the BB's exploitative strategies. The BB's shoving frequency depends on both the SB's raise-calling and raise-folding ranges. The more the SB is raise-folding, the more profitable the BB's shoves become. On the other hand, a little bit of extra SB raise-calling can discourage BB shoves, but a lot of SB raise-calling will lead the BB to expand his shoving range in order to profit from getting it in versus his opponent's weak holdings. This situation should appear much like that facing the SB in the shove/fold game. The only difference is in the range of his opponent. Indeed, if the SB is minraising 100% of buttons, then the situation becomes exactly analogous to the shove/fold situation and we can get the BB's maximally exploitative shoving ranges from the SB's shove/fold game solutions in Figure 3.8 using the divide-stack-size-by-two trick. As it is, the trick provides an upper bound on the BB's shoving frequency. From there the trend is simple: the more the SB open-folds his button, the less the BB should be shoving over raises.

For reference, we provide charts in Figures 3.14 and 3.15 describing the BB's maximally exploitative reshoving frequencies at stack depths of 8, 12, 16, and 22 BB with respect to the SB opening and calling frequencies. These stack sizes span those where playing shove-or-fold versus a SB min-raiser might be reasonable. Certainly, a strategy which involves flat-calling out of position with some hands at these stack sizes will be best versus many opponents.

Exploitative BB shoving frequencies 8 BB deep

SB open %	SB shove-calling %																			
	5	10	15	20	25	30	35	40	45	50	55	60	65	70	75	80	85	90	95	100
100	1.00	1.00	1.00	1.00	1.00	1.00	1.00	1.00	1.00	1.00	1.00	0.92	0.84	0.76	0.71	0.70	0.70	0.70	0.70	0.70
95	1.00	1.00	1.00	1.00	1.00	1.00	1.00	1.00	1.00	1.00	0.97	0.86	0.76	0.69	0.69	0.66	0.65	0.65	0.66	
90	1.00	1.00	1.00	1.00	1.00	1.00	1.00	1.00	1.00	1.00	0.90	0.78	0.70	0.65	0.62	0.62	0.62	0.63		
85	1.00	1.00	1.00	1.00	1.00	1.00	1.00	1.00	1.00	0.94	0.81	0.68	0.62	0.60	0.60	0.60	0.60			
80	1.00	1.00	1.00	1.00	1.00	1.00	1.00	1.00	0.99	0.84	0.70	0.59	0.57	0.56	0.55	0.55				
75	1.00	1.00	1.00	1.00	1.00	1.00	1.00	1.00	0.88	0.73	0.60	0.55	0.54	0.51	0.52					
70	1.00	1.00	1.00	1.00	1.00	1.00	1.00	0.96	0.78	0.59	0.52	0.49	0.49	0.49						
65	1.00	1.00	1.00	1.00	1.00	1.00	0.82	0.61	0.51	0.46	0.44	0.44								
60	1.00	1.00	1.00	1.00	1.00	1.00	0.91	0.65	0.48	0.44	0.42	0.42								
55	1.00	1.00	1.00	1.00	1.00	1.00	0.71	0.49	0.43	0.38	0.38									
50	1.00	1.00	1.00	1.00	1.00	0.80	0.51	0.38	0.36	0.35										
45	1.00	1.00	1.00	1.00	0.96	0.56	0.35	0.32	0.32											
40	1.00	1.00	1.00	1.00	0.66	0.36	0.29	0.28												
35	1.00	1.00	1.00	0.82	0.35	0.27	0.26													
30	1.00	1.00	1.00	0.39	0.26	0.23														
25	1.00	1.00	0.58	0.23	0.19															
20	1.00	0.98	0.19	0.14																
15	1.00	0.17	0.10																	
10	0.57	0.06																		
5	0.03																			

Exploitative BB shoving frequencies 12 BB deep

SB open %	SB shove-calling %																			
	5	10	15	20	25	30	35	40	45	50	55	60	65	70	75	80	85	90	95	100
100	1.00	1.00	1.00	1.00	1.00	1.00	1.00	1.00	0.91	0.78	0.66	0.60	0.59	0.58	0.59	0.60	0.60	0.60	0.60	0.63
95	1.00	1.00	1.00	1.00	1.00	1.00	1.00	0.99	0.85	0.70	0.61	0.58	0.56	0.56	0.55	0.56	0.59	0.59	0.60	
90	1.00	1.00	1.00	1.00	1.00	1.00	1.00	0.94	0.76	0.63	0.56	0.53	0.53	0.53	0.54	0.54	0.54			
85	1.00	1.00	1.00	1.00	1.00	1.00	1.00	0.82	0.66	0.55	0.50	0.49	0.49	0.49	0.51	0.52	0.53			
80	1.00	1.00	1.00	1.00	1.00	1.00	0.94	0.72	0.56	0.49	0.47	0.48	0.48	0.48	0.49	0.50				
75	1.00	1.00	1.00	1.00	1.00	1.00	0.82	0.60	0.49	0.44	0.44	0.44	0.44	0.46	0.48					
70	1.00	1.00	1.00	1.00	1.00	0.95	0.70	0.50	0.44	0.42	0.41	0.42	0.43	0.44						
65	1.00	1.00	1.00	1.00	1.00	0.79	0.54	0.42	0.39	0.38	0.39	0.40	0.40							
60	1.00	1.00	1.00	1.00	0.96	0.63	0.44	0.37	0.37	0.36	0.36	0.37								
55	1.00	1.00	1.00	1.00	0.77	0.46	0.35	0.33	0.32	0.33	0.34									
50	1.00	1.00	1.00	0.99	0.57	0.36	0.31	0.30	0.30	0.30										
45	1.00	1.00	1.00	0.76	0.36	0.29	0.28	0.27	0.27											
40	1.00	1.00	1.00	0.47	0.28	0.26	0.25	0.26												
35	1.00	1.00	0.78	0.29	0.25	0.23	0.23													
30	1.00	1.00	0.38	0.21	0.19	0.18														
25	1.00	0.80	0.19	0.16	0.14															
20	1.00	0.24	0.11	0.11																
15	0.88	0.08	0.08																	
10	0.10	0.06																		
5	0.03																			

Figure 3.14: Exploitative BB shove frequencies for the minraise/shove game. The "SB shove-calling %"s indicate the percent of preflop starting hands with which the SB calls a shove (not the percent of his open-raising range).

Exploitative BB shoving frequencies 16 BB deep

SB open %	SB shove-calling %																			
	5	10	15	20	25	30	35	40	45	50	55	60	65	70	75	80	85	90	95	100
100	1.00	1.00	1.00	1.00	1.00	1.00	0.94	0.76	0.60	0.54	0.50	0.49	0.49	0.51	0.52	0.53	0.54	0.56	0.57	0.60
95	1.00	1.00	1.00	1.00	1.00	1.00	0.85	0.67	0.54	0.49	0.48	0.48	0.49	0.49	0.50	0.52	0.53	0.53	0.55	
90	1.00	1.00	1.00	1.00	1.00	0.99	0.78	0.59	0.49	0.47	0.45	0.46	0.47	0.48	0.49	0.50	0.51	0.53		
85	1.00	1.00	1.00	1.00	1.00	0.90	0.66	0.50	0.46	0.43	0.43	0.44	0.44	0.47	0.48	0.49	0.50			
80	1.00	1.00	1.00	1.00	1.00	0.79	0.55	0.46	0.43	0.41	0.41	0.42	0.44	0.44	0.46	0.47				
75	1.00	1.00	1.00	1.00	0.99	0.69	0.48	0.40	0.38	0.38	0.40	0.40	0.41	0.42	0.44					
70	1.00	1.00	1.00	1.00	0.83	0.55	0.40	0.37	0.37	0.36	0.37	0.38	0.39	0.41						
65	1.00	1.00	1.00	1.00	0.70	0.43	0.35	0.33	0.34	0.34	0.35	0.37	0.38							
60	1.00	1.00	1.00	0.94	0.52	0.35	0.31	0.31	0.32	0.32	0.34	0.34								
55	1.00	1.00	1.00	0.74	0.38	0.30	0.28	0.30	0.30	0.30	0.32									
50	1.00	1.00	1.00	0.52	0.31	0.27	0.27	0.27	0.27	0.30										
45	1.00	1.00	0.85	0.35	0.26	0.25	0.25	0.26	0.27											
40	1.00	1.00	0.57	0.27	0.25	0.24	0.24	0.23												
35	1.00	1.00	0.33	0.21	0.19	0.20	0.21													
30	1.00	0.68	0.19	0.18	0.15	0.16														
25	1.00	0.26	0.14	0.13	0.13															
20	0.98	0.11	0.10	0.10																
15	0.31	0.07	0.08																	
10	0.05	0.05																		
5	0.03																			

Exploitative BB shoving frequencies 22 BB deep

SB open %	SB shove-calling %																			
	5	10	15	20	25	30	35	40	45	50	55	60	65	70	75	80	85	90	95	100
100	1.00	1.00	1.00	1.00	0.99	0.74	0.54	0.46	0.43	0.43	0.42	0.44	0.44	0.47	0.48	0.49	0.51	0.53	0.53	0.57
95	1.00	1.00	1.00	1.00	0.91	0.65	0.49	0.41	0.40	0.40	0.41	0.42	0.44	0.44	0.48	0.48	0.50	0.52	0.53	
90	1.00	1.00	1.00	1.00	0.82	0.57	0.42	0.38	0.38	0.38	0.40	0.40	0.42	0.44	0.46	0.47	0.49	0.50		
85	1.00	1.00	1.00	1.00	0.72	0.47	0.38	0.36	0.37	0.36	0.38	0.39	0.41	0.42	0.44	0.47	0.47			
80	1.00	1.00	1.00	0.99	0.62	0.41	0.35	0.35	0.35	0.35	0.36	0.38	0.39	0.41	0.42	0.43				
75	1.00	1.00	1.00	0.85	0.50	0.35	0.32	0.32	0.32	0.33	0.35	0.37	0.38	0.39	0.41					
70	1.00	1.00	1.00	0.71	0.39	0.31	0.30	0.30	0.32	0.32	0.34	0.35	0.37	0.38						
65	1.00	1.00	1.00	0.56	0.34	0.29	0.28	0.30	0.30	0.31	0.32	0.34	0.35							
60	1.00	1.00	0.90	0.40	0.29	0.27	0.28	0.27	0.29	0.30	0.32	0.33								
55	1.00	1.00	0.74	0.32	0.26	0.25	0.26	0.26	0.27	0.29	0.30									
50	1.00	1.00	0.50	0.27	0.25	0.25	0.25	0.26	0.27	0.27										
45	1.00	1.00	0.34	0.24	0.22	0.23	0.23	0.23	0.26											
40	1.00	0.78	0.25	0.19	0.19	0.19	0.21	0.22												
35	1.00	0.46	0.17	0.16	0.16	0.17	0.18													
30	1.00	0.20	0.14	0.13	0.14	0.15														
25	0.91	0.11	0.10	0.11	0.11															
20	0.36	0.07	0.09	0.10																
15	0.09	0.06	0.08																	
10	0.04	0.05																		
5	0.02																			

Figure 3.15: Exploitative BB shove frequencies for the minraise/shove game. The "SB shove-calling %"s indicate the percent of preflop starting hands with which the SB calls a shove (not the percent of his open-raising range).

3.3 Bet Sizing Considerations

We now return to the case where the SB's initial raise size is larger than a minraise. It is easy to see that this is worse than minraising for any particular BB shoving range. Consider the three ways the SB can play all the parts of his range: open-folding, raise-folding, and raise-calling. The SB's open-folding hands have the same value regardless of his open-raising size – he profits –0.5 BB. His raise-calling hands do the same as well for any particular BB shoving range. His raise-folding hands, however, lose more money when he opens larger and the BB shoves. Thus, the open-minraising strategy is always the better choice against any BB shoving range.

Of course, this analysis is a bit deceptive. There is no reason to think that the BB will shove with the same range regardless of the SB's open size, and indeed he should not. We saw previously that if Hero minraises the button, the BB has to shove 50% of the time to keep us from making money with our raise-folding range. However, if we make pot-sized raises from the SB (i.e. raises to 3 BB total), Villain has only to continue 37.5% of the time to have the same effect since he steals more chips each time we raise-fold. Basically, when the SB open-raises to a larger amount, it lets the BB be more selective with his shoving hands while not giving up his blind too much. Since larger SB preflop raises are good for the BB, the SB should not make them.

The operative concept here is known as *stack leveraging*. Because of the definition of the raise/shove game, a raise of any size puts the BB to a decision for all of his chips. By using as few chips as possible to accomplish this, we maximize the BB's risk-reward ratio. This example is somewhat unrealistic since the BB has no option to call, and smaller bets will make the BB's option to just call more attractive in real HUNL. However, the principle here does apply to many real situations – bets which force an opponent into an all-in-or-fold position regardless of their sizing should generally be kept as small as possible.

Exceptions to this rule can occur when you hold a hand which is strong enough to bet-call versus the stronger shoving range but is still weak enough to prefer that Villain folds rather than gets all-in, even with his weaker shoving range. That is, you hold a hand which has decent equity versus almost everything but does not have great equity versus anything. This situation is rare in preflop-only games, but the hand 22 exactly satisfies these criteria in the minraise/shove situation at certain stack sizes. Postflop, this description applies perfectly to drawing hands. Indeed this observation provides the basis for the semi-bluff – a move which involves playing a draw aggressively to force an opponent to fold as many hands as possible in the knowledge that you still have good equity when he continues but that you prefer him to fold many of his mediocre made hands that have a lot of equity versus your draw.

We saw in our study of preflop-only games that the player putting in the last bet was generally at a disadvantage if stacks were such that he had a bad risk/reward ratio on his all-in bets. It can sometimes be worthwhile to make a bigger bet in a spot if doing so will cause a Villain to play shove-or-fold where going smaller would have allowed him to play more profitably by having a re-raise-folding range.

All that said, many weak players will sometimes open raise for full pot on the button at low stacks even when their opponents are mostly playing shove-or-fold in the BB. Although Hero will profit at least as much versus this strategy by continuing to shove the exploitative ranges shown in Figures 3.14 and 3.15 as he would versus a button minraiser, he can often do better by exploiting the SB's imbalances. One common exploitable tendency is for the SB to raise larger with hands which tend to have good equity all-in preflop but which are hard to play postflop such as weak aces and small pairs. Other players might just raise larger with some very strong and very weak hands but few in between.

Splitting your opening range in this way is not good when facing an observant, adjusting opponent. However, small variations in your bet sizing can make it a lot harder for thinking opponents to get a good read on your tendencies. As we have shown in this chapter, situations which are approximately preflop-only games arise very often in short-stacked HUNL, and furthermore, they are relatively easy to analyze. Once a player has accurate knowledge of your ranges, it is fairly easy for him to come up with a counter-strategy. One way to avoid this is to vary your play slightly. For example, instead of raising only to 2 BB when you enter a pot from the SB, try opening to 2.02 or 2.10 BB occasionally so that your opponent might incorrectly try to assign you different ranges for each slightly-different action. Consider just calling on the SB even if you plan to play exclusively raise-or-fold afterwards so that Villain might think your raising range is stronger than it is. Perhaps flat call a raise in the BB when planning to play shove-or-fold versus raises in the future for similar reasons.

3.4 Trends and Lessons

We began our study of real HUNL games in this chapter by discussing preflop-only games. These are simple and relatively easy to analyze, and they provided a good opportunity to see some applications of the game theoretic material we covered in Chapter 2. However, preflop-only analyses are also sometimes applicable to real play situations. In particular, the shove/fold and raise/shove games approximate real dynamics that often arise in short-stacked play. To prepare for these situations, we spent some time solving for and detailing GTO and exploitative strategies for these games. We will use the same techniques in studying more complicated multi-street games. In general, a player's options are limited to folding, checking, betting, raising and calling. In our study of preflop-only games, we have made detailed evaluation of the first four of those five. The option to call with money left behind is what makes postflop play more complicated.

Indeed, we will see that the option to call changes the nature of GTO play, and this must be kept in mind in order to apply the specific strategies developed in this chapter to short-stacked situations. For example, if Hero is playing minraise-or-fold on the button, and Villain is sometimes shoving over the raise, sometimes folding, and sometimes calling, the minraise/shove solution tables in Section 3.2 do not apply. Generally, this is because Villain is using a strategic option which was not included in the approximate game we solved to find those results. More specifically, the fact that Villain is sometimes flat calling out of position allows him to make his shoving range stronger without giving up his blind too frequently. Since his shoving range is tighter, Hero's calling range must be tighter as well. That said, just because a SB is sometimes limping or minraising at short stacks does not necessarily mean his open-shoving range is particularly strong. Similarly, a BB could tend to shove over minraises with hands that do not play very well postflop while playing most of his genuinely strong hands differently.

To effectively develop exploitative strategies, it is important to pay careful attention to how opponents' preflop strategies change with changing stack sizes. There are usually a few stack sizes at which players begun using certain strategic options. Suppose Hero is in the BB. At very short effective stacks, his opponent is often playing shove-or-fold from the SB. As stacks get deeper, the SB will start including non-all-in open raises. It is very important to take notice of the stack size at which this transition occurs. Additionally, a SB might begin shoving some hands and minraising others or he might just eliminate open-shoving altogether and switch to a minraise-or-fold approach. We will also see later that limping can be a viable option for the SB in many cases. Characterizing the SB's play in this way is a critical first step towards developing an exploitative short-stack strategy.

On the other hand, suppose Hero is in the SB. The BB will usually play shove-or-fold versus open raises at sufficiently short stack sizes. In this case, the charted SB strategies can be used. The equilibrium frequencies will perform alright, but it is certainly better to attempt to estimate his frequencies and then take an exploitative approach. As stacks continue to get deeper, Villain will begin to incorporate calling into his BB play, and the stack size at which this transition occurs is important to notice as well.

Accurately estimating frequencies is necessary for implementing good exploitative strategies. A quick example can show the magnitude of edges we can obtain even at the very short effective stacks of 8 BB. Suppose first of all that Hero is in the BB, and the SB is playing shove-or-fold. At the equilibrium, the SB is jamming about 62% and Hero should call about 45%. This earns Hero about 0.4 BB per 100 hands, a small edge. As you can see in Figure 3.6, 8 BB is right around the point where the shove/fold game is a break-even proposition for both players. (By the way, at 8 BB deep, the SB actually has a positive expected profit when playing the minraise/shove game.) However, if the SB is jamming a bit tighter, say, with the top 50% of hands, the BB should call about 35% of the time. This strategy pair wins Hero about 3 BB per 100 hands. On the other hand, if SB is too loose and is shoving 80%, then calling with about 55% of hands earns Hero an expectation of almost 6 BB per 100 hands. These are not huge edges, but these situations come up very frequently in some HUNL formats. In these games, it is certainly worth trying to play these spots as well as possible. To do this, consider keeping a running tally of your opponent's preflop actions in short-stacked situations.

Some other transitional stack depths are less important but still useful information to have when characterizing an opponent's play. A SB should notice the stack sizes when the BB opens up a 3-bet-folding range. If the BB is never just calling an open but is playing (non-all-in) 3-bet-or-fold, then the solutions to the minraise/3-bet/shove game can be easily found and applied, but this is not too common. Even if he is sometimes just calling preflop, the stack size at which he becomes capable of 3-bet-folding is an important piece of data to have. Certainly it will influence your approach to 4-betting. Similarly, the stack size at which a SB opens up a 4-bet-folding range is important to notice.

After our detailed analysis of the shove/fold and raise/shove games, we found some more general concepts that are applicable to many HUNL situations. In discussing the exploitative minraise/fold game strategies, we found that there were some hands which were folded by the BB at the equilibrium which he should shove if the SB was playing poorly. This led us to observe that there can be value in making decisions simply because they lead to parts of the game tree where Villain plays poorly, and this can lead to some unintuitive results. Poker authors like to list reasons for betting. For example, it has been said that the only reasons to bet are for value (i.e., to get called by worse hands) and as a bluff (i.e., to make better hands fold). Hand protection and the gain of information are also sometimes given as reasons for betting. However, this discussion reminds us that there is only one fundamental reason to choose to bet a hand: because it is more profitable on average than calling, checking, or folding (or betting another size). We will sometimes find a bet to be our most profitable option when it is not clearly a value bet or a bluff but simply because it leads to a part of the decision tree where Villain employs a poor strategy or is otherwise unable to play well.

Another concept arose when we considered the stack sizes at which Hero might want to stop playing shove-or-fold from the button and incorporate a raise-folding range into his strategy. We considered his other option – minraising buttons – and tried to estimate (by solving the minraise/shove game) the stack size at which raise-folding should no longer be part of his SB strategy. At this point, we reasoned, since he can not fold to the BB's shove after minraising, he should just shove himself with any hands he wants to raise. The reason for this is straightforward. Suppose Hero is minraising his button but calling all shoves. Now, if just playing the shove/fold game is most advantageous for Villain in the BB, then the BB can effectively force play of the shove/fold game by just shoving over the minraise with any hands that would have called a shove. In this case, the SB's minraise was effectively a shove since he is never folding to the all-in, and the BB's shove is effectively a call. However, suppose that just calling the minraise is sometimes advantageous to the BB. Then by minraising instead of shoving, the SB gives him the ability to take advantage of this. By minraising his buttons, the SB gives his opponent another strategic option which he can use if it helps him and effectively avoid using if it does not. In this way, the strategic option is guaranteed to have non-negative value for the BB. In general we should avoid making moves or sizing our bets in a way that gives Villain strategic options without giving ourselves any – an important exception occurs when Villain is a weak player, and we expect that he will make bad decisions.

This idea can be applied at all stack sizes and in postflop situations as well. For example, suppose Hero is out of position 20 BB deep and flat calls a minraise. The flop comes 7♠-6♦-5♠. There is 4 BB in the pot and 18 BB behind. Should Hero have a check-raise-fold range on this flop? Likely not. This flop connects in some way with a very large number of hands. In fact, almost anything in a reasonable preflop defending range has at least 5 outs versus top pair and tons of hands have lots more with two over-cards and some flush or straight possibilities. So, there is no reason for Hero to check-raise the flop with hands with little equity – there are plenty of reasonable draws from which he can choose his check-raising hands. However, after check-raising, these hands will generally have the odds needed to call all-in. Since Hero can not check-raise-fold the flop, he should probably just check-raise all-in when he does want to raise. Having a small-raising range which includes no hands which fold to a shove allows Villain to profit by taking advantage of the option to get it in on the flop all the time if it is to his benefit but to see cheap turns otherwise.

Again, important exceptions to this arise when Villain is likely to make mistakes. For example, he could be prone to calling a small raise and then folding to the turn jam too frequently. Giving your opponent more decisions to make can be wise if he is going to make them poorly. Alternately, suppose your opponent simply plays too tight versus the small raises. Then, it may be that there is a lot of value in bluff-raising but you do not have the equity needed to call once your opponent 3-bet jams. In this case, some raise-folding might be appropriate.

Now, to run a bit further with this example for the sake of completeness, it is not impossible that the BB is sometimes check-raise-folding this flop, even at the equilibrium. In particular, it might be good to raise small on the flop with especially strong flopped hands in order to try to get action.

Of course, if our small-raising range consisted only of the flopped nuts, Villain would be very tight against it, and then we would have a lot of incentive to bluff that way as well. In other words, if we play our nut hands that way, then at the equilibrium, we will also play some bluffs by small-check-raising, for balance-related reasons. In this context, perhaps Villain's flop 3-bet shoving range will be strong enough that we should fold our weaker semi-bluffs to the shove, and there we have it – a flop raise-folding range. On the other hand, perhaps it would be best to keep our nut holdings combined with the bulk of our holdings which are either calling or jamming on the flop. There are some trade-offs involved, and we're certainly getting ahead of ourselves. We will come back to this spot when we consider flop play.

Lastly, we found the related principle of stack leveraging which states that, generally, if you make a bet which forces your opponent into a shove-or-fold decision, you want to use few chips. By using as small a bet as possible to put him to his decision, you give him as little value as possible when you bet/fold. At the same time, you force him to jam with a high frequency in order to keep you from profiting with your bluffs. If you chose a larger bet size, it would allow him to get all-in with a tighter range while still protecting himself against your bluffs. Although this is almost always a good thing in preflop-only games, we saw that it can be undesirable in certain situations – especially postflop with drawing hands.

3.5 You Should Now...

- ♠ Be very, very familiar with unexploitable and exploitative play of the shove/fold and raise/shove games

- ♠ Understand the conditions under which these strategies can be used in real play

- ♠ Understand the role of card removal effects, stack leveraging, and the value of strategic options in these games, and have some idea how each of these might be important in more realistic HUNL games

Chapter 4

The Indifference Principle

It's not whether you won or lost, but how many bad-beat stories you were able to tell. – Grantland Rice

4.1 More Preflop Bets and the Indifference Principle

Calling a non-all-in bet is not an option in preflop-only games, so we can only make these situations more complicated by adding re-raises or allowing players to use different bet sizings. After a while, looking at games with more preflop bets is also no longer useful, since these games will not represent real play at any stack sizes. A SB can realistically play jam-or-fold with a particularly short stack, and a BB can play shove-or-fold facing open raises with a somewhat deeper one, but once a BB starts making non-all-in 3-bets, the SB will almost always want to have a flat-calling range because of his postflop positional advantage. So, we will not chart out detailed solutions for more complicated preflop-only games. However, we will look at one more in order to motivate and present an important concept, the Indifference Principle.

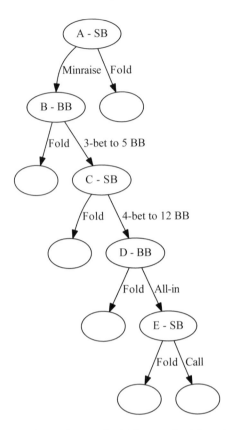

Figure 4.1: The minraise/3-bet/4-bet/shove decision tree.

Consider the minraise/3-bet/4-bet/shove game shown in Figure 4.1. The SB can raise or fold first to act at decision point *A*. If he raises, the play moves to point *B* where the BB can 3-bet or fold. At point *C*, the SB can 4-bet or fold. Finally, facing a 4-bet, the BB can shove or fold at *D*, and the SB can then call or fold at *E*.

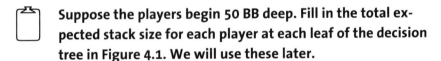 **Suppose the players begin 50 BB deep. Fill in the total expected stack size for each player at each leaf of the decision tree in Figure 4.1. We will use these later.**

What does GTO play of this game look like? As you might guess, at many stack sizes, the SB will start out raising a lot of hands and folding some bad ones. The BB will then 3-bet with good hands and fold some worse ones. The SB will 4-bet a tighter range of good hands and fold others, and so on.

However, it turns out that we can do a lot better than this without resorting to the brute-force methods which we have used so far.

Recall something we learned in Chapter 2 about equilibrium strategies. By definition, they are maximally exploitative strategies when facing an opponent who is playing his own GTO strategy – in this case, every hand is played as profitably as possible. So, the only way a hand can be played in two different ways at the equilibrium is if both of those actions have exactly the same EV, that is, if the player is indifferent to his choice of actions. This is known as the Indifference Principle: *if a player plays a mixed strategy with a hand at the equilibrium, then it must be that all of the actions he takes with a nonzero frequency have the same EV.* This is a powerful statement, because it tells us something about the GTO strategy of the player's opponent. If a player is indifferent between two options, it must be that his opponent is playing in such a way as to a make him so. We will be able to leverage this constraint on the opponent's strategy to learn a lot about GTO play in many situations.

This principle is intimately connected with the idea of balance. For example, think back to our discussion of balance in Section 2.3.1. We talked about the play of small pocket pairs from the BB when facing a raise 35 BB deep. We saw that there is good reason to think that just going all-in with these hands would be part of a GTO strategy. Those hands have good hot-and-cold equity versus most calling ranges preflop but can be difficult to play profitably postflop. We saw, however, that if our entire jamming range in that situation consisted of small pocket pairs, Villain's counter-strategy would involve calling all-in with a wide variety of rather mediocre holdings, over a third of all hands in total. At this point, Hero's counter-counter-strategy involved jamming over open raises with all strong hands – this would almost certainly be the most profitable way to play premium holdings since the SB is calling all-in so often. But, if Hero is jamming preflop with all of these, Villain's re-adjustment is to tighten up his calling range, probably to the point that all-in is no longer Hero's best option with many of his strong hands.

Here comes the important point. Assume we know for a fact that unexploitable play with small pocket pairs from the BB at 35 BB is to go all-in.

Focus on Hero's play with the high-card hands (such as, perhaps, A-Ko) that might also be jammed for balance-related reasons. If Hero is always shoving these high-card hands, then Villain's counter-strategy incentivizes him to stop. So, his equilibrium strategy can not be to always shove. However, if he is not shoving at all, then Villain's counter-strategy incentivizes him to start. Thus his equilibrium play can not be to never shove. This is the sort of argument that tells us that Hero must be playing a mixed strategy at equilibrium. Since he can not be always shoving nor can he be never shoving, his equilibrium play must involve doing both with non-zero probability. Since he is taking both actions, we know from the Indifference Principle that they must have the same EV at the equilibrium. To make this as clear as possible, imagine that Villain was playing so that shoving had slightly higher EV than not-shoving. In this case, Hero would start shoving more, but then Villain's adjustment would cause shoving to become less profitable, thus incentivizing Hero to move back towards his unexploitable mixed strategy. And vice-versa. The only stable situation is where the two actions have the same EV. This observation gives us some information about Villain's equilibrium play – his equilibrium strategy, whatever it is, must make the EVs of Hero's two options equal.

To begin to see how we can use these ideas to address the minraise/3-bet/4-bet/shove game, recall some observations we made about the minraise/shove preflop-only game in Section 3.2. We found that the SB's equilibrium strategy at many stack sizes involved both open-folding and raise-folding some hands. Since neither of these actions results in going to showdown, the particular hands the SB chose to make these plays with were not important. (This is not precisely true due to card removal effects, but these are relatively small and will be neglected in the following discussion.) So, hands which were open-folded could just as well have been raise-folded, and vice versa – all that mattered were the overall frequencies of open-folding and raise-folding. Thus, in the case of the minraise/shove game, at stack sizes where SB is sometimes open-folding and sometimes raise-folding, the SB is indifferent between the two actions with his weak hands at the equilibrium. Furthermore, the BB's equilibrium strategy must involve shoving over the SB's opens with just the right frequency to make it so.

Write down the SB's EVs of raise-folding and open-folding in the minraise/shove game at 20 BB as a function of the BB's 3-betting frequency. Find the BB jamming frequency that makes them equal. Is this re-raising frequency the one which is used at the equilibrium?

We can use reasoning based on this principle to essentially solve the min-raise/3-bet/4-bet/shove game shown in Figure 4.1. There are multiple situations in this game where one of the players is indifferent between two actions with some hands, and the other player must be playing in such a way as to make him indifferent. We will list them now and work out the consequences which each indifference has for the GTO strategies. Suppose, for concreteness, that starting stacks are 50 BB, the 3-bet is to 5 BB and the 4-bet is to 12 BB.

To see where the following indifferences come from, again think back to the SB's situation in the raise/shove game. When he played his open-folding and raise-folding lines, his holding was unimportant because he never got to showdown. And so, with any hand which was not good enough to take to showdown, he would take both lines with some frequency. Knowing this, we applied the Indifference Principle to conclude that the EVs of both actions were equal. In this game, there are a number of lines that both players can take with hands they have no intention of getting all-in. The SB can open-fold, raise-fold, or raise-4bet-fold. If he is indeed taking all of these actions with non-zero frequencies, then the EVs of all three must be equal, since the actual holdings used to take these lines are interchangeable. As for the BB, he can fold or 3-bet-fold with the hands he is unwilling to get all-in, and if he is doing both at the equilibrium, the SB's strategy must make him indifferent to the choice.

Of course, at sufficiently deep stack sizes in the raise/shove game, the BB was not able to shove often enough to discourage the SB from opening all his buttons. Then, the indifference was not satisfied, and the SB's open-folding frequency was 0. However, this was not really the case at any stack sizes where it made sense to think in terms of the raise/shove decision tree in real play. We will find some similar breakdowns here at extreme stack sizes, but we will start out by assuming that the players are indeed taking all their non-showdown lines with some non-zero frequencies.

The SB is indifferent between raise-folding and open-folding.

It must be the case that the BB is 3-betting enough that those two ranges have the same EV. We can set those two EVs equal in order to solve for the 3-bet frequency, *X*, that makes this happen. We have

$$EV_{SB}(\text{open-fold}) = EV_{SB}(\text{raise-fold})$$
$$49.5 = 48X + 51(1 - X)$$

since we necessarily end up with 49.5 BB if we open-fold, but if we raise-fold, we end up with 48 BB the *X* of the time the BB 3-bets and 51 BB the (1-X) of the time he does not. This equation is satisfied by X=0.5. That is, the BB will 3-bet half of the hands with which he reaches decision point *B*, and fold the other half. This is the same as in the minraise/shove game since the calculation really depends only on the SB's open raise sizing.

The BB is indifferent between 3-bet-folding and folding to the SB's first raise.

It must be the case that the SB is 4-betting with a frequency such that those two plays have the same EV. We can solve for the SB's 4-bet frequency, *X*, that makes this possible. We have

$$EV_{BB}(\text{fold}) = EV_{BB}(\text{3-bet-fold})$$
$$49 = 45X + 52(1 - X)$$

which is satisfied by X=3/7. So, the SB will 4-bet with 3/7 of the hands with which he gets to decision point *C* and fold the other 4/7.

After getting to decision point C, the SB is indifferent between raise-folding and raise-4-bet-folding.

It must be the case that the BB is 5-bet shoving enough that these two actions have the same EV. Let us solve for the shove frequency, *X*, that makes this happen.

$$\text{EV}_{\text{SB}}(\text{raise-fold}) = \text{EV}_{\text{SB}}(\text{4-bet-fold})$$
$$48 = 38X + 55(1 - X)$$

which is satisfied by *X=7/17*. Thus, it must be that the BB is shoving with 7/17 of the hands with which he gets to decision point *D*.

What have we found so far of the solution to this game? Consider the BB's strategy. First, facing a SB open, he 3-bets 50% of the time. Then, when facing a 4-bet, he 5-bet shoves 7/17 of that 50% so that his total 5-bet shoving range includes 7/34 or about 20.6% of hands. We see that the constraints arising from the Indifference Principle completely specify the BB's frequencies in this game!

What about the SB's strategy? At the beginning of the hand, the SB can basically divide his holdings into two categories: hands which are able to to call all-in profitably once they get to decision point *E* and those which are not. If a hand is more profitably played by raise-4-bet-calling than raise-4-bet-folding, then raise-4-bet-calling is also better than open-folding and raise-folding, since the EVs of the lines ending in a fold are all equal at equilibrium. So, those which are able to call all-in at point *E* will constitute his raise-4-bet-calling range. Finding these hands, at least approximately, is easy. At point *E*, the SB will have to call a raise of 38 BB to win a pot which will total 100 BB, so his calling range will just be all hands that have at least 38% equity versus the BB's shoving range. We know that the BB's shoving frequency is 20.6%. Assuming the BB's shoving range is the top 20.6% of hands, the range of SB holdings which have 38% equity is {22+, A2s+, K9s+, QTs+, JTs, T9s, A2o+, KTo+} which is about 25.5% of hands.

The other 74.5% of hands held by the SB will be folded at some point, either by open-folding, raise-folding, or raise-4-bet-folding. We are still neglecting card removal effects, so if a hand is a folding hand, it does not matter where it is folded as long as we get the correct folding frequencies at each point.

So we know how many hands the SB is calling all-in with at point *E*. Let us find his frequency of folding to the BB's all-in. This requires us to make one last application of the Indifference Principle. Consider the last BB decision: to shove or fold to the SB's 4-bet. The weakest hands in the BB's shoving range are not profitable if they have to get it all-in – shoving these is only profitable since the SB sometimes folds to the shove. Furthermore, even with the SB sometimes folding, the very worst hand in the BB's shoving range is essentially breaking even. That is, the EV of shoving it is more or less the same as the EV of folding it. The same can be said of the strongest hands in the BB's folding range at point D.

The idea here is this: both the worst hand in the BB's shoving range and the best hand in his folding range are effectively indifferent between shoving and folding. In fact, there is often a real indifference here – the hand on the borderline between a shove and a fold is often played with a mixed strategy at the equilibrium. The BB's shoving range is comprised of 20.6% of all hands, so his range might look like {55+, A3s+, K8s+, QTs+, A7o+, K9o+, QJo} and A-6o is a good representative of the bottom of his shoving range and the top of his folding range. (It turns out that A-6o is actually played with a mixed strategy in this case.)

Thus, the BB must be indifferent between jamming and folding A-6o, and the SB must be folding enough to the shove to make it so. What SB folding frequency does this imply? A-6o has equity 0.4214 versus the SB calling range. Let the SB's folding frequency be X. Then, at the equilibrium:

$$EV_{BB}(\text{fold A6o at point D}) = EV_{BB}(\text{shove A6o at point D})$$
$$45 = 62X + (2 \cdot 50 \cdot 0.4214)(1 - X)$$

which is satisfied by $X=0.144$. So, at decision point E, the SB will be folding about 14.4% of the time and calling the shove the other 85.6% of the time.

Let us find the rest of the SB's frequencies. We have already estimated the range with which the SB is calling the shove (25.5% of all hands), and taken together with his last folding frequency, we can find how many hands in total the SB brings to point E where he faces the shove, that is, the total fraction of hands he raises and then 4-bets. If this total number of hands is X, then 85.6% of X is 25.5% of all hands, so he must be getting to decision point E with 29.8% of all hands.

Working the SB's frequencies back up the tree, we see that he raise-4-bets with 3/7 of the hands he raises, so he must raise with 7/3 x 29.8% = 69.5% of all hands. This means that he open-raises 69.5% of hands in total, and he must open-fold the remaining 30.5% of hands at the equilibrium.

We have now, to good approximation, found the equilibrium frequencies of the game. To find the BB's frequencies, we made no reference to things like individual hand strengths or equities. We just found the bulk volume of hands necessary to make the SB indifferent between the various lines he takes with his weak hands.

There is an additional important point to be made about the solutions to the minraise/3-bet/4-bet/shove game. Remember how we found the SB ranges. We found what hands he is actually willing to get it all-in with. Then, we found how many other hands he had to reach each decision point with in order to be unexploitable. What are these other hands? Bluffs, of course! With 50 BB stacks and the bet sizings given, the SB is willing to get all-in with 25.5% of holdings. So, at the beginning of the hand, he raises with those 25.5% and also another 44% of hands which are bluffs. If he gets 3-bet, he continues by re-raising all of the 25.5% as well as a smaller chunk of bluffs which comprises about 4.3% of all hands.

These frequencies are the exact ones needed to make the BB indifferent to having bluff-raising ranges himself. For example, if the SB neglected to include the 44% of bluff hands in his opening range, then the BB would no longer be indifferent between folding at point *B* and 3-bet-folding. He would never 3-bet-fold – since the SB is never raise-folding, 3-bet-folding would be burning money. In fact, if the SB included even slightly less than the GTO number of bluffs in his opening range (but kept his other ranges the same), the BB's best response 3-bet-folding frequency would still be zero.

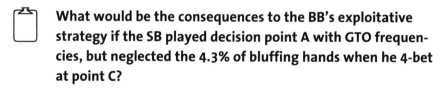 **What would be the consequences to the BB's exploitative strategy if the SB played decision point A with GTO frequencies, but neglected the 4.3% of bluffing hands when he 4-bet at point C?**

As we will see, when designing equilibrium and exploitative ranges, it is often best to think in terms of frequencies first and then find hands to add up to those frequencies second. In the minraise/shove game at 20 BB, the BB is 3-bet shoving right around 50% of hands at the equilibrium. Any range that wide contains lots of hands that many players would consider too weak to go all-in in that spot. However, from the Indifference Principle, it is clear that he needs to be shoving with that frequency to avoid being exploited. We will see the use of this frequency-based thought in a post-flop application of the Indifference Principle shortly.

First, however, let us look at the actual solutions to the minraise/3-bet/4-bet/shove game. Our calculations so far have been only approximate since they ignored card removal effects and occasionally assumed ranges where we only knew frequencies. The exact equilibrium frequencies are shown in Figure 4.2a. It is easy to see the stack sizes for which our estimates of the BB's frequencies (that BB 3-bets 50% and shoves 20.6% of hands) hold, and Figures 4.2b and 4.2c show some of the more complicated correspondences.

Minraise/3-bet/4-bet/shove game GTO Frequencies

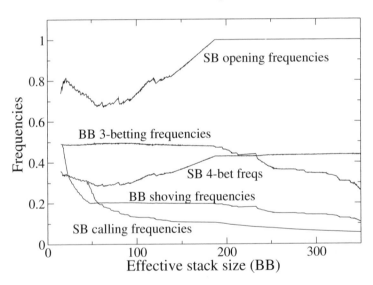

Minraise/3-bet/4-bet/shove game GTO SB frequencies

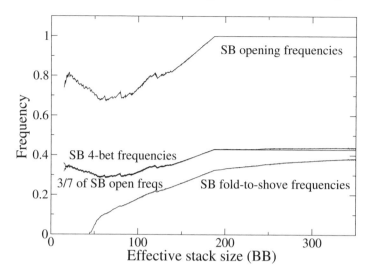

Minraise/3-bet/4-bet/shove game GTO BB frequencies

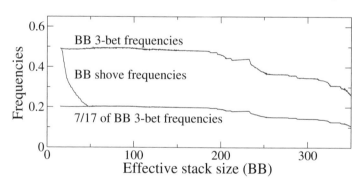

Figure 4.2: GTO frequencies in the minraise/3-bet/4-bet/shove game versus stack size. The 3-bet is to 5 BB total, and the 4-bet is to 12 BB total.

Our estimates based on the Indifference Principle hold for a lot of stack sizes but seem to break down above approximately 185 BB and below about 45 BB. What is going on here?

First consider the deep-stacked regime. As we get deeper and deeper, the BB's all-in shove with 20.6% of hands becomes less and less profitable. He simply has to risk too many chips to move all-in over a 12 BB 4-bet. The In-difference Principle tells us that at the equilibrium, as stacks get deeper, the SB must start raise-4-betting with more and more hands that will fold to a shove so that the top of the BB's folding range is indifferent to shoving. This is why we see the SB open-folding less and less around 175 BB. He is shifting those weak hands to fold at point *E*.

At around 185 BB, however, the SB's open-folding frequency hits 0%. At this point, he is open-raising 100% of the time and is 4-betting with 3/7 of those hands, and so this is as far as he can go to increase his folding frequency at point *E*. Thus, at larger stack sizes, the weakest of the 20.6% of hands which the BB was shoving can no longer be profitably jammed. The BB can no longer maintain the same shoving frequency and has to decrease his shoving range. To shove less at decision point *D*, he could either just start folding more to the 4-bet, or he could get to D with fewer hands in the first place. Consider these two options. If he just starts folding more (and thus disrupts his 7/17 : 10/17 jam-to-bluff ratio), then the SB will no longer be indifferent between raise-folding and raise-4-bet-folding. He will be able to make more money with the latter.

If, on the other hand, the BB just gets to D with fewer hands (i.e. he folds more facing the SB's first raise), then the SB is no longer indifferent between open-folding and raise-folding. It turns out that giving up the edge when the pot is smaller is the more profitable choice, so this is what happens. The BB maintains the 7/17 shoving fraction at point *D* (as we see in Figure 4.2c), but gets to that spot with fewer hands by 3-betting less than 50 percent. As soon as the BB is 3-betting less than 50%, raise-folding becomes better than open-folding for the SB with any two cards, and indeed we see his open-folding frequency go to zero. As we consider even larger stack sizes, the SB continues 4-betting with a frequency that makes the BB indifferent between folding and 3-bet-folding but decreases his calling range on the end. In the limit of very large stacks, the SB is opening 100%, 4-betting around 3/7 of that, and calling the shove with only A-A. In this case, the BB is opening very tightly, 3-betting with A-A and some A blockers, and only shoving with A-A.

Now consider the short-stacked regime. The simple explanation here is that, at sufficiently short stacks, some of the players' re-raises put enough chips in the pot that they are then getting odds to put the rest in with their entire ranges. At around 43 BB, the SB can no longer 4-bet-fold. At 16 BB, the BB can no longer 3-bet-fold, and so the game has essentially reduced to minraise/shove. However, we can benefit from taking a closer look.

Let us start by looking at the GTO frequencies at around 100 BB. Here, two things are happening simultaneously. First, as the stacks are getting shorter, the SB is getting better and better odds to call all-in, so his shove-calling range is getting wider and wider. The BB's shoving range is more or less fixed by the Indifference Principle at 20.6%, however, so as the SB calling range weakens, the SB needs fewer and fewer folding hands at point *E* to make the bottom of the BB's shoving range indifferent to folding. So, the SB's fold-to-shove and total 4-bet frequencies are decreasing as well.

At around 45 BB, the SB's shove-calling range has gotten wide enough that the BB no longer needs the SB to fold at all for shoving the 20.6% of hands to be profitable, and in fact, he can even start shoving more. Of course, as soon as he starts shoving more than that, the SB is no longer indifferent between raise-folding and raise-4-bet-folding. This is why we see the SB's raise-4-bet-folding frequency go to zero and the BB's shove frequency break above 20.6% at the same time, right around 45 BB deep.

Consider still shorter stacks. The BB's shove frequency continues to increase. Since the SB is calling all-in with all hands he 4-bets, we can think of his 4-bets practically as shoves, and the actual BB shove as simply a call all-in. So, similarly to before, as the BB "calling" range gets wider and wider, the SB needs him to be folding fewer hands at point *D* to make a profitable 4-bet "shove" at *C*. Eventually, at around 16 BB deep, he is able to "shove" profitably with all the hands he gets to *C* without the BB ever folding. Below this point, he finds profitable 4-bets with even more than the 3/7 of his range he was 4-betting with before, and the BB no longer ever 3-bet-folds.

> **How might the addition of options to flat-call bets preflop change these solutions? What indifferences are maintained at the equilibrium in this case? This is a tricky question, and we will come back to it in detail when we look at preflop play. For now, here's an easier one...**

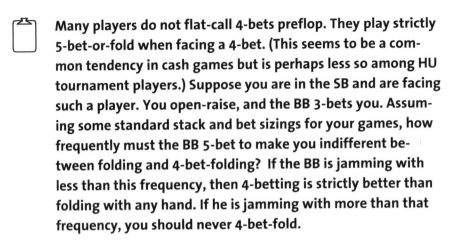

Many players do not flat-call 4-bets preflop. They play strictly 5-bet-or-fold when facing a 4-bet. (This seems to be a common tendency in cash games but is perhaps less so among HU tournament players.) Suppose you are in the SB and are facing such a player. You open-raise, and the BB 3-bets you. Assuming some standard stack and bet sizings for your games, how frequently must the BB 5-bet to make you indifferent between folding and 4-bet-folding? If the BB is jamming with less than this frequency, then 4-betting is strictly better than folding with any hand. If he is jamming with more than that frequency, you should never 4-bet-fold.

4.2 Asymmetric Ranges and Breakdown of Indifference

The Indifference Principle says that if a player is taking multiple actions with one hand at equilibrium, then those actions have the same EV. We have used this fact to draw conclusions about his opponent's equilibrium strategy. Sometimes, however, in a spot where we expect an indifference equation to hold, it will turn out that one line is just always more profitable. We saw this happen above in a preflop-only game with a fixed number of re-raises at extreme stack sizes. In the large-stack case, the fact that the BB had to make such a huge bet to go all-in caused problems. It was a lot of money to risk, and he could not do it with a high enough frequency to keep the SB from opening 100% of buttons. In real play, however, the BB could avoid the issue in this case by making non all-in 5-bets as stacks got larger or by just calling preflop.

There is a more important reason that an indifference we expect to hold can break down. It has to do with the strength of the players' hand ranges. For example, suppose that Hero's range is simply a lot stronger than Villain's. As we will see, we expect that in many cases, Villain will call bets enough to keep us indifferent between bluffing and not bluffing with weak hands. If our range is too strong, however, Villain may not be able to continue versus a bet often enough to discourage us from bluffing all the time. This scenario is uncommon preflop since both players start preflop play with the same range of hands, and, in particular, it is a very wide range containing lots of different types of hands. The situation is different postflop. As a hand proceeds, players make decisions that narrow and define their ranges. Even good players with well-balanced strategies can find themselves in spots where a rare card comes off that happens to help one player's range a lot more than his opponent's.

We will look at an example to help clarify this issue. Consider the following situation. The SB minraises his button with 30 BB effective stacks, the BB 3-bets to 5 BB, and the SB calls. We see an 8♥-6♣-5♦ flop. The BB can either check-fold or continuation-bet 1/2 pot. If he bets, the SB can jam or fold. The tree representing the flop subgame is shown in Figure 4.3. We have labeled the expected SB stack sizes at each leaf. What is the equilibrium play here?

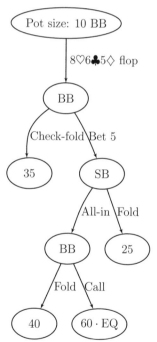

Figure 4.3: A decision tree representing a simple subgame where the BB is deciding between betting and check-folding after making a 3-bet. We have labeled the leaves with the SB's payoffs, and EQ is the SB's equity versus the BB's calling range once they get all-in.

First of all, this tree should look familiar. It is almost exactly the same as the minraise/shove game! The player first to act can bet or fold, and the other player can shove or fold when facing a bet. There are differences. Stack and pot sizes are different, the hand ranges which the players start with are different, and the hand strengths are greatly affected by the flop.

Before we say anything about the flop or the players' preflop ranges, let us see how things work out if we suppose that the BB is both check-folding and bet-folding with a non-zero frequency at the equilibrium. In this case, the EV of the two moves must be the same, and we can find the consequences that this has for the SB's shoving range. Try it yourself.

Find the SB shoving frequency that makes the BB indifferent to check-folding and bet-folding the flop.

If the critical SB jamming frequency is X, then

$$EV_{BB}(\text{check-fold}) = EV_{BB}(\text{bet-fold})$$
$$25 = 20X + 35(1 - X)$$

which is satisfied by X=2/3. So, SB can jam 2/3 of the time to make the BB indifferent between check-folding and bet-folding. In other words, the SB must jam 2/3 of the time to keep the BB from wanting to bet 100% of his range. If the SB folds to the bet more than a third of the time, then the BB should never check-fold. On the other hand, if the SB folds to the bet less than a third of the time, the BB strictly prefers check-folding to bet-folding.

To find the BB's strategy, we need to specify the players' preflop ranges. Suppose first of all, for simplicity, that they both reach the flop this way with the top 35% of preflop hands, {44+, A2s+, K3s+, Q7s+, J9s+, T9s, A2o+, K6o+, Q9o+, J-10o, J♣-8♣}. Then, the top 2/3 of these hands (ranked by equity versus the range that the BB starts with on the flop) is

44+, A4s+, K5s-K9s, Q7s-Q8s, A4o+, K6o-K9o, A♣2♣, A♣3♣, K♣Q♣, J♣8♣, A♣3◇, A♣3♡, A◇3♣, A◇2◇, A◇3◇, K◇Q◇, A◇3♡, A♡3♣, A♡3◇, A♡2♡, A♡3♡, K♡Q♡

So, this is a reasonable estimate of the range of hands the SB will shove over a c-bet at the equilibrium.

To estimate the BB's calling range, we just find all hands that can profitably call all-in versus that range, that is, those that have at least 33.3% equity versus the SB's shoving range. These are

44+, A5s+, K5s-K8s, Q7s-Q8s, A5o+, K6o-K8o, A♣4♣, K♣9♣, Q♣9♣, J♣8♣, J♣9♣, T♣9♣, A♢4♢, K♢9♢, Q♢9♢, J♢9♢, T♢9♢, A♡4♡, K♡9♡, Q♡9♡, J♡9♡, T♡9♡

which is 19.23% of all hands.

Then, to find the BB's bet-folding range, we solve for the frequency he needs to fold to the SB's shove so that the weakest of the SB's jamming range is indifferent to jamming and folding. From looking at the SB's jamming hands, we can guess that a borderline hand is Q♠-9♥ (which is actually played with a mixed strategy by the SB at the equilibrium in this spot). This hand has equity 0.319 when his shove is called by the BB. Let us set the SB's EV of folding equal to that of shoving this hand to find the BB's fold-to-shove frequency, X.

We have

$$EV_{SB}(\text{fold } Q♠ \, 9♡) = EV_{SB}(\text{shove } Q♠ \, 9♡)$$
$$25 = 40X + (60 \cdot 0.319)(1 - X)$$

which is satisfied by X=0.280. Thus, at the equilibrium, the BB is folding to the SB's shove 28% of the time. Since he is calling with 19.23% of all hands, he must be betting the flop with 26.73% of hands in total. This means that he is bet-folding with a bluff range comprised of 26.73%–19.23%=7.50% of all hands. Finally, the BB is getting to the flop with 32.58% of all hands (that is, a top-35% preflop range less those hands containing 8♥, 6♣, or 5♦), so he must be check-folding with 32.58%–26.73%=5.85% of all hands. We have now estimated equilibrium frequencies for each range in this game, and it turns out they are correct to within a percent or two.

> **We went through the algebra above quite quickly as it is similar to things we have done before. Work out the details yourself to make sure you understand it. Perhaps choose some more realistic preflop BB 3-bet and SB 3-bet-calling ranges.**

Now we can go back through this reasoning and look for places where it can break down. First, we simply used the bet and stack sizes in the hand to find the SB's jamming frequency and to estimate his range for doing so. We then found the BB's bet-calling range which is just all hands which had the correct odds to call all-in versus the SB's shoving range. Finally, we found the BB's bet-fold range by finding how often he needed to fold to the shove to make the SB indifferent between shoving and folding with the strongest of his folding hands.

Now, this line of reasoning made several implicit assumptions. For them to hold, we need the SB's range to be strong enough so that he can jam 2/3 of the time and still break even (with respect to folding) with his weakest jamming hand. The BB might have to be bet-folding a lot to make this true if the SB's cutoff hand is weak. However, the BB only has so many hands to bet-fold before he runs out and the indifference can not be satisfied. In other words, if the BB is betting the flop with his whole range, and the SB still can not profitably shove 2/3 of his hands, then the BB will not be indifferent between check-folding and bet-folding at the equilibrium – he will always prefer to bet-fold.

On the other hand, what happens if the strength of the SB's range is at the other extreme? Suppose the SB's range is so strong that he can profitably jam more than 2/3 of his hands even if the BB is never bet-folding. Then, he will do so – there is nothing the BB can do to stop it. In this case, the BB will always prefer check-folding to bet-folding with his weak hands.

So, the BB's bet-folding frequency is key. It goes to zero when the SB's range is too strong and to the other extreme when the SB's range is too weak. Let us solve for it in general. Let T be the total fraction of all hands with which the BB gets to the flop (0.3258 of all hands in the example above), let C be the total fraction of hands with which BB is bet-calling the flop (0.1923 in the example), and let F be the total fraction of hands with which the BB is bet-folding the flop (we estimated 0.075 above). Then, if we let EQ be the equity of the borderline hand between the SB's shoving and folding ranges (Q♠-9♥ in the example) versus the BB's shove-calling range, we can find F.

$$\mathrm{EV_{SB}(fold\ borderline\ hand)} = \mathrm{EV_{SB}(shove\ borderline\ hand)}$$
$$25 = 40\frac{F}{F+C} + 60EQ\frac{C}{F+C}$$
$$F = \frac{5-12EQ}{3}C$$

This gives us the proportion of hands the BB needs to be bet-folding to make the SB appropriately indifferent. Does this value of *F* agree with the one we found earlier?

We can now look at the requirements for the indifference equations to be satisfiable. Firstly, *F* needs to be at least 0 since bet-folding a negative number of hands makes no sense. Secondly, *F* can be no greater than (*T–C*). That is, the BB's bet-folding hands and bet-calling hands taken together can not add up to more hands than he gets to the flop with in the first place. Let us look at the consequences of these constraints. First, we have

$$0 \le F$$
$$0 \le \frac{5-12EQ}{3}C$$
$$EQ \le \frac{5}{12}$$

So, if *EQ*>5/12, it means that *F* is negative. In other words, the BB would have to be bet-folding a negative amount of hands to make the SB indifferent between shoving and folding the bottom of his shoving range. This can not be, and so this indicates that the SB's range is too strong – even if the BB is never folding to the shove, the 33rd percentile hand in the SB's range is still more profitable to shove than to fold. In this case, the SB will be shoving over 2/3 of the time, and the BB will not be indifferent between check-folding and bet-folding – he will always prefer check-fold. In this case, the BB's overall range is simply too weak for him to get away with *any* bluffs on the flop.

Consider the other constraint on *F*. We have

$$F \le T - C$$
$$\frac{5-12EQ}{3}C \le T - C$$
$$EQ \ge \frac{2}{3} - \frac{1}{4}\frac{T}{C}$$

Notice here that *C/T* is the fraction of hands that the BB is bet-calling out of those with which he gets to the flop, and *T/C* is just its reciprocal. So, if $EQ < 2/3 - 1/4 \times T/C$, it means that the BB would have to be bet-folding more hands than he can possibly have given the number of hands he gets to the flop with and bet-calls. Our interpretation of this result is that the SB's range is too weak. No realizable amount of BB bet-folding can make the SB's 33rd percentile hand a break-even jam. In this case, the SB will be shoving less than 2/3 of the time, and so the BB will always prefer bet-folding to check-folding. The SB's range is just too weak to jam often enough to keep the BB from bluffing with all of his weak hands.

How do these criteria change with different stack and bet sizes?

When the BB can be indifferent between bet-fold and check-fold

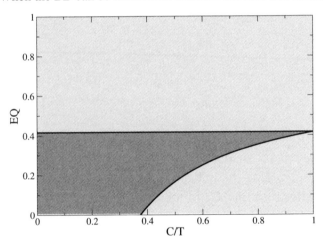

Figure 4.4: The bottom left region represents the combinations of SB and BB range strengths that make it possible to reach an equilibrium where the BB is sometimes bet-folding and sometimes check-folding.

In Figure 4.4 we have plotted these two inequalities with *EQ* on the vertical axis and *C/T* on the horizontal axis. *EQ* is the equity of the 33rd percentile hand in the SB's preflop range versus the BB's bet-calling hands, so it can be thought of as a measure of the strength of the SB's range. *C/T* is the fraction of hands the BB can profitably bet-call, so it can be thought of as a measure of the strength of the BB's range.

We can see in the figure the regions where both inequalities are satisfied. Above the horizontal line, the SB's range is too strong. He will be jamming more than 2/3 of the time, and the BB should never bet-fold. Below the curved line, the SB's range is too weak, and he will not be able to jam enough to keep the BB from betting the flop with his entire range. Only between the curves (i.e. the bottom left part of the figure) will the game reach an equilibrium where the BB is sometimes check-folding and sometimes bet-folding with hands that are not strong enough to bet-call.

It is interesting to note exactly what passes for hand strength here, that is, what factors actually have an effect on the GTO strategies. First of all, only the tops of the players' ranges matter – the hands they are actually willing to get all-in. Whether the hands the players are folding at some point are very weak or just slightly too weak to get all-in is unimportant. They do not come into play. Then, for the SB, the equity of his 33rd percentile hand is of particular importance (given the bet and stack sizes in the example). His strategy basically revolves around the question of whether or not this hand is strong enough that he can happily jam it over the c-bet even if BB is never bet-folding or weak enough that he can not jam it even if BB is never check-folding. If neither of those special cases holds, then the SB is jamming his top 67% of hands, and that's that. It is nice if his stronger shoving hands are particularly strong – it increases his expected profit – but it does not affect his strategy. On the other hand, the whole of the SB's jamming range affects the set of hands the BB can get all-in. His strategy is to bet-call with all of these and then just include enough bet-folding bluffs to balance.

In the previous example, we assumed that the players got to the flop with the same ranges. In this case, we are likely to find the indifferences satisfied at the equilibrium, at least at stack sizes which are conducive to the SB shoving over a flop bet, since the players both hold a lot of relatively strong and weak hands. On the other hand, in real play, it may well be true that the BB's range is strong enough that he can get away with bluffing with all his weak hands or that it is weak enough that he should bluff with none. In particular, it is common in 3-bet pots to assume that the BB has the stronger range by virtue of more aggressively preflop play. Thus, many BBs will bet the flop after 3-betting with a very high frequency. That said, being aware of this, a BB could easily overdo it and end up c-betting too much in some spots.

Of course, this is not just a question of the BB's overall c-betting frequencies – the particular board is very important here. Some flops connect much more strongly with one player's range than his opponent's. In fact, the 8♥-6♣-5♦ board we have been looking at is stereotypically one of these. Putting in some time away from the tables looking at how various flops interact with different preflop ranges and the consequences this has for proper flop play can be very beneficial. We will gain an additional analytical tool in the next chapter that will help us think about and visualize these issues more easily.

While players can end up with ranges with somewhat different strengths preflop, this situation is rare and minor compared to the asymmetries which arise postflop. Spots where one player's range is much stronger than his opponent's often arise in later-street situations where players' earlier actions have narrowed down their hand ranges. Fairly mild differences on early streets can be exacerbated when board cards come to help one player and hurt the other. Opportunities often arise to take advantage in these spots. In general, identifying as accurately as possible the ranges involved in any situation will take us a long way towards playing profitable HUNL..

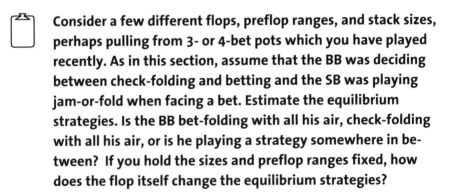 **Consider a few different flops, preflop ranges, and stack sizes, perhaps pulling from 3- or 4-bet pots which you have played recently. As in this section, assume that the BB was deciding between check-folding and betting and the SB was playing jam-or-fold when facing a bet. Estimate the equilibrium strategies. Is the BB bet-folding with all his air, check-folding with all his air, or is he playing a strategy somewhere in between? If you hold the sizes and preflop ranges fixed, how does the flop itself change the equilibrium strategies?**

4.3 Lessons

In this chapter, we introduced the Indifference Principle. It arose from the observation that unexploitable play can involve making more than one choice with a single hand in certain spots. This was the case when hands were being used as bluffs in preflop-only games. These hands were always folded if their bluffs were unsuccessful – it was just a question of when. In this case, neglecting card removal effects, the particular hands used for each bluffing line did not matter. Only the bulk bluffing frequencies were of import. So, for example, the SB's EVs of playing a bluff hand by open-folding, raise-folding, and raise-4-bet-folding had to be equal at the equilibrium. We found that this equality allowed us to solve for the BB's equilibrium frequencies.

The Indifference Principle is an extremely important idea for estimating GTO frequencies in various spots. There is an alternate way of thinking about certain applications of the principle that is especially useful for performing estimates at the table. Consider the flop subgame we studied in Section 4.2. We found the SB shoving frequency that made the BB indifferent between check-folding and bet-folding his bluffs. If the SB had folded to a bet more than 1/3 of the time, then the BB would have automatically profited with a bluff relative to check-folding, regardless of his holding. In other words, the 2/3 jamming frequency was the minimum necessary to keep the BB from bluffing with 100% of his weak hands.

This suggests something about the case where Villain bets with a range whose bluffs always lose when they do not bet. In this situation, unless Hero's range is just too weak to keep Villain from always bluffing, Hero should continue facing a bet, either by calling or raising, frequently enough that Villain can not profit with his bluffs. This result of the Indifference Principle is useful in a variety of spots. A corollary is also true: if Villain is not continuing enough versus a bet to keep Hero from profiting with his bluffs, then Hero should bluff 100% of the time. Of course, it is important to keep in mind the reverse as well. If Villain is continuing versus a bet more than the equilibrium frequency, we can essentially profit by never bluffing and always giving up with weak hands. This is not as sexy as the more aggressive case, but it is just as important.

In the context of the minraise/shove game, we found that Hero does better by minraising the button than by open-folding if Villain shoves from the BB less than 50%. This result carries over to more general HUNL situations where the BB might just call out of position preflop as well. In this case, even if Hero loses the pot every time the BB continues, he will still prefer to minraise 100% of his buttons until the BB is continuing (either by calling or raising) more than 50% of the time. The fact that Hero could improve to win with even his weakest hands if the BB flat calls is an extra bonus.

Lastly, we discussed situations where extreme stack sizes or differing range strengths could make it so that a player was unable to keep his opponent from bluffing profitably. In this case, the EV of bluffing was not equal to that of not-bluffing, so simple Indifference Principle arguments could not be used to estimate GTO frequencies. For example, it very well may be the case that the BB should defend less than 50% at certain stack sizes when facing an open-minraiser due to his postflop positional disadvantage. However, if this is the case, then the SB should be opening 100% of buttons. Identification and analysis of these sorts of situations will factor greatly into proper postflop play. We will see applications and refinements of these ideas throughout the book. We will discuss a few more important analytical tools in Chapter 5, before we begin a broad overview of how to approach full-game play in Chapter 6.

4.4 You Should Now...

♠ Be able to state the Indifference Principle and understand its connection to balance

♠ Be able to identify spots where a player is likely to be indifferent between two options with a particular hand at the equilibrium

♠ Be able to find the consequences Hero's indifference has for Villain's GTO strategy and understand how Hero can adjust exploitatively if Villain deviates from unexploitable play

♠ Understand how we used the Indifference Principle to essentially solve the minraise/3-bet/4-bet/shove game and the 3-bet/c-bet flop situation

♠ Understand how the indifference relationships broke down in preflop-only games due to extreme stack sizes and in the postflop situation due to asymmetric distributions

Chapter 5

Equity Distributions

Hold'em - like life itself - has its defining moment. It's the flop. When you see the flop, you're looking at 71 percent of your hand, and the cost is only a single round of betting. – Lou Krieger

A range is a list of hands, possibly with some associated frequency information. It is useful to know the ranges of hands held by opponents in various spots. To make strategic decisions based on players' ranges, we have to go a step further and evaluate the strengths of those various hands, both current and potential. To this end, we might colloquially speak about the strength of a range. A *strong* range is one which contains a lot of strong hands, a *weak* one contains mostly weak hands.

However, this is too inexact a description on which to base our strategic thought processes. A more fine-grained way to think about the strength of players' ranges relative to our own is needed. Of course, if we can narrow an opponent's holding to just a few possibilities, then thinking about his range in terms of those specific hands can lead to the best results. However, this can be difficult in HUNL where players can often show up with many different holdings, even on later streets.

In this chapter, we will introduce two graphical tools that we can use to visualize the strengths of various hands in a range. Ultimately, you will want to develop your hand-reading technique to the point that you do have a good idea as to whether or not your opponent can be holding any particular hand in a given spot and thus have a guess as to the specific list of hands in his range. However, as we will see, these tools will still be very useful for performing some quantitative strategizing since they abstract out some non-essential details of particular situations.

5.1 Hand Distributions

Hand distributions give us a simple way to visualize the strengths of all the hands in a player's range. Consider, for example, the distributions shown in Figure 5.1. These represent several possible BB preflop 3-betting ranges. All 1,326 hold'em starting hands are lined up on the horizontal axis, starting on the left with the nuts and ending on the far right with the nut low. On the vertical axis we show the fraction of each hand contained in the range.

To make these plots, we assume that we have some way to rank all of the BB's hands from best to worst. For example, we might measure strength of his 3-bet holdings according to their equity versus the SB's range at that point in the hand, that is, versus the SB's preflop opening range. It might be even better to rank hands according to their equity versus the range with which the SB continues versus a 3-bet, since that is what really matters. However, those two choices will lead to fairly similar results. More important is the general observation that the strengths of various parts of the BB's range depend on the SB's strategy. In any reasonable hand ranking, A-A is going to be the best hand and 2-3o will likely be the worst, but the strengths of many holdings in between depend on the SB's ranges. Notice that there is no (or, at least, much less) ambiguity in relative hand rankings on the river. The nuts is the best hand, the second nuts is the second best hand, etc., regardless of the other player's range. We will come back to this point in detail later. Anyhow, the reality is that on-the-fly visualization of hand distributions is an inexact science which we will only use to get a qualitative feel for players' ranges.

Now, consider the hand distributions shown in the figure. We will focus mostly on reading what the graphs say and leave in-depth evaluation of the 3-betting strategies they represent for later. Hand distribution 5.1 shows a 3-betting range consisting only of the strongest hands. The strongest hands are almost 100% in the range. This implies that the ranges associated with BB's other possible actions at his decision point, such as folding or calling, do not contain those hands at all. On the other hand, this distribution contains 0% of most weaker holdings.

Distribution 5.1b is similar to the previous one. Hero is again 3-betting with some of the strongest hands, but only 50 percent of the time each. Presumably he is calling with these holdings the other half of the time. Distribution 5.1c represents a different sort of range. Hero is 3-betting the top several percent of hands all the time and some chunk of hands in the middle half the time each. Distribution 5.1d represents a range only containing weak hands and, indeed, containing many of them. When might this represent a reasonable 3-betting range? Finally, distribution 5.1e represents a range containing only strong hands but none of the strongest or premium hands. Do you find that some opponents 3-bet this range? When might it be appropriate?

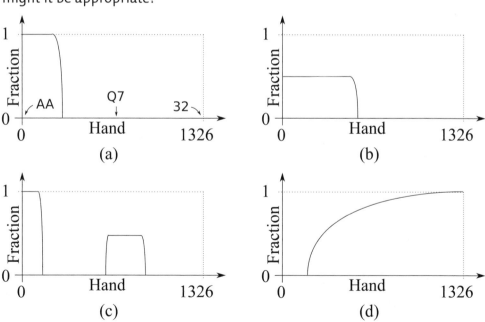

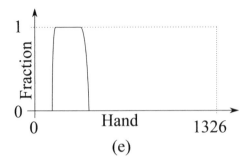

(e)

Figure 5.1: Example hand distributions representing various 3-betting ranges.

Visualizing ranges in terms of their distributions is often very helpful for formulating counter-strategies. Not to get ahead of ourselves, but as an example, consider how each of the 3-betting ranges diagrammed above might respond to a small preflop 4-bet. Would frequent small preflop 4-bets be a good exploitative strategy versus each of the 3-betting ranges shown?

Now, some terminology is very useful for describing hand distributions. Visualizing the details of entire distributions can make for the most accurate decisions, but roughly describing a distribution's qualitative features can make it easier to organize your thought processes, especially when making decisions very quickly. If you make an effort to think of your opponents' ranges in terms of the following descriptors, it will aid you in making more accurate decisions.

The concepts *strong* and *weak* refer to the overall average strength of the entire distribution. A *wide* distribution or range is one which contains many hands, and a *tight* distribution or range contains few hands.

A distribution is *capped* if it contains none of the strongest hands. We say it is *capped high* if there are relatively few of the strongest hands absent from it such as in Figure 5.1e. A distribution is *capped low* if a relatively large number of the strongest hands are absent, e.g. Figure 5.1d. In practice, if a player takes a line he would never take with the nuts, then his range is capped. We will see that this often happens on boards where the nuts changes significantly on turn and river cards and also that it can have large strategic consequences.

In practice, words describing the details of the strong ends of opponents' distributions tend to be more important for strategic decisions. However, it is sometimes useful to have analogous words for the bottom ends of ranges. We will refer to a range that contains none of the worst hands as *bounded below*. For example, a player's range is bounded below if he "definitely has something".

A *polarized* distribution is one which contains some relatively strong hands and some relatively weak ones but few or none in between. Figure 5.1c is a good example of this. Polarized ranges might often arise when a player plays a hand very aggressively: his range might contain strong hands and bluffs but little in between. Of course, a range can be polarized but still capped or bounded, etc. Polarization will be a particularly important concept for us.

In visualizing hand distributions, it is important to avoid fuzzy thinking as much as possible. The conclusion that a range is polarized is often useful in and of itself, but it is usually still important to know more details of the distribution. How big, relatively, are the strong and weak parts of the range? How strong is the strong? How weak is the weak?

Now, we will often want to formulate strategies like, "raise with the top X% of my range". However, even many strong players lack good intuition for which hand actually is their Xth percentile holding, especially in post-flop situations. So, let us take some examples. Figure 5.2 shows the 98th, 95th, 90th, 75th, 50th, and 25th percentile hands on some flops facing an any-two-cards (ATC) range.

Samples from some hand distributions

Percentile	2♠2♡2◊	J♠5♡3◊	K◊J♠7♡	T♠9♠8♠
98	7♡2♣	J♣3♠	K♣7◊	Q♠2♠
95	K◊K♠	A♣J◊	K♡Q◊	7♠6♣
90	A♣K♡	J◊6♠	K♣6◊	J♠8♡
75	A◊3♣	9♣5♣	T♡T♣	Q♠6♡
50	Q◊3♠	A♠6◊	A♣6◊	Q♡4♠
25	9◊7♣	7♣6♠	9♣6♠	A♡K◊

Figure 5.2: The 98th, 95th, 90th, 75th, 50th, and 25th percentile hands on some flops facing an any-two-cards (ATC) range.

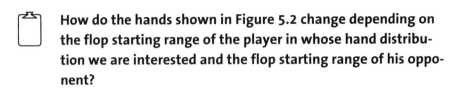

How do the hands shown in Figure 5.2 change depending on the flop starting range of the player in whose hand distribution we are interested and the flop starting range of his opponent?

Notice that, e.g., A-high is quite close to the top of the distribution on the 2♠-2♥-2♦ board but near the bottom on 10♠-9♠-8♠. We refer to "A-high" as the *absolute strength* of the holding, and it is the same on both boards. However, the hand's *relative strength* is very different, that is, the strength of a holding relative to an opponent's range. The discussion in this chapter should convince you that relative strength is what really matters from a strategic standpoint. How might you take advantage of players who focus a bit too much on the absolute strength of their hands, especially on some of the more extreme boards such as 2♠-2♥-2♦ or 10♠-9♠-8♠?

Visualizing ranges in terms of hand distributions can be helpful for making accurate strategic decisions quickly when facing opponents with wide ranges. In less common spots where an opponent's range is very tight and can be narrowed to just a few hands, it will be better to think about play versus those individual hands. However, wide ranges occur often in heads-up play, especially on early streets, in short-stacked situations, and when facing commonly-used lines. In these cases, it can be more useful to think of ranges in terms of hand distribution shapes and consider strategizing in terms of play against bulges in the distributions instead of against specific hands.

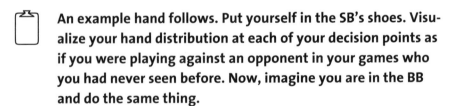

An example hand follows. Put yourself in the SB's shoes. Visualize your hand distribution at each of your decision points as if you were playing against an opponent in your games who you had never seen before. Now, imagine you are in the BB and do the same thing.

Effective stacks: 100 BB
Preflop:
SB raises to 3BB, BB raises to 10BB, SB calls 7BB
Flop: 10♣ 8♥ 2♦ (20BB)
BB bets 10BB, SB calls 10BB

Turn: 6♠ (40BB)
BB bets 22BB, SB calls 22BB
River: 3♠ (84BB)
BB bets 58BB and is all-in

Many players effectively visualize ranges in terms of hand distributions. However, as we saw, the mere ranking of hands according to their equity does not tell the whole story. In particular, we would also like to think about precisely how much equity hands have and how that might change on certain cards on later streets. For example, on some boards, a good hand will be pretty much a lock versus any worse hand. On other boards, there may be draws which have good equity even versus the current nuts. This motivates the use of equity distributions which can show more of the story.

5.2 Equity Distributions

The equity distribution is another way to visualize the strength of various parts of your range versus your opponent's. These are graphed similarly to the hand distributions. Again you plot all of the hands in your range on the horizontal axis. However, instead of plotting all 1,326 hands, you only include hands which are actually in the range. Furthermore, each hand does not get a whole 1 unit of horizontal space; it only gets as much as it is in the range. For example, a hand which is only 5% in the range only gets 0.05 horizontal width. Then, on the vertical axis is the equity of each hand versus Villain's range. In this way, an equity distribution shows how large a range is: the total width of the plot along the horizontal axis.

The average height of the graph is the average equity of the range. However, there is a big difference between holding a range where all of your hands have mediocre equity and holding a range where some of your hands are particularly strong and some are particularly weak, and this difference shows up in the graph. That is, an equity distribution shows you how your equity is distributed throughout your range. An example will help to make this clear.

Consider Figure 5.3 which shows the equity distribution of an "any two cards" (ATC) range versus ATC preflop. The horizontal axis goes from 0 to 1,326 since 100% of hands are included in the range. Equity values on the vertical axis range from about 0.85 to 0.323, the all-in preflop equities of AA and 32o, respectively, versus ATC. After the few premium-type hands on the left side of the graph (hands with greater than 65% equity are, in order, A-A, K-K, Q-Q, J-J, 10-10, 9-9, 8-8, A-Ks, 7-7, A-Qs, A-Js, and A-Ko) the graph declines fairly slowly – there are many hands close in equity.

Preflop equity distribution of ATC versus ATC

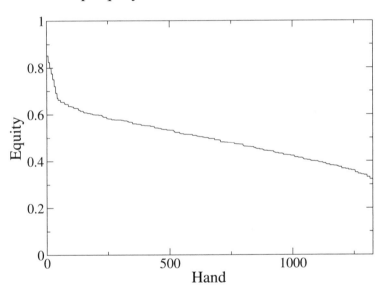

Figure 5.3: Equity distribution of ATC vs ATC preflop.

Although hand distributions rank hands in order according to their equity, they do not show how much equity various parts of a range actually have. Equity distributions present this information very clearly. Let us consider a few postflop examples.

Recall the four flops we considered in the previous section: 2♠-2♥-2♦, J♠-5♥-3♦, K♦-J♠-7♥, and 10♠-9♠-8♠. If Hero is opening the top 80% of hands from the SB and his opponent is defending the top 40%, we can plot Hero's equity distribution on each board at the beginning of flop play. We will not dwell on this choice of ranges as it is not particularly important for the example, but it represents reasonable strategies for both players at certain stack and raise sizes with the exception of our neglect of preflop re-raising. The SB's equity distributions at the beginning of flop play are shown in Figure 5.4. Each of these equity distributions contains between 900 and 1,000 hands. There are the most hands on 2♥-2♠-2♦ since that board overlaps the least with the SB's opening range.

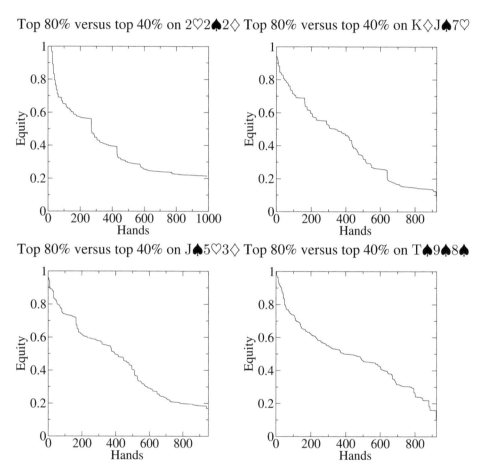

Figure 5.4: Equity distributions of the top 80% of hands when facing the top 40% on several flops.

If we start by looking at the top left corner of each graph, we can see how much equity the top of the SB's range (i.e. its best hands) has. On 2♥-2♠-2♦, there is a small number of hands that have very near 100 percent equity – they are more-or-less complete locks. These are, of course, the flopped four-of-a-kind hands. Big pocket pairs are also near-locks for the SB on this board since the BB's preflop defending range contains few deuces and bare under-card hands have no outs. On the other hand, on K♦-J♠-7♥, the top of the SB's range, K-K, only has around 94% equity. This is because there are draws on board, but no straights or flushes are actually yet possible.

Let us move slightly to the right in each plot towards the 100th best hand which is around the 90th percentile. Hands' equities on the dry 2♥-2♠-2♦ board drop off very quickly. The 90th percentile hand is A-Qo. It only has 65 percent equity since even when it is the best hand, the BB's two cards have a substantial chance to improve to a full house by the river. Thus, even a top-10% hand on this board such as A-Q can be awkward to play since it has a lot to worry about unless it improves.

These two properties of the 2♥-2♠-2♦ board have significant strategic im-port. First, the good hands have high equity – they are nearly invulnerable. Second, there are relatively few of these hands. If a player plays this flop very aggressively, the hands he is *representing* (that is, the hands that he holds or is pretending to hold) are more or less invulnerable, but it is hard to have one of these hands. This contrasts with the situation on the other three boards where there are more hands with more equity but no hands which have such complete locks on the flop. On the 2♥-2♠-2♦, it is very hard for his opponent to have a hand with which he wants to fight back. This can make good spots to bluff on this sort of board. Although 2♥-2♠-2♦ is an extreme case, paired boards and boards with a single high card and no draws are much more common flops that also have this property to a degree.

As we will see, at least on the river, the ideal equity distribution is, in some sense, a straight line. That is, the 90th percentile hand has 90 percent eq-uity, the 70th percentile hand has 70 percent equity, etc. It is hard to over-state the strategic importance of deviations from the ideal. These consid-erations form the basis of exploiting many players.

The thing is that players tend to have a good feel for their equity with a par-ticular holding. They have a lot of experience counting outs and using the "rule of 4 and 2", or working with computational equity calculators, etc.

Players tend to be much worse at estimating the percentile at which a hand falls within their own range and incorporating that information into their strategies. However, the second skill is often at least as important as the first. For example, in Chapter 4, we saw that minraise-folding a SB preflop was always better than open-folding as long as the BB would fold to the raise at least half the time. That is, the SB can "automatically profit" by raising no matter what his actual holding is, if the BB does not prevent him from doing so.

Now, people have a lot of experience regulating their preflop frequencies since preflop situations come up often and are all more or less the same insofar as no community cards have yet been dealt. However, these "automatic profit" opportunities come up all the time postflop. In fact, the possibility should be considered at every decision point where we have a chance to bet or raise. We will frequently be able to take advantage of them when facing opponents who are focused too much on their particular holding and not enough on their whole range by identifying boards on which they have few hands with significant equity. So, players are good at figuring out their equity. What they often need to know, however, is where a hand fits into their entire range in a situation. The equity distribution shows the connection between those two numbers.

Additionally, the situation with the 65% equity hand A-Q on 2♥-2♠-2♦ does not have to be as awkward as some players might feel. On the K♦-J♠-7♥, the 90th percentile hand is K-8o. It has about 71% equity. This demonstrates the strength of the approach of viewing hands by their spot in an equity distribution. Insofar as 71% equity is not too much different from 65% equity, A-Q on the 2♥-2♠-2♦ should be viewed and played much like a weak king on the K♦-J♠-7♥: they are both relatively strong hands on their respective boards, they are ahead of the same amount of Hero's own range, and hands which they are ahead of but which continue versus a bet likely have between 3 to 6 outs.

On the other hand, it is relatively easy to tell which turn and river cards might connect with the straight draws that Villain is bluffing with on the K♦-J♠-7♥ but less obvious which cards might improve his bluffs on the 2♥-2♠-2♦. Or at least it is somewhat more player-dependent. For example,

Villain might feel that it is best if his bluffing range is composed primarily of high-card type hands. However, weak opponents will decide to bluff those boards when they feel like it whereas stronger ones will tend to bluff when they have the good hands for it.

But we digress. Weak kings may be thought of as similar to A-Q on the respective boards for strategic purposes. That said, a 5-6 percent difference in equity is nothing to sneeze at. It certainly is significant in many cases. It is just that the psychological difference between having top pair in the situation where only a few well-defined cards need be feared and having only a high card where all cards must be feared but in reality no particular card is that likely to help Villain leads people to overestimate the difference in relative hand strengths between the situations. This effect is an additional reason why bluffing these 2♥-2♠-2♦-like boards can be profitable.

Moving further to the right on each plot in Figure 5.4, we see a few "step" type features where there are a lot of hand combinations with about the same equity before a sharp drop-off. On the K♦-J♠-7♥ flop, the first step is the top-pair-weak-kicker hands and the second step is second-pair hands. On the 2♥-2♠-2♦, the two steps correspond to A-high and K-high holdings.

On the J♠-5♥-3♦, the first step is the jacks, but the fives do not make a step. To see why this is, consider that A-5o has about 63% equity versus the BB's preflop range whereas A♥-K♥, with overs and some straight and flush possibilities, has 61% – about the same. This is for two reasons. Firstly, since the second pair on this board is so low, it is very vulnerable. Most of the BB's holdings have two overcards if they are not already ahead. Secondly, if the BB does not yet have a pair (a likely scenario since there are few fives or treys contained in his OOP defending range), then the A-K is likely to be good, and it also has a decent amount of equity when behind. We might refer to these holdings as *weak made hands*.

The 10♠-9♠-8♠ board is a bit different in this respect. Since it is so drawy, tons of hands have a least a little equity. It turns out that it is necessary to have some sort of draw to go along with a made hand to actually be in good shape. For example, a draw-less top pair-top kicker hand such as A♥-10♥, is actually in the 70th percentile of hands and only has 54% equity versus the BB's entire preflop defending range! On the other hand, A♠-10♥

is in the 93rd percentile and has 77% equity. Also, J♠-J♥ has more equity than 10♣-10♥ versus the BB's defending range (but possibly not versus his get-it-in range on the flop or on a variety of turn and river cards). For this reason, there are no well-defined "steps" associated with made hands. The made hands are all mixed in with all the draws since many draw-type hands have more equity than the made hands.

Finally, we will consider the overall shapes of the graphs. They all look somewhat similar as will most equity distributions which compare wide-range versus wide-range on early streets. We will see that, as more cards come out and/or ranges become tighter and more defined, the structure of these equity distribution plots can become more telling. We will see plenty of examples like this when we consider equity distributions on the river, so there is no reason to delve into that here just for the sake of an example – discussion of these flop equity distributions should give plenty of intuition as to how they work.

However, the overall shape of the graphs in these early-street spots is very important in itself as we can see if we think about them slightly differently. For example, what is the average equity of SB's top-80% range facing BB's top-40% range on each of these flops? We expect the BB to usually be ahead since he is playing a stronger preflop range, but how much on each board? These numbers are shown in Figure 5.5, and we include the preflop range versus range equity for comparison. Of course, the BB's equity in these spots is just 100% minus the SB's equity.

SB equities

Board	Preflop	2♠2♡2◇	J♠5♡3◇	K◇J♠7♡	T♠9♠8♠
SB Equity	42.4%	38.7%	44.1%	39.9%	48.3%

Figure 5.5: Equity of a top-80% SB opening range versus a top-40% BB defending range on several flops.

Firstly, as you might have guessed, the BB's stronger preflop range is holding up the best on the 2♠-2♥-2♦ flop. If a hand was the best preflop, it is very likely to have stayed that way on a flop which improves so few holdings. At the other extreme, the 10♠-9♠-8♠ flop has almost equalized the situation. That board has such a huge effect on the relative equities of different holdings that hands' preflop strengths matter little.

This is probably something we could have guessed before looking at all these plots: the BB has a bit more equity on the flop and how much exactly depends on how the flop interacts with players' ranges. However, for strategic purposes, it is very important not just how much average equity the players' preflop ranges have versus each other on different flops, but how that equity is distributed between different hands in their ranges. Notice that, graphically, the average equity is just the average height of the equity distribution curve. (For the mathematically-inclined, this is the integral of the distribution curve normalized by its width.) At the most basic level, situations where many of your hands have a bit of equity each can be much more difficult to play than situations where some hands have a lot of equity and some hands have very little. This has been discussed a bit in terms of bluffing on the dry boards, but we will come back to these ideas frequently in the next couple of chapters.

There are two things which equity distributions do not tell us when considering ranges on early streets. Both have to do with the presence of draws. To see these issues, it is important to understand the difference between made hands and draws. Although most people have an intuitive understanding of the difference, it is helpful to nail it down in terms of the essentials.

Take an example. Suppose you defend a raise in the BB versus an opponent who is opening the top 80 percent of hands. The flop comes A♥-8♥-2♠. Consider two hands you could hold: 5♥-4♥ and 5♦-5♣. The 5♥-4♥ has 53.7 percent equity and the 5♦-5♣ has 53.6 percent. These two hands look pretty much the same on the equity distribution plot, yet there are significant strategic differences between them. The two things the equity distribution plot neglects to show us are:

1. The equity of the draw is going to change drastically on later streets depending on which cards come off.

2. The draw has about the same equity versus almost all of the SB's hands on the flop, whereas the pair is either significantly ahead of or pretty far behind most particular holdings in the SB's range.

We can see this graphically by looking at things from the SB's point of view. Figure 5.6 shows the equity of the SB's top-80% range when the BB has either the 5♥-4♥ or 5♦-5♣ on the A♥-8♥-2♠ flop. When facing the draw, the only hands in SB's range with better than 60% equity are sets and dominating draws, but even the SB's complete air hands like 7-6o have about 40% equity. On the other hand, when facing the made hand, the ma-jority of the SB's range is in one of two groups: hands with greater than 80% equity and hands with less than 35%. There is very little in the middle. Thus, the difference between these two BB holdings is great, but it is not represented in the equity distribution.

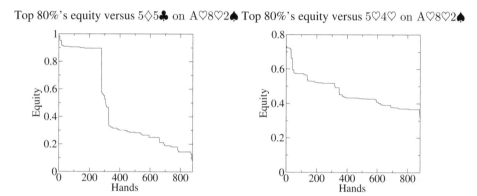

Top 80%'s equity versus 5♦5♣ on A♡8♡2♠   Top 80%'s equity versus 5♡4♡ on A♡8♡2♠

Figure 5.6: Equity distribution of the top 80% of hands when facing a draw and a made hand on A♥-8♥-2♠.

A full discussion of the strategic consequences of these issues would be get-ting ahead of ourselves. However, readers might recognize this as the basis for the semi-bluff play. Playing aggressively on the flop with the draw is likely profitable since the SB will fold a lot of the hands that have good eq-uity against it (such as the 7-6o), and the SB's good hands that do continue still only have mediocre equity versus the draw. On the other hand, playing the weak made hand aggressively would likely just cause the SB to fold all of his worse hands and continue with better ones, an unprofitable result. The point here is that the equity distribution does not give all the information needed to make strategic decisions, at least on boards with draws present.

However, equity distributions do capture a lot of important information and can help a player make sound strategic decisions. Most notably, the approach provides a natural way to consider individual holdings in the context of all the hands you might hold in a spot and how they stack up versus an opponent. They abstract many details of the situation away from the cards. This makes it relatively easy to draw parallels between different boards and aids the development of a mental framework within which we can view different boards and integrate knowledge about various situations' similarities and differences.

In fact, some players use this situation-abstracting power of equity distributions to help learn new games. Unsure how to play a spot in a new poker game? Find a spot in a game you know better (which has a similar betting structure) in which you hold a similar equity distribution and then play similarly. Equity distributions' power is in presenting most of the essential information without the extra baggage associated with the specifics of the cards. The plot throws away all absolute hand information and just gives most of the strategically-important relative hand strength, freeing you to think about play. On the river, it even does somewhat better than that.

5.3 Equity Distributions on the River

Equity distributions on the river are something of a special case. They have properties in addition to those had by distributions on the earlier streets that make them especially useful. We will refer to the equity distribution constructs extensively in our analysis of river play, so it is good to go ahead and mention these issues.

First, remember we noted that equity distributions do not effectively capture the differences between made hands and draws. This is no longer an issue since there are no more draws on the river.

The easiest way to see the second simplification that occurs on the river is to consider the problem of ranking hands. Recall that, preflop, J-10s is ahead of 2-2 which is ahead of A-Ko which is ahead of J-10s. The same thing happens when considering the equity of individual hands versus specific ranges. There are some ranges against which A-K is much better preflop than 8-8, and others against which 8-8 does a lot better than A-K. That is, there is no absolute ranking of hands possible – hand strengths are situationally-dependent.

However, the ranking of all possible hands from strongest to weakest on the river is the same no matter what range they are put up against (almost). The nuts is the strongest hand, the second nuts comes next, etc. The second nuts is better than the third nuts regardless of the range which it is up against. If we are on the river, and J-10s is better than 2-2, and 2-2 is better than A-Ko, then it is necessarily the case that J-10s is better than A-Ko, too. Let us drive this home with a concrete example.

Recall the hand discussed in Section 2.2.3 where we reached the river on J♠-6♥-3♠-J♦-2♦. J♥-J♣ is the best hand possible. The various J-6 combinations tie for second. The J-3 hands tie for 8-13th place, the J-2 for 14-19th place, and so on. This ranking does not depend on Villain's range of holdings.

The specific equities of hands still depend on Villain's range, of course. However, even the interpretation of equity becomes simpler on the river. A hand's equity on the river is just the fraction of Villain's hands it is ahead of (plus half of those with which it ties, if any). That is, if your opponent on the river holds a range with 100 hand combinations, and your hand beats 30 of them and loses to 70, then you have 30% equity.

So, what does this mean for equity distributions? To make an equity distribution, we simply plot each hand according to its ranking in our range and its equity versus our opponent's range. What exactly does this mean on the river? On the horizontal axis, each of our hands is plotted based on how many hands in our own range that it beats. On the vertical axis, each hand is plotted based on the fraction of hands in Villain's range that it beats.

This leads to a certain symmetry between Hero's distribution versus Villain's range and Villain's distribution versus Hero's range. Hero's distribution is just a plot which shows, for each hand, the number of hands in Hero's range which it is ahead of versus the number of hands in Villain's range it beats. Villain's distribution is just the reverse: a plot of each hand according to the number of hands in Villain's range it beats versus the number of hands in Hero's range it beats. Thus, to find Villain's equity distribution, we can essentially just flip the graph of Hero's equity distribution. This is illustrated in Figure 5.7 where we show the two players' equity distributions with ranges as described in Section 2.2.3 on the J♠-6♥-3♠-J♦-2♦ board.

In order to emphasize this symmetry, we will sometimes normalize the horizontal axis so that instead of going from 0 up to the number of hands, it goes from 0 to 1. In this case, each hand is essentially allotted space on the horizontal axis equal to the fraction of the range which it makes up. We will discuss this further when we use it in the context of river play in Chapter 7.

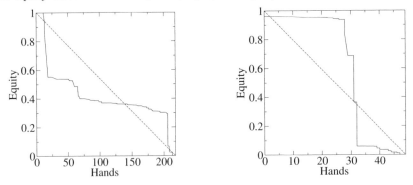

Figure 5.7: SB and BB equity distributions on the river of J♠-6♥-3♠-J♦-2♦. Flipping the SB distribution about the straight line plotted gives us the BB equity distribution except for some some card removal effects.

Now, there are a couple a slight exceptions to all of this. The first has to do with card-removal effects. Consider the following example. Suppose Hero reaches the river on a board of K♠-7♠-2♠-3♥-8♣ and that Villain's range is {A♠-5♥, A♠-5♠, J♥-J♦}. If Hero holds A♥-A♦, then he has the best hand 2/3 of the time. If he holds A♠-K♦, then he has the best hand all of the time. This may be a bit unintuitive since a pair of aces is stronger than a pair of kings, but of course the reason for this is that when Hero's hand contains the A♠, Villain's range becomes exactly J♥-J♦. This is a card-elimination or card-removal effect: Villain's range depends slightly on Hero's holding. The second issue arises when multiple hands have the same value on the river, i.e., they chop. For example, in the most extreme case, the nuts are on board and all hands chop. In this case, all hands will have 50% equity, and the players' distributions are not mirror images of one another. More commonly, various one-pair hands with kickers too low to play will end up chopping.

These issues can make the graph flipping construction imprecise. Because of these effects, the number of hands in Villain's range that a particular Hero holding is ahead of divided by the total number of hands in the Villain's range is not quite the same as Hero's equity in the hand. The reader may have noticed that the two graphs in Figure 5.7 were not quite mirror images of each other as claimed. A more direct way to visualize this issue is to consider the river distribution of ATC versus ATC. Since the two players' ranges are the same, flipping one player's distribution graph has to give you the same graph you started with, and a straight line along the mirror axis is the only curve which satisfies this symmetry constraint. The ATC versus ATC distribution is plotted for two rivers in Figure 5.8, and it is clear that they are not straight lines. They lie near the line but deviate from it slightly. These equity distributions have been plotted by assigning each of Hero's hands a number between 0 and 1, as described above, in anticipation of our approach during our discussion of river play.

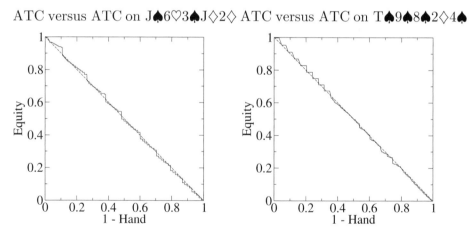

Figure 5.8: Equity distributions for ATC vs ATC on two rivers. A straight line representing the ideal is also drawn for comparison.

We mention these points for the sake of completeness, but they are fairly minor issues in most situations, far outweighed by the value we will gain from framing much of our discussion in terms of equity distributions. The card removal effects are only particularly important when considering narrow ranges on the river, and we will address these situations specifically. Thus, most of our river discussion will be in terms of the players' distributions, and we will take advantage of the symmetry between them.

5.4 You Should Now...

♠ Know how to visualize the strength of the hands making up a range through hand distributions

♠ Be familiar with the words used to describe hand distributions and the associated ranges

♠ Be able to estimate where a particular hand might fall in the context of your entire range

♠ Understand how the relative strengths of all hands in a range can be visualized with an equity distribution

♠ Understand how flops interact with players' ranges using equity distributions

♠ Understand the relationship between two players' equity distributions on the river

Chapter 6

Postflop concepts

Poker's a day to learn and a lifetime to master. – Robert Williamson III

6.1 Introduction to Postflop Concepts

In this chapter, we will start to introduce the concepts needed to strategize about full HUNL (i.e. postflop) play. This will set the stage for the remaining chapters which focus on the river, the turn, the flop, and, finally, the pre-flop betting round, in that order. This sequence, from the end of a hand to the beginning, may seem counter-intuitive. There are some fairly compelling reasons to think that the opposite is more natural. Of course, when we actually play a hand, we start with preflop and end on the river. Proper play on one street depends strongly on the hands you get there with, i.e., how you played the previous streets. Thus, it is somewhat difficult to talk about later streets before talking about earlier ones.

However, this straightforward dependence of prior streets on future ones is intuitive and fairly well understood by most players. Much less appreciated, and in many ways more important and fundamental to playing strategically, is the dependence of early street play on that of the later ones. When strategizing, it is important to keep in mind where the money comes from in poker, that is, where the payoffs are in the game. The payoffs come at the end of the hand – at the leaves of the decision tree, after a fold or at show-down. The only purpose of early-in-the-hand decisions is to lead the play towards the most profitable end-of-hand situations, that is, to get to the leaves of the decision tree with the highest pay-offs (on average).

To see this point more clearly, remember the way we actually solved for exploitative strategies in Section 2.2. Our EV at any given decision point depended on those directly below it in the decision tree. In turn, the EVs at those lower points depended on the EVs at the ones below them, and so on down to the leaves at the end of the hand. Thus, estimating the value of various holdings towards the end of a hand is a necessary prerequisite for evaluating decisions earlier in the hand. In particular, understanding the value of various river situations is necessary to even start thinking about turn play. Knowing the EV of having a hand on the turn is necessary to evaluate the merits of any flop decisions which can lead to the turn. And so on. This dependence of early decision points on the later ones is both more fundamental to game-theoretic strategizing and less understood by most players than the naive progression, so we have chosen to focus on it here.

Still, our analyses of river play must make some assumptions about the players' *river starting ranges* – the hands they get to the river with. This is not actually a major disadvantage of our approach: discussing "correct" flop and turn play before river play would not necessarily lessen the number of river situations we need to consider. Insofar as we are interested in playing exploitable opponents, knowing what hands the players "should" get to the flop with does not help simplify our analysis too much – we still want to consider play against a variety of opponent strategies.

That said, a little discussion of the big ideas of early-street play is called for to justify some of our assumptions in the following chapters, especially our justifications for starting ranges on later streets. For this reason and also just to get our feet wet thinking about postflop situations in general, we will give a brief overview of postflop play from the beginning to the end of hand before proceeding with the more advanced approach.

That is the first goal of this chapter – to start developing some intuition for what players' hand distributions on postflop streets might look like. This will give us a good foundation and context in which to understand the next few chapters. This chapter might read more easily than past ones as it is less technical – there is little math. However, this appearance is deceiving. We cover some very important ideas here, and it is especially important that less experienced players read carefully and supplement the discussion with examples of players' ranges in various spots from their own experience to get the most out of the discussion.

The second major purpose of this chapter is to drill home the practice of range-based thinking. We will constantly be considering all the hands with which players might take various actions and not just some particular holdings. It is extremely important to make this a habit that carries over to the tables. This may be hard at first since it takes much more mental effort than lazier decision making methods, but the reward is great, and it becomes easier with practice.

Keep in mind that range-oriented thinking requires you to keep two players' ranges in mind. The majority of modern HUNL players have developed the habit of thinking about their opponent's range. Almost everyone knows that his opponent can have a variety of different hands in most spots and makes some effort to play in a way that does best on average versus all of those. The skill in which many players are still relatively weak is keeping their own range in mind as well and in properly incorporating that information into their decision making processes. We will see that doing so is critical to strategizing and to deciding on the most profitable ways to play individual hands versus thinking opponents.

The third purpose of this chapter is to start thinking about the style of play which is considered "standard" or "solid" in many games at the time of writing. Of course, this style varies dramatically from cardroom to cardroom, buy-in level to buy-in level, player to player, and, indeed, month to month. The dynamic nature of this material makes a book a poor format for discussing it. Therefore, this book's focus is on the theory which will not change. However, there are some ideas built up from players' long experience that that are useful in their own right. More importantly, an awareness of some of the basic thought processes which players might be using to reason about the game is important for interpreting your opponents' play and for understanding how they might view your own actions.

Thus, much of the discussion in this chapter revolves around strategies which are not necessarily GTO nor generated to exploit any particular opponent's tendencies. The focus here, however, is less on the ranges themselves than on an awareness of the thought processes that lead to them. We will make only a little mention of exploitative responses to the strategies we describe in this chapter, but many of the ideas lead to play which is certainly exploitable, so it is a good idea to be thinking about it.

6.2 Postflop Concepts and Board Texture

We want to discuss the ranges with which we might take different postflop lines on different boards, and we want to do so in a way that emphasizes thought processes and concepts more than the specific ranges. This is convenient – specific ranges depend strongly on things like stack depth and preflop tendencies, but to demonstrate these concepts, we can just pick a representative example and run with it.

So for concreteness, assume we are playing 100 BB deep, and both players are competent. Additionally, for the sake of discussion, we will suppose that Hero is in the SB. Assume he is open-raising almost all hands preflop and Villain is capable of defending a fairly wide range made up of hands with high-card strength as well as those with some degree of suited and/or connectedness. Perhaps Hero's standard open is a minraise, and Villain is folding about half the time.

We will consider play in singly-raised pots and focus the discussion on situations when the BB is primarily check-calling down. Of course, the BB's options to lead and raise preflop and postflop (not to mention the use of different bet sizings) are extremely important strategically, but again, this is more of an example of the kinds of things to think about than a comprehensive guide to postflop play. Anyhow, we will consider, for example, the threat of the check-raise when discussing Hero's SB options, but will not explore the results of those lines in much depth. In this way, we can cover many common lines while limiting the scope of discussion but retaining a rich enough framework in which to present some important concepts.

So this will be a discussion of how many and which streets Hero will bet in situations when Villain is check-calling down. In this case, since Hero has two choices when checked to on each of the three postflop streets, there are only eight different lines he can take. A little bit of notation will make discussing them easier. If, for example, Hero bets the flop and then checks back the turn and river when checked to, we will say something like Hero went "bet, check, check", and call his line simply *bcc*. If Hero bets flop, checks turn, bets river, we will call it the "bet, check, bet" or the *bcb* line, and so on. By the way, shorthand notation like this can be very useful when making notes about opponents at the table.

Now, how should SB decide which line to take in a particular hand? There are just a few primary variables we will use here to distinguish between different situations:

- ♠ Our hand and range
- ♠ Villain's range
- ♠ The flop texture
- ♠ Turn and river cards

Board texture is a general term referring to how the different community cards interact with each other and are likely to interact with players' holdings. We say very generally that a board is especially textured if it "has a lot going on" in terms of possible draws or ways of connecting with players' hands. However, we can be much more specific than this.

Let us dive right in by talking about various possible board textures. First, in broad terms, there are two primary issues.

- ♠ How is the current board likely to interact with or improve hands in the players' starting ranges?
- ♠ Given the current board, how are future cards likely to further interact with the hands with which the players make it to the future streets?

Clearly these questions have different answers depending on certain properties of the board.

6.2.1 Flop Texture

Strength

Let us focus now on the flop and take the first question first – how do various flops interact with the ranges with which players see them? The general terms *strong* and *weak* are used to describe the degree of likelihood that the flop has "hit" or improved a player's hand in some way. A flop is strong for a player if it is likely to have hit him and improved his hand, and a weak flop is the opposite.

It is important to be clear about what we mean by hand strength. We mentioned the difference between absolute and relative hand strength in Section 5.1. Absolute strength refers to the simple mechanical ranking of a particular holding (high card, one pair, two pair, etc), while relative strength refers to a hand's value relative to an opponent's range. Relative strength is much more important for strategic purposes, but it is important to keep in mind issues surrounding absolute strength as well, if for no other reason than to deal with weak players who get very excited to make two pair despite the fact that the board is 4♠-5♠-8♠-10♥-7♠.

To be specific about our meaning, we call a board *absolutely strong* or *absolutely weak* for a player if it is likely or unlikely to improve his absolute hand strength, and we call a board *relatively strong* or *relatively weak* for him depending on its effect on his relative hand strength. Notice that a board can be absolutely strong for both players – some boards just connect with a lot of hands. Similarly, some boards tend to be absolutely weak for both players. However, a board which is relatively strong for one player is necessarily relatively weak for the other. If the board improves Hero's range when compared to Villain's, then it has weakened Villain's range when compared to Hero's.

So, it is important to keep in mind the difference between absolute and relative board strength since the terms themselves can be a little misleading. If it is said that a board is absolutely strong for a player, it might give the impression that that is a more weighty statement than saying the board is relatively strong for him. However, the second is far more important for strategic purposes. Occasionally, we might refer to a board as strong or weak for a player without specifying absolute or relative strength. In this case, we mean relative strength.

These terms do not say all there is to be said about how boards affect ranges. Perhaps a player's range and a particular board is such that half of his range is made to be quite strong and half very weak. None of the terms we have coined so far really describe this situation. In these spots, it is necessary to be thinking in terms of hand distributions to get the most accurate picture possible. In fact, it is really always best to be thinking in terms of the details of the distributions when you have the mental energy, but the ability to make quick evaluations is a useful skill in itself. And the general concepts of strong and weak can be useful on their own – think for example about the 3-bet/continuation-bet example in Section 4.2 where we saw that some very large-scale features of a player's range dictated equilibrium play.

We can demonstrate these ideas with some examples. Consider the board J♠-10♠-9♠, and, suppose the BB gets to the flop with the top 40% of hands. In this case, the flop gives him a made hand, pair or better, 52.5% of the time and, additionally, a draw gutshot or better 67.1% of the time! So, the BB will have "something" on this flop a significant majority of the time. The same flop will give the SB's 100% opening range a pair or better 46.4% of the time and a gutshot draw or better with a frequency of 64%. These are all big numbers – this board just connects with a lot of hands. So, this board is absolutely strong for both players. Now consider the flop K♠-7♥-2♦. The BB's range makes a pair or better 45.3% of the time whereas the any-two-cards (ATC) range has a pair or better with a frequency of 38.8%. Additionally, neither player can ever have any real draw. It is significantly harder to hit this board.

There are a couple of things to notice here. First, some boards just tend to be absolutely strong for almost all ranges (like J♠-10♠-9♠). Some tend to be absolutely weak for almost all ranges (the K♠-7♥-2♦). Some flops are just much more likely than others to give an opponent, say, a reason to want to continue in the hand facing a bet. It is a bit of sloppy wording, but we might refer to these boards as strong or weak in general without bothering to consider the players' ranges. Successful play in these extreme cases revolves around analysis of relative hand strengths.

Now, it is important to notice that board texture is not just an inherent property of a board but also depends strongly on the ranges involved. For example, consider the 6♠-5♣-4♦ flop. It is quite coordinated, and many draws and made hands are possible. However, the top-40% BB range only makes a pair or better 28.1% of the time and a gutshot or better about 30% of the time. These numbers are even less than on the K♠-7♥-2♦ (an exemplary weak board)! This is simply because the flop starting range we gave the BB contains primarily high cards and relatively few sixes, fives, and fours. The ATC range, on the other hand, has a pair or better 43% of the time and a gutshot or better 51%. So, the SB's opening range, although weaker preflop, is significantly more likely to connect with this particular flop. Thus, the 6♠-5♣-4♦ flop is quite strong for the SB. The big idea here: ranges matter when considering issues of board texture.

Volatility

The second primary aspect of board texture is in how future cards are likely to affect hands in the players' ranges. In particular, the turn and river can improve or devalue players' hands and do so to different degrees. On some boards, there is the possibility for hands to improve to be very strong, whereas on others, many hands can only improve to a middling pair. On some boards, such improvement is likely, and on some, it is not.

Most obviously, if a flop has flush or straight draws, then those draws can either come in or not on the turn and river. When they come in, old made hands (i.e., 3-of-a-kind or worse) are relatively weakened. Conversely (and just as importantly!) those made hands increase in strength versus an opponent's range on turn and river cards that do not complete draws. Flush and straight cards are not the only ones that devalue many made hands. High cards can do this as well – especially *over-cards*, those which are higher than the highest card on the flop.

For example, suppose Hero holds Q♥-J♥, and our players saw a Q♠-8♠-4♦ flop. Top pair, third kicker is a strong hand in many situations, but turns such as the K♥ and the 2♠ can improve a number of Villain's holdings to beat it. After the K♥ turn, there are 135 unique king-containing hands possible (3 other kings times the 45 other cards with which they could each be paired), but after a 2♠ turn, there are only 45 ways Villain can hold spades. So, the overcard could be quite a bit worse than a spade for Hero's Q♥-J♥. Now, in some situations, Villain might have folded a K earlier in the hand where he would not have folded spades, and Hero still has equity versus a king but none versus a flush. Nevertheless, in situations where ranges are wide, over-cards can affect relative hand strengths in a significant way. Of course we should not forget the second- or bottom-pair hands either. Relative hand values on boards on which the lower cards are still quite high are generally less prone to change than on those on which they are not.

So, the second important texture-related property of a flop is how likely future cards are to change the relative values of players' hands. This likelihood is a property of the flop in combination with players' ranges. We will call boards on which hands are very likely to change in value by the river *volatile*. Boards on which good hands are likely to stay good and bad hands likely to stay bad are called *static*. Let us take some more examples.

Consider again the 6♠-5♣-4♦ board. We showed earlier that it is relatively weak for the top 40% of preflop hands and strong for the ATC range. Now, is it static or is it volatile? With respect to most ranges, it is clearly going to be quite volatile. There are very few hands which do not have to be "worried" about being hurt by future cards, and even the weakest hands on this board have a significant likelihood of improving. A hand as "strong" as top pair-top kicker (A-6o) is actually not as valuable as it may seem since any turn and river card except an ace or a 6 will make either a one-card straight possible, a higher pair possible, or improve lower pairs to three-of-a-kind. Of course, it is important to keep in mind that these possibilities are already 'built-in' to the equity of these hands on the flop. Top pair on a 6-high board does not have nearly the equity against most Villain ranges as does top pair on many other boards. Thus, the hand's average equity (its relative strength) will improve on some turn cards that do improve some of Villain's hands to better as long as the new card does not improve Villain's range as much as the average turn card would have.

So, on some boards, the relative hand strengths of many holdings are very likely to change significantly on later streets, and on some boards that is not the case. The other aspect of board volatility is the degree to which improved hands improve. On the 6♠-5♣-4♦ board, it is rare that a hand improves to second pair or the like. If a hand does improve on the turn, it is almost always going to have improved to beat the flopped top pair. In contrast, on a static board like A♣-7♥-2♦, it is very unlikely for a hand which is unpaired on the flop to improve to beat top pair.

In general, the lower or more connected (in rank and suit) the cards on the flop, the more volatile it is with respect to most ranges. On the other hand, flops composed of high cards and with fewer draws tend to be static. This is because, in general, if Hero makes a high pair or better, fewer overcards and other draws are available to come in and devalue those hands. And, of course, we should not focus too much on top pairs. The board K♠-J♥-3♣ is less volatile than K♠-6♥-3♣ in a very important way: the second pair on board is far more likely to be devalued on the turn on the second board. So, for example, if Hero is in the small blind, he can often expect to have both more equity and to find more profitable bluffing opportunities on the turn after the BB check-calls on the K♠-6♥-3♣ flop than on the K♠-J♥-3♣.

It is important to think carefully about how the ranges of particular opponents interact with a flop, because these general considerations can be deceiving. As an example, think again about the 6♠-5♣-4♦ flop and consider hands with a pair and a straight draw such as 7-6, 7-5, 8-6, 7-4, etc. These are often known as combination or combo-draws since they have a draw in combination with a pair. (The term can also refer to hands which have more than one type of draw, and indeed if we hold 7-4 and a lot of money goes in on this flop, our 4 is probably not good, and we can think of our hand as a straight draw in combination with two-pair and three-of-a-kind draws.) Now, these hands are fairly strong on the flop. Then, on future cards which are near the flop in rank such as a 3, 7, or 8, these hands tend to improve in value by becoming a straight or two pair whereas most other one-pair hands would have decreased in value significantly. On future cards which are not near the board (i.e. a card 9 or higher), these hands still have a good amount of strength and equity given that they have a pair in a situation where draws missed. So, the values of these hands are actually quite resilient. Their strength often stays more or less constant on what is usually a very volatile board.

Now suppose the BB is, as is common, playing a fairly tight range preflop consisting of high cards and low cards with some suitedness or connectedness. His high-card hands will miss this flop, but the low-card hands which are in his range tend to be connected in rank. That is, the BB will usually not pair the board, but when he does, he very often has a combo-draw. Now, he still has his over-cards, but this 6♠-5♣-4♦ flop can actually be a lot more static than you might think for the BB's flop starting range.

6.2.2 Turn and River Texture

Many of the same sorts of ideas apply when we want to evaluate the effect of turn and river cards on players' ranges. In addition to thinking about strength of ranges on later-street boards as a whole, it is also useful to describe individual turn and river cards as strong or weak depending on how they affect the players' ranges. This extension of the strength concept to later streets is fairly straightforward. Given a player's range, it is usually easy to say something about how much a card helped it.

Judging volatility, however, is relatively tricky. Even more so than on the flop, it requires careful consideration of the ranges involved. Players generally get to the flop with wide ranges that are easy to estimate and visualize, but this is not true of players' *turn starting distributions*, the distribution of the players hands at the beginning of turn play. The flop play often changes ranges drastically.

Note that even if both players check on the flop, this still has a large effect on the ranges. The BB now holds only those hands with which he does not lead the flop, and the SB has only the holdings with which he does not continuation bet (or c-bet – so-called because he raised preflop and is now continuing to represent strength on the flop). Of course, if the BB never leads flops (a common enough tendency), his action does not narrow his range, but missing a c-bet almost always says a lot about a SB's holding.

To get a taste for the subtle effects that this sort of narrowing of postflop ranges can have on our evaluation of board texture, consider the following example. Our hero in the SB raised and was called preflop, and the BB check-called the flop. Generally this indicates that the BB has some sort of hand whereas the SB could have been value betting with something or bluffing because he had nothing. The flop was particularly static, K♣-7♥-2♦, but the turn brought the J♥. How volatile is the board now, given players' ranges? That is, how likely is the river card to affect the relative strengths of the hands in the ranges?

Well, the K and J are relatively high-ranking cards so the threat of over-cards is not so great, but there are now a number of draws on board. Any two hearts now have a draw to the flush, and there are many straight draws possible: A-Q, A-10, Q-10, Q-9, 10-9, 10-8, and 9-8. Thus, it might seem that many river cards will change the relative values of many of the players' hands. However, you will overestimate this likelihood if you do not think carefully about the players' likely holdings. In particular, the BB flat-called preflop and then check-called the flop. Insofar as he is likely to 3-bet preflop with A-Q and is unlikely to check-call the flop two random cards like 10-9o, he probably does not hold any of the possible straight draws on the turn. Perhaps he can have A-10 exactly. It is conceivable that he might flat-call with it preflop and not fold to the flop c-bet, but he also could have played differently at either of those decision points. Furthermore, the only hearts the BB is likely to have are those which have something else as well to let him continue on the flop, e.g., A♥-2♥, and there are just not that many of these hands.

So, the BB is unlikely to have picked up a draw on the turn and thus draw-completing river cards are quite unlikely to improve his absolute hand strength. Still it is relative hand strength that matters. If turn and river cards are likely to affect the SB's absolute hand strength, then they still af-fect both players' relative hand strengths. It is certainly possible that the SB turned a straight or flush draw. He may very well have bet the flop with many of those hands as a bluff. On the other hand, if he bets the flop with those hands, then he also does so with many other bluffs which did not pick up a draw on this specific turn. So, he still has mostly unimproved hands in his range on the turn.

There are a couple of lessons here. First, when hand ranges get narrowed on the flop, it makes draws that come on the turn much less relevant. If a draw comes on the flop and gets there on the river, it is a much bigger deal than if it comes on the turn and gets there on the river. So, this J♥ turn is less volatile than you might think since it is unlikely to lead to rivers which change relative hand strengths. It is certainly less volatile than it would be if the flop play was such that the players' turn starting ranges were wider.

That said, the J♥ can help the SB much more frequently than it helps the BB. That is, it is relatively strong for the SB. This observation provides a hint as to one use of these concepts in this sort of spot, something we will discuss further in the next few sections: changing board textures are generally bad for a player with a range narrowly defined on early streets. That is, if a board is volatile, then many turn and river cards will be strong for the player with the wider and less defined range. This effect is tempered by the fact that he has a wider and weaker range in the first place.

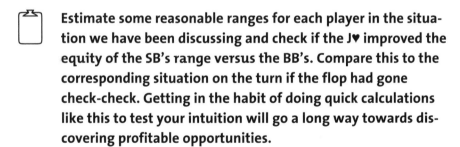

> **Estimate some reasonable ranges for each player in the situation we have been discussing and check if the J♥ improved the equity of the SB's range versus the BB's. Compare this to the corresponding situation on the turn if the flop had gone check-check. Getting in the habit of doing quick calculations like this to test your intuition will go a long way towards discovering profitable opportunities.**

Now, it is important to keep in mind that the threat of changing hand values is always less severe on the turn than on the flop for the simple reason that there is only one card to come instead of two. Similarly, we can think of the river as the case when all boards are static – there are no future cards coming to change things up. We will see in Chapter 7 that effective river play rests on careful consideration of strength of different parts of players' ranges. In extrapolating lessons from the relatively simple river play to earlier streets, it is helpful to keep in mind this context – early-street play will be similar to river play insofar as hand values are static and different when hand values are more volatile.

Finally, it is worth making some comments about the differences between straight and flush draws that can be helpful to keep in mind when evaluating players' later-street ranges. Suppose we have seen a 10♦-8♠-2♥ flop. There are a variety of straight draws possible, the highest of which is Q-J. So, if all the straight draws completely miss by the river (i.e., no Q, J, 9, or 7 comes), then all of those draws have become unpaired hands with very little showdown value. However, if any of those four cards came, then it is still the case that a lot of the straight draws did not make straights, but most of them did not completely miss either. Most of the straight draws which did not improve to straights made at least a pair. So, it is easy to see when straight draws are likely to have turned into completely worthless hands on the river and when that is not the case.

Flush draws work a bit differently. First, it is a lot easier to see if a flush draw gets there. If there are two hearts on the flop and another comes on the turn, then all flopped flush draws now have a flush. This is obvious, but it is an important difference when compared to straight draws. On the other hand, it is much harder than with straight draws to tell if flush draws are likely to have picked up pairs. There is a relatively small and well-defined set of cards which give pairs to straight draws on most boards, but almost any card can pair up a flush draw. Finally, the monotone or 3-flush flops are a bit different. Players tend to only continue with one-card flush draws if that one card is of high rank. So, if the board bricks off after a monotone flop, then missed flush draws generally at least have some high-card value which is enough to lead many players to want to go to showdown rather than bluff on the river.

These considerations are often helpful in accurately identifying players' river starting distributions and have a lot of bearing on correct river play.

6.3 Barrelling on Static Boards

We noted earlier that bcb, bbc, bbb, cbb, ccc, ccb, cbc, ccb are all of Hero's possible lines from the SB when the BB check-calls down. We now have some ideas about the things which are important to consider when trying to differentiate between various postflop situations. Issues of board texture are the one of the primary metrics with which to evaluate situations and group them into categories of spots which are strategically similar. In this section, we will focus on situations on generally static boards. Because hand values will be relatively unlikely to change on later streets, it makes sense to start planning all our actions in the hand on the flop. That is, we can go ahead and think about how we will likely want to play each part of our range on later streets, assuming we do not face a raise or lead and no particularly interesting cards come off. Thus, with issues such as texture in mind, we can start partitioning Hero's flop range into different lines. That is, we will consider the group of hands with which he will take each line. Hero's first decision is whether or not to continuation-bet. In fact, Hero can find a reason to c-bet with most of his hands. He can bet *for value* because he has a good hand (i.e., with the hope of being called by worse), or he can bet because has a bad hand, as a *bluff* (i.e., with the hope of making a better hand fold). Indeed many players only check back the flop with those hands in between, so-called weak showdown hands, which are not good enough to bet for value but not bad enough to bet as a bluff. By checking these back on the flop, they hope to control the size of the pot and get closer to showdown. On later streets, there is often the option to continue towards showdown or to put in a value-bet if appropriate.

Let us focus on the more common case where the SB c-bets. How should the turn and river play go after Hero c-bets on a static board, is called, and is checked to on the turn? Now, since Villain called the bet on the flop, he likely has something. This is not necessarily the case for Hero whose range is still very wide. Hero might group his own hands at this point loosely into several categories: strong hands (say, he would like to bet all three streets if Villain keeps check-calling), middling hands (say, he would like to put one more bet in for value), weak hands (he would like to go to showdown but is probably not good if he bets again and is called), and pure air (some of which will be turned into bluffs). Experience should provide some guide as to how to categorize particular hands and how to choose holdings to turn into bluffs. We will give more attention to these topics in later chapters.

So how might Hero want to play each of these groupings on the turn and river? First, his strong hands are probably the easiest to play. He will often want to play bbb with these to try to get the most value for his big hands. Conversely, with the weak hands, which are worth taking to showdown but with which he wants to put no more bets in, will try to do just that: Hero will try to take the bcc line with these.

Now, with our middling hands, we want to make one more bet. Our choice is whether to bet on the turn or on the river. Which is best? The answer is generally the river, for two main reasons. First, by checking back the turn with middling made hands, we control the size of the pot. That is, checking back the turn allows us to be more sure of being able get to showdown without having to put more money than we want to into the pot. In particular, it eliminates Villain's chance to check-call the turn and then lead the river or to check-raise the turn. If Villain leads the river after we check back the flop, we can simply call the bet and have successfully gotten one bet in with our middling hand. The only remaining danger is that Villain can check-raise our bet on the river, but even in this case, it is easier for us to call the raise on the river and get immediately to showdown than to have faced the raise on the turn with the implicit threat of an additional river bet.

A second reason to play bcb rather than bbc with middling made hands is that by checking back the turn and value-betting the river, we can expect to get called by weaker hands more often. If Villain has a weak holding which is considering a call when facing a turn bet, he has to be scared of facing a big river bet also. In particular, by taking a weak-looking turn line, he might be scared giving away the fact that his hand is weak and made, in which case he is very vulnerable both to a wide value-betting range as well as bluffs on the river. There is, however, no such threat of future bets to discourage his paying us off on the river.

Finally, what about our air? As you probably expect from the earlier chapters, some of these hands can be profitably turned into bluffs. With some bluffs, we will want to bet twice just as if we had one of our strong hands. However, what if we just want to bluff once on the turn and river? In this case, it is probably best to bet only the turn for reasons similar to above. Our bluff will be most effective on the turn since Villain must fear the possibility of a river bet. Additionally, betting the turn is how we play our strong value hands. (Keep in mind that we are talking about static boards – how might these considerations change if more draws were possible?)

At this point we have outlined a moderately reasonable approach to betting on static boards versus a check-calling opponent in the BB. Many competent players will play a strategy very similar to this one, at least before they start making reads. They will also tend to think in terms of these sorts of strategies. For example, they will tend to expect you to have many weak showdown value hands after you check back the flop. However, this strategy is certainly not the final word, especially against good opponents. Before we move on to how these ideas must change to accommodate changing hand values on volatile textures, we should at least mention how this approach could be exploited by a smart BB and if and how the SB should adjust his strategy to avoid such exploitation.

First, consider the SB's tendency to check back weak-showdown hands (and only weak-showdown hands) on the flop. By defining his hand as not strong, he makes himself vulnerable to the BB leading the turn and river aggressively. The BB can do this both with bluffs and with a very wide range of value hands since he can be confident that even many of his mediocre hands are better than the SB's holding.

This is a serious threat, but the danger is partially offset by two things. First, by virtue of his position, the SB will have more information available to him at each of his decision points, and he can try to use it to call down when appropriate and fold when appropriate. Second, since he checked back the flop, there are only two rounds of betting left. This limits the amount of pressure the BB can apply, at least with standard-sized bets. Players in the BB will often decline to begin a bluff facing a missed c-bet, since they are unable to fire three streets, and they know that the SB has something that is likely to call at least once.

Still, defining his range so narrowly early in the hand can lead to problems for the SB when facing a good, aggressive opponent. The equilibration exercise can be used to identify the SB's proper adjustment in this case. If the BB is leading turns and rivers very frequently after a missed c-bet to take advantage of Hero's presumably-weak range, checking back the flop with stronger hands becomes more profitable than it would have otherwise been and may very well become more profitable than c-betting in the first place. So, the SB will definitely want to be capable of checking back some hands strong enough to confidently call down two streets. He may also want to be able to raise the turn and river with some frequency both for value and as bluffs (and especially the river so as to allow the BB to put as much money in as possible with weak holdings).

One interesting adjustment which is likely underutilized at the time of writing is for the BB to incorporate leading turns and rivers for over-bets (that is, betting larger than the size of the pot) when facing a SB who checks back exactly weak-showdown value holdings. The BB can do this with many hands for value since the SB's range is capped low, and so he can also do this with many bluffs. In the next chapter, we will analyze river spots where a player's range is defined as weak showdown value, and we will see that his opponent's most profitable response involves going all-in with many hands, regardless of the current pot size. Intuitively, this move lets him get the most value from his made hands as well as having the most effective bluffs. However, this sort of analysis does rest on assumptions about the SB's range – it is easy to imagine that if the BB starts to over-bet leading turns and rivers with too high a frequency, then checking back the flop with strong hands becomes a very attractive option for the SB. Thus, overbetting in this spot is a great example of a play which is highly exploitative in that it takes maximum advantage of the strategy described earlier but can also be very exploitable itself.

Now, take the case that the SB c-bets and the BB calls. The basic outline of the SB strategy above was to bet the turn and river with strong value hands and some bluffs, to bet the turn but give up on the river with other bluffs, and to check the turn and bet the river with middling-strength value hands. The logic leading to this strategy is reasonable, and it is a good strategy against many inexperienced opponents. However, we can also see how a BB aware of the strategy would be able to take advantage of it.

Consider first the situation after the SB bets the flop and turn. He holds in this case both strong hands and bluffs with little in between since he is checking his middling hands on the turn. Thus, his range is polar. So, to some degree, most of the BB's middling strength hands have the same value against this polarized range. However, insofar as the SB has a good ratio of value bets to bluffs, it is hard for the BB to take advantage of this knowledge. We will see in future chapters that the BB must just play "check-and-guess" with most of his range in this kind of spot.

But what about the times that the SB checks the turn and bets the river? He only does this with middling strength value-betting hands. Since his range is so well defined, the BB will very often know if he has the best hand and can thus play very well. He can avoid incorrectly calling down with weak hands that only beat a bluff since the SB is not bluffing. If the BB starts folding to too many river bets, however, it is easy for the SB to start including some bluffs in his bcb range.

The more serious problem with the SB's strategy is not that the BB might call and fold well but rather that he might raise. This is due to the fact that the SB's range is capped when he bets the river at the end of the bcb line. As when he checked back the flop, having a capped range makes him quite vulnerable to a counterstrategy involving wide value-betting and bluffing ranges. These can come both as river leads and as river check-raises, both of which can be over-bets if the BB wants to apply maximum pressure.

Whereas the BB check-folding to river value bets too much led to a simple solution for the SB (bluff more), this issue leads to problems which are a bit harder for the SB to fix. We noted that after the SB bcb, the BB could play well by check-calling and check-folding most of his hands intelligently. What if, on the other hand, the BB still check-calls the river with those same hands with which he can profitably do so, but check-raises with his weakish hands and moderately strong ones? If the SB checks back the turn and bets the river with the above ranges (weak value and maybe some bluffs), he may never have a hand strong enough to happily call the river check-raise. This sets up a very profitable situation for the BB.

Now, if necessary, the SB can begin to address this problem by either checking back the turn with stronger hands or by just calling down light sometimes. Against a particularly aggressive opponent, the SB might find it profitable to do both. Against a more passive player, it might not be worth it to do either even if this means being exploited occasionally. (Recall the discussion of the appropriate use of the balance concept in Section 2.3.1.) In any case, these adjustments have serious consequences for other parts of the SB's strategy. These sorts of considerations form the basis of the discussion in the following chapters.

 Neglecting variations in bet sizing, there are just eight lines possible to the SB when the BB plays passively. Which are unused in the "standard" strategy described above? Do you think this is problematic? In other words, under what conditions could the SB increase his expectation by taking some of the unused lines?

6.4 Distributions on Volatile Boards

The reasoning which led to the strategies discussed in Section 6.3 generally relied on the assumption that hand values were not likely to change much on future streets. Two primary issues arise in play on volatile boards that complicate execution of these strategies.

1. Sometimes players' relative hand strengths suddenly get weaker from one street to the next.

2. Sometimes players' relative hand strengths suddenly get stronger from one street to the next.

These issues have significant consequences for the way we play our hands.

First of all, it is clear that turn and river cards can only improve players' absolute hand strength. (A hand can not decrease from two pair to one pair because of an additional community card.) However, it is important to keep in mind that we are talking about changes in *relative* hand strength. Hands can certainly decrease in strength relative to an opponent's range.

In fact, there are a couple of reasons that any new card that does not improve your hand in some way could have weakened it relatively. First, it does improve some of your opponent's hands, and second, the chance that a turn card would come to help your hand did not pan out. This is the case on even the most static of boards, but has a much more pronounced effect on the play of hands on more volatile boards where hand equities can sometimes change drastically from street to street. You should keep in mind that your equity on an early street already incorporates the chance that future cards will come and change hand values. So, to judge whether your equity was increased or decreased by, e.g., a turn card, you really need to think about how much it improved your hand or your opponent's range as compared to the average turn card.

Accurately identifying players' hand distributions and how they interact with and are affected by the board cards is one of the most subtle and important parts of HUNL strategy. Discussion of these issues will certainly fill much of the rest of this book. In this section, we will get a taste of some of these issues by way of an example.

Consider the flop 8♠-7♠-3♥. Given wide preflop ranges, almost any turn and river cards will improve some hands to straights, flushes, or good pairs. It is impossible to have flopped a hand that is not threatened by these draws since no straights or flushes are currently possible. Almost all hands which are good but not extraordinary (e.g. A-8o) will face so-called *scare-cards* on almost all turns and rivers. Finally, the drawing hands themselves will usually become either very strong or very weak by the river. Thus, we can expect the equities of most hands to change drastically as the board develops. The flop 8♠-7♠-3♥ is quite volatile.

We will now consider several possibilities for the flop action and estimate the associated ranges. We will look at the players' equity distributions at the end of the flop action and after several of the possible turn cards and discuss the strategic consequences of these cards in terms of the distributions.

For context, we will assume that stacks are 100 BB deep and that the SB minraised his button preflop and the BB called. For concreteness and simplicity, we will also assume that the SB gets to the flop with 100% of hands and that the BB gets to the flop with the range

AA, 22-99, A2s-ATs, K2s+, Q2s+, J4s+, T6s+, 96s+, 86s+, 75s+, 65s, 54s,
A2o-ATo, K6o-KJo, Q8o+, J8o+, T8o+, 98o

which is approximately the top 50% of hands less those which will almost
always be included in a BB's value 3-betting range. The specifics of this section's analysis will of course change if these assumptions are modified, but
we will focus on the big ideas rather than the specific results.

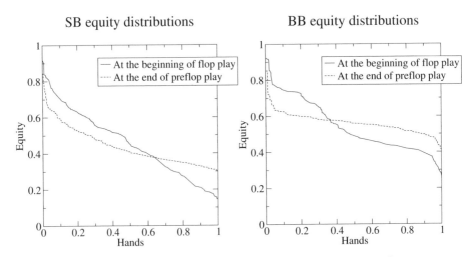

*Figure 6.1: Players' flop starting distributions plotted according to
their preflop equities as well as their equities at the beginning of play
on the 8♠-7♠-3♥ flop.*

The players' equity distributions at the beginning of flop play are shown in
Figure 6.1. They are useful for establishing a baseline from which to appreciate how the players' distributions change as we move down the decision
tree. The equity distributions take both the player's and his opponent's
range into account, so it is easy to see changing relative hand strength.
How does the flop affect the players' distributions in Figure 6.1? Is the flop
particularly strong for either player? For one thing, it appears that the
players' strongest hands have gained equity while their weaker hands have
lost it. This is almost always the case on the flop. (Why is this?) For reference, here are the equities of several of the SB's holdings at this point: K-K
has 78%, A-8o has 73%, and A-3o has about 52% equity. This should give

you an idea of the equities of hands which you might consider worthy of a value c-bet.

The volatility of the board is also apparent in these plots. Most flops will have improved some hands drastically and crushed the hopes of others. This will be reflected in the equity distributions: some hands will have very high equity (indeed, some may be locks or near-locks), and others will have very low equity. This is not the case on the 8♠-7♠-3♥. The players' best hands have a bit more equity than the best hands preflop, and the distribution drops off quickly. Similarly, the worst hands here only have a bit less equity than the worst preflop. In this way, volatile boards actually play a bit like preflop situations. Indeed you can think of preflop play as the ultimate volatile situation: hand equities always change a lot on later streets. Strategic considerations on volatile boards will resemble those of preflop play to some degree.

6.4.1 A c-bet on 8♠-7♠-3♥ is Check-raised

Now assume the SB c-bets with his entire range (only his check-raise-calling range will really matter for this section) and is check-raised. We will consider two possible check-raising ranges for the BB which represent different degrees of aggression and, in particular, how he plays his draws. We will assume that both raising ranges contain all made hands top-pair-top-kicker or better for value

$$AA, 77\text{-}99, 33, A8s, 87s, A8o$$

but that the more aggressive BB also check-raises with K8-J8 as well as many draws: all his flush draws, open-ended straight draws, over-card plus gut-shot straight draws, and various over-card plus runner-runner draw holdings. In total, this raising range is

AA, 77-99, 33, A♡T♡, A♡9♡, A8s, K♡J♡, K♡T♡, K8s, Q8s, J8s+, T9s, 96s, 87s, 65s, A♠T♣, A♠T♢, A♠T♡, A♠9♣, A♠9♢, A♠9♡, A8o, K♠J♣, K♠J♢, K♠J♡, K♠T♣, K♠T♢, K♠T♡, K8o, Q8o, J8o+, T9o, A♠2♠+, K♠2♠+, Q♠2♠+, J♠4♠+, T♠6♠+, 9♠6♠+, 8♠6♠+, 7♠5♠+, 6♠5♠, 5♠4♠

We will refer to the first BB strategy as *P* (for passive) and the second one as *A* (for aggressive). Note that the first is a moderately tight value range, and even most passive players will occasionally throw in a bluff. Even the aggressive strategy *A* mostly just includes hands that do have a reasonable chance of improving on later streets. There are enough of these hands on a board like this that a BB never really needs to bluff-raise with worse.

In reality many players will fall around or in between these two cases, but these two stereotypes will make it easy to demonstrate the important concepts. Additionally, in the case of the drawing hands in particular, many weak players do tend to draw either passively by calling or aggressively by raising (or leading) with less mixing-it-up than you might think. As we will see, if Villain does one or the other with a high frequency, it makes a big difference for later-street strategic play. Thus, it is important to take note of how your opponents play their draws.

As an aside, even many strong players have a core set of tendencies that define their style. These are the things they do almost all of the time and would probably just describe as good, solid play if you asked them. For many, these include raising Q-10o preflop, 3-betting A-K, c-betting top pair on the flop, and for some players, certainly – check-raising the flop with flush draws. Most players have a relatively small set of frequencies they are in the habit of adjusting in response to particular opponent tendencies.

Anyhow, the BB check-raises the 8♠-7♠-3♥ flop with either strategy *A* or *P*, and the SB calls. We will assume that the SB's calling range is any 2nd pair or better or any flush draw, open-ended straight draw, or gut-shot straight draw plus over cards:

77+, 33, A8s, A7s, K8s, K7s, Q8s, Q7s, J7s+, T7s+, 96s+, 82s+, 72s+, 65s, A8o, A7o, K8o, K7o, Q8o, Q7o, J7o+, T7o+, 96o+, 82o+, 72o+, 65o, A♠2♠+, K♠2♠+, Q♠2♠+, J♠2♠+, T♠2♠+, 9♠2♠+, 8♠2♠+, 7♠2♠+, 6♠2♠+, 5♠2♠+, 4♠2♠+, 3♠2♠

Whether or not this represents approximately correct play depends on many factors. In particular, from an exploitative standpoint, it matters greatly whether his opponent is playing *P* or *A*, but perhaps the SB is unaware of his opponent's strategy. Let us see how he does, but first, try some quick checks to see if these strategies are reasonable.

Find the SB's calling frequency in the above situation. Choose some reasonable bet sizings. Suppose the BB is considering check-raising with a complete bluff, i.e., with a hand which will put no more money into the pot and will always lose if he gets called. Assuming the SB folds with hands not listed in his calling range, is the SB calling enough to keep the BB from profitably raising with such a hand? If not, how many of his bet-folding hands does the SB have to quit c-betting to keep the BB from profiting in this way? If the SB is c-betting 100% and his SB's continuing range does not change depending on the raise size, what is the smallest raise size such that the BB can profit with such a move?

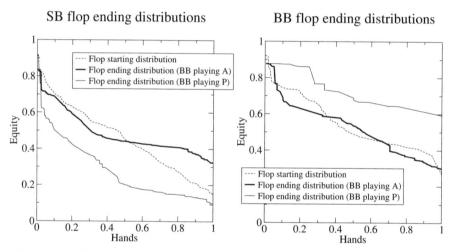

Figure 6.2: Players' flop ending distributions for each of the BB's two check-raising strategies plotted according to their equities on the 8♠-7♠-3♥ flop.

The equity distributions for each player and each of the BB strategies after the SB bet-calls are shown in Figure 6.2. Consider first how the SB's distribution changes due to the flop play when the BB is playing *P* (see Figure 6.2). The distributions indicate that his range is quite weak across the board. While nearly half of his hands had at least 50% equity at the beginning of flop play, not even a tenth of his range has that much at the end.

The reason, of course, is that the BB in this case is only raising with quite strong hands and no bluffs or draws. If the BB is only raising with strong made hands, then the SB's medium-strength made hands all fare very poorly. So, in this case, it is actually the SB's own drawing hands that give him most of his equity.

If the SB knows that the BB is playing a strategy like *P*, he probably should not call the flop raise so much. His maximally exploitative play would likely involve folding so much of his c-betting range to the check-raise that the BB could profit by raising with all of his pure bluffs. (You did work out the previous exercise didn't you?) This SB strategy would thus be highly exploitable as well as maximally exploitative. The situation would be a poor one for the BB who would have to wait a long time to find a hand strong enough to raise and then rarely get much value when he did. And, of course, if he did start to take advantage of the situation by check-raise bluffing, then the SB could widen his calling range to include those second-pair type hands.

Now consider the SB's situation when the BB is raising with strategy *A* (Figure 6.2a). His distribution appears to have stayed about the same over the course of the flop play. This is because the BB is now raising enough weak hands along with his strong ones that all of the SB's continuing range still has good equity. The biggest change in this case is that, at the end of flop play, the weakest hands in the SB's range have increased equity. Intuitively, the reason for this is that the aggressive BB has a number of especially speculative draws in his range, whereas the SB, after calling the raise, almost always has something at least a little more reasonable.

Now look at the BB's end-of-flop-play distributions in Figure 6.2b. It is easy to see that there are no real bluffs included in his *P* raising range. All of the hands in the range have good equity. Notice that the curve corresponding to the BB's strategy *P* is pretty much the same as the first 40 percent or so of his graph with *A*. This is because they represent the same hands – the aggressive check-raising range is the passive one plus a bunch of other stuff, and the SB's range is the same in both cases. His *A* strategy, however, includes a lot of weaker hands too. It turns out that in this case his equity distribution looks about the same before and after the flop play. So, what did he accomplish by raising here?

SB turn starting distributions (BB playing A) SB turn starting distributions (BB playing P)

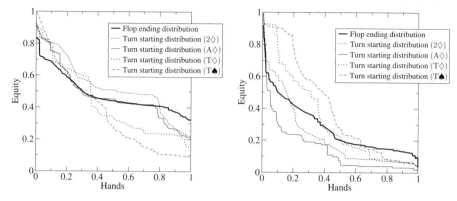

Figure 6.3: SB turn starting distributions for each of the BB's two check-raising strategies.

BB turn starting distributions (BB playing A)   BB turn starting distributions (BB playing P)

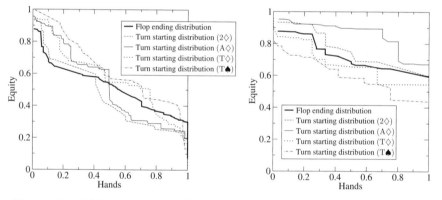

Figure 6.4: BB turn starting distributions for each of the BB's two check-raising strategies.

We will now consider a couple of turn cards and see how they affect the players' distributions: an off-suit A, 2, and 10, and a suited 10. The SB's starting distribution on each turn is shown in Figure 6.3 for each of the BB's strategies. Consider first the right-hand column which corresponds to the situations when the BB is playing *P*. We noted earlier that a lot of the SB's equity in this case comes from his draws since his middling made hands rarely improve to beat the BB's stronger made hands. On the 2♦ turn, all of the draws miss. Indeed we see that many of his hands were approximately halved in equity from the end of flop play to the beginning of turn play since there are now only half as many chances left to try to hit. However, about a fifth of the SB's hands actually improve in equity on the 2♦. A few of these hands actually hit the deuce, but most of them have just become relatively stronger by virtue of the fact that the 2♦ could not have helped the BB at all.

Compare this situation to the second possible turn, the A♦. This is still a bad card for the SB's draws since they all missed, but in this case, it is also a bad card for his made hands. The weakest hand in the passive BB's check-raising range was A-8, and this hand makes up a decent fraction of his range besides. The SB, on the other hand, has relatively few aces in his range. Thus, the A♦ turn is very weak for the SB. All of his draws missed, and it increases the absolute strength of many of his opponent's holdings so that even improving to two-pair on the river is less likely to give him the best hand.

Now consider the 10♦ and 10♠ turns, when some draws get there and when a lot of draws get there, respectively. These are both quite strong for the SB since the BB does not have many draws in his range. The plot corresponding to the 10♦ turn can be divided cleanly into four sections by comparing the SB's end-of-flop distribution to that at the beginning of the turn. From left to right, we first have about 10% of hands which improved to near-locks. These are all straights. Then, there are about about 25% of hands which improved more modestly on the turn, mostly flopped straight draws which paired the 10 itself. The next 30% of hands appear to have not really changed in equity much, but actually, these are all draws that had more equity on the flop. The strongest of them, such as Q♠-J♠ and A♠-3♠, still have over 40% equity. Finally, the rest of the SB's range is composed of his weak made hands such as a pair of sevens. These lost about half their equity from the flop on this turn. In fact, these are essentially weak draws since they are losing to all of the BB's hands and they must improve to two-pair or three-of-a-kind to win.

Compare the SB's distribution on the 10♠ to that on the 10♦ which we just discussed. The spade promotes many more of his hands to near-nut strength. Notice, however, that these are not quite as strong as straights on the ♦ turn since, now, more of the BB's range has redraws to higher flushes. He has fewer very weak hands on this turn, too. Many of his weak made hands have become combo-draws by virtue of having a single spade. This particular turn is extremely strong for the SB when the BB does not hold any draws.

The left-hand column of Figure 6.3 corresponds to the cases when the BB is playing *A*, and we can understand it similarly. Here, the distributions do not change quite as much on any turn cards. This is simply because the players' ranges are more similar – both contain a variety of made hands and draws – so the changes in texture affect them more evenly. Missed draws do not hurt the SB nearly as much since the BB has many missed draws in his range also. However, his range as a whole is also not helped as much when draws do come in.

First of all, let us find the specific differences between the players' ranges and try to get an idea of which turn cards might be volatile or particularly strong for each of the players. Given the ranges we chose, there are several hundred hand combinations that the SB has that the BB does not. The strongest of these include over-pairs that the BB would have 3-bet preflop. It also includes many weak eights, a bunch of sevens, and weaker spade draws. There are many fewer hands that the BB holds and the SB does not. These are just his speculative semi-bluffs: weak combo-draw holdings such as K♥-10♥ and A♠-9♦. Given this, a second 7 is very strong for the SB. In general, low cards are strong for the SB and high cards are strong for the BB. A low spade decreases the SB's equity only a little on average, but this card has very different effects on different parts of the players' ranges.

Now study the distributions for the four turn cards given. Of these, the strongest turn card for the SB is the 2♦ since the SB has many more middling made hands than does the BB, and these gain in strength when the draws miss. The second most notable feature from these plots is in the bottom left graph. The 10♠ is extremely bad for the weaker half of the SB's range, that is, for his sevens and eights. Those hands were already behind the made hand part of the BB's raising range, and now they are behind most of his flopped draws as well.

Now, how do these various turn cards affect the BB? These distributions are shown in Figure 6.4. In some sense, most of the trends are just the reverse of those for the SB. Consider first when he is playing *P*. The changes in these distributions are the easiest to interpret since his range really consists of just one type of hand: medium to strong made hands. It is clear that the 2♦ is strong for him, the A♦ is very strong for him, the 10♦ is somewhat weak for him, and the 10♠ is very weak for him. That is, cards that change the absolute strengths of many holdings are bad for him. In particular, since he can not have any of the straights or flushes when he is playing *P*, his range is capped quite low on these turns. We will see in the future that this puts him in bad spots.

The situation is a little more interesting for the BB when he is playing *A*. In this case, his range is those same strong made hands, plus various draws. Almost all of this range fares fairly well when the draw-completing 10♦ and 10♠ turns come in. But, something else happens on the A♦ and 2♦ turns. In these cases, his distribution divides more or less cleanly in two. The made hands get stronger and the draws get weaker. This is plain to see in a sharp drop-off in equity about halfway through his distributions. That is, these cards have a polarizing effect on the BB's distribution. We will see that this has significant strategic consequences.

The last note here is to keep the big picture in mind. The distributions for the players are all very different on these various turn cards. That is, the strengths of different parts of the players' ranges change a ton! This is the most immediate consequence of the volatility of the board. Flop play can be very challenging when you have little idea how strong your hands will be on the turn. The idea for now is to just start to really understand how cards can affect the relative strengths of different parts of your distribution. Hopefully going over this example graphically has helped you to visualize these effects.

> There exist various free online tools that let you visualize players' equity distributions given a board and some ranges. Find one and pick a situation involving an especially static board texture. How do various turn cards affect strengths of various parts of the players' ranges in this case? What cards are particularly helpful for each players range? Which ones turn much of a player's range into middling hands and which have a more polarizing effect?

6.4.2 A c-bet on 8♠-7♠-3♥ is Check-called

Now suppose the BB check-calls the flop c-bet. What has changed, and what has stayed the same? To avoid an explosion of plots and to focus on the big ideas, we will just go over the intuition behind the differences in distributions after the flop is check-called rather than check-raised.

First of all, in real situations, it is critical to understand how the BB's flop raising and calling ranges interact. For example, we assumed in the previous section that the BB raised with all of his strong hands. Certainly some players play this way, and it significantly limits the hands they can hold after check-calling. This has significant strategic implications – their calling ranges are capped on many turn and river cards and are thus vulnerable to frequent turn and river bets. However, that assumption in the previous section was for convenience as much as anything. (It would have been inconvenient to specify a percentage for each hand in his raising range.) So, we will assume there is really no contradiction when we consider the possibility that the BB might be check-calling to slow-play with some of his strong hands.

Now, of course, the pot size is different if BB calls the flop versus when he raises, but when it comes to the players' distributions, there are really just a couple of big differences that tend to hold true for most players. First, consider the SB's range. If the BB just calls his c-bet, then the SB gets to the turn with his whole c-betting range. For most players, this will be a much wider range than that with which he calls a check-raise. There are some exceptions. Some players may only c-bet with those hands which are strong enough to call a raise. Alternately, the SB could just be the type to call a raise with many hands, either because he is loose in general or because he expects to be able to win frequently with a later bluff given the board texture.

As for the BB, he may tend to either call or raise with strong made hands on any particular board. Different players also may also tend towards either action with draws. The consistent difference between calling and raising ranges for players in the BB is really in how they play weak made hands (second and third pair). Almost all players will find these too strong to fold but too weak to raise (at medium to deep stacks) and will tend to just call.

So the main differences in the turn starting ranges after check-called flops as opposed to check-raised ones are: the SB has many more very weak holdings in his range, and the BB has more middling value holdings. The BB's range is often somewhat capped as well, but the rest of the details are fairly opponent- (and board-) dependent. Now, these differences have consequences for how various turn cards affect the turn starting ranges. The sorts of general considerations which arise, however, are analogous to those we talked about in the previous section, so we will leave this as an exercise.

Test Yourself

1. Think of an opponent you have played recently.

2. Write down your c-betting range on the 8♠-7♠-3♥ flop (you should know this) and estimate his check-calling range (write it down!).

3. Sketch what you expect the equity distributions to look like at the end of flop play and 10♠,10♦,A♦, and 2♦ turns. Check your answers computationally.

4. Assuming they check to you on the turn with all of their flop check-calling hands, estimate how likely they are to call a second barrel on the turn.

5. How much equity do they need to have to call, according to your estimate of their range (i.e. how much equity does the weakest calling hand you gave them have)?

6. What do your bluffing prospects look like on each turn? Can you bluff profitably even if you lose whenever you are called? If not, how much do you have to win when called to make a semi-bluff profitable?

Use the discussion from the check-raised flop as your guide, but remember that the pot is smaller in this case at the beginning of the turn, so there is more room to play.

6.4.3 Adjusting the SB's Strategy for Volatile Boards

This brings us to a slightly different take on the difference between static and volatile boards. On the river, if you hold a hand with 75% equity, then (neglecting chops) it means that exactly 25% of Villain's range is ahead of you, and you have 75% of it beat. This is nearly the case on earlier streets on static boards, too, since it is the case on the river, and static means that hand values do not change between the flop and the river. It is not nearly true, however, on volatile boards. For example, if you are in the BB with A♦-8♣ on 8♠-7♠-3♥ facing a SB with any two cards, then you are ahead of more than 90% of the SB's holdings, but you only have about 74% equity. This is because it is a volatile board and there are many hands with some chance to improve to win.

As we have hinted and will continue to see, this has significant consequences for how we should play. Recall our discussion of barreling on static boards in Section 6.3. We divided our range on the flop into hands with which we would like to put one more bet in, two more, etc. We can not really do this on volatile boards since we do not know how strong our hand will be on later streets.

However, insofar as we want to take various actions on the flop, we still have to partition our range somehow. How do we do it? Well, for one thing, we argued that on static boards, bcb did best to get value with the SB's weak holdings because it was easier for the BB to call the river bet than a turn double barrel. On volatile boards, however, it might be better to bet a lot of these weak value hands on the turn to get value from draws. A BB might also check-call wider on the turn since he can assume that the SB is betting some draws. On the other hand, if the BB is particularly aggressive or the draws in his range are weak, it might be better for the SB to check back on the turn in order to induce a river bluff that he can pick off when a safe card comes. Thus we see that we can still sort of plan ahead, but we have to consider more possible future situations. Dealing with changing hand strengths is a broad and yet nuanced topic. For now – let's talk about bluffing.

Changes in board texture strongly impact many players' bluffing ranges on later streets. Cards which are strong for the SB are seen as good for him to bluff and those which are strong for the BB are not. It is relatively easy to identify these cards by focusing on the BB's range. The issue is that after c-betting on the flop, the SB can still have many different kinds of holdings, whereas the BB's range is perceived as somewhat more defined. He likely has one of the draws or pairs which were possible on the flop. Thus, it is relatively easy to predict how turn and river cards will interact with this range.

So, suppose the SB c-bets the flop and the BB check-calls and checks on the turn. You should always keep in mind that strength depends on the ranges involved and are thus player dependent. However, there are certain stereotypes that often hold true that you should be aware of, if for no other reason than that many players choose their bluffing opportunities very consistently based on these considerations. In particular, turn and river cards which are higher than the top pair on the flop are seen as strong for the SB and good for him to bluff. The BB likely discarded unpaired overcards when facing the flop c-bet, but the SB could certainly still have them. It is often the case that the higher the card, the better it is for the SB. However, a K may be better for the SB to bluff on than an A depending on whether the BB can check-call the flop with A-high and whether the SB is perceived to check back A-high on the flop. A draw which only becomes possible on the turn and then comes in on the river, such as the flush on 10♠-7♣-5♦-K♦-2♦, is also seen as particularly strong for the SB since the BB would have had no reason to call the flop with many diamond-diamond holdings.

On the other hand, many cards are stereotypically good for the BB's range after he calls a c-bet and are particularly unlikely to be bluffed. Suppose a turn or river card pairs one of the cards on the flop. The BB is more likely to have improved to three-of-a-kind than is the SB, and his other hands that were able to call on the flop can often call again on the turn. For example, suppose a board comes out Q♠-9♣-5♥-Q♦. The BB's nines and fives improved relatively on this turn since it made it less likely that the SB holds a queen.

Next, suppose a turn card comes which coordinates strongly with those on the flop in some other way. For example, imagine we see a 9♦ turn after a 10♥-7♠-2♣ flop. Since he called a bet, the BB is more likely to have a holding which was coordinated with the flop, and since the 9♦ is also in that neighborhood, it will often improve his hand further. In particular, many of the BB's draws will have picked up pairs (or a straight), and many of his pairs will have picked up draws. This is not generally seen as a good turn to bluff since the BB will tend to call again.

In addition to betting on cards that are strong for you and not on those which are strong for your opponent, there are several other properties of the board on which many players base their decisions to bluff. First, many players choose to begin bluffs on the flop with hands that have the possibility of picking up a draw on the turn. In this way, they can continue their bluffs on the turn those times that they do actually pick up some equity. For example, with this line of reasoning, if you are in the BB on a Q♥-7♠-2♥ flop, J♠-10♠ might be a good hand to turn into a bluff since it is not really strong enough to check-call, but if your bluff-raise gets called, a lot of turn cards give you a straight or flush draw which may allow you to profitably continue bluffing on the turn. Certainly, you should usually have some bluffing hands in your range when you raise the flop, and having some equity is better than not. However, players who rely exclusively on this sort of consideration to choose bluffing hands are in danger of having too few or many bluffing hands on different turn cards.

Next, some boards lend themselves particularly well to firing one, two, or three streets with bluffs. For example, A♥-K♠-2♦ is often a good board for the SB to just stab at once with his bluffing hands. It is quite likely that the BB simply has two unimproved cards between the K and the 2 which will easily fold to one bet. However, if he calls, he is likely to have an A or a K which is likely to continue calling on future streets. However, this line of reasoning does lead to a severely unbalanced turn betting range and also leaves the SB very vulnerable to the out-of-position float play.

On the other hand, on a board such as 9♠-6♥-2♦-7♣-K♦, many players will never bluff earlier streets without following through on the river. As on the 10♥-7♠-2♣-9♦ that we mentioned above, many weak-pair-plus-straight-draw type hands are possible on the turn which are very likely to call a bet. However, on the river, all those hands are now just weak pairs. Thus, it is generally expected that a check-calling BB will rarely fold to two bets but will often give up when facing a third. Many players just decide not to bluff the turn, but if they do, they continue on the river with the expectation of seeing a lot of folds.

Lastly and perhaps most importantly, there is the issue of continuing bluffs on rivers when obvious draws miss. Semi-bluffs do make up a large amount of a lot of most players' bluffing ranges on early streets, so when the draws miss, they end up on the river with a range that contains lots of missed draws. On the other hand, when all the obvious draws come in, players are perceived to have many fewer weak hands in their range to use as bluffs even if they wanted to. The consequence is that some players are significantly more likely to call down on the river if some draws missed. On the other hand, knowing this, some players are extremely hesitant to continue bluffing on the river after obvious draws miss. They only continue in such spots with value hands. A quick application of the equilibration exercise here should allow you to convince yourself that the GTO strategy involves continuing with bluffs here *sometimes*, but many players fall into one camp or the other, or at least are quick to make an extreme adjustment after seeing one or two showdowns in such a spot versus a new opponent.

These are all good things to consider when playing later streets. Certainly you should be more prone to bluff on cards which are good for your range (and you are generally value-betting more frequently in these spots, too). However, some people take this too far. Even many smart, aggressive players with good average bluffing frequencies are in fact bluffing way too often on over-card turns but perhaps never at all on board-pairing ones. Looking for spots that an aggressive opponent is likely to see as good for bluffing can help you identify good opportunities to call down light. Too strictly following any relatively simple "system" can make you quite vulnerable to exploitation when playing versus an observant opponent.

This is particularly the case on volatile boards. It is important to keep in mind the results we found when the BB was playing his passive strategy *P* on the volatile board. Since he had only one type of hand after check-raising, it was easy to see how later cards affected his distribution and thus to play against him. There was real danger in defining his range early in the hand on volatile boards since on many turn and river cards, he simply was not able to have any particularly strong hands, and as we will see, this can be very exploitable. These considerations are not nearly as hard to deal with on static boards.

So it is much harder to make long-range plans for a hand and to otherwise know quite what to do on volatile boards. Basically, play on static boards is relatively intuitive for most players. This is not so on volatile ones. So what are we to do? As we have seen, the first step is to just think hard during the hand about the players' ranges and how they are affected by each new card. It is often necessary to significantly reevaluate your view of the situation from street to street.

From an analytical standpoint however, the key is to remember that nothing has really changed that much. To devise maximally exploitative strategies, our method is still to evaluate the EV of each of our strategic options at each decision point and then to simply go with whichever one is the biggest. The challenge with volatile boards is in estimating the value of holding various hands on later streets. Remember that this is just the expected value averaged over all the possible cards that can come. But, insofar as a board is static, it does not matter what card comes – hand values will not change much since that is what static means. So, it is easy both to plan ahead and to think about the EVs on later-street play. On volatile boards, however, your EV and your play may be wildly different depending on the cards that come, and thinking of all the possibilities and then weighting and averaging them to find the EV of, e.g., calling a non-all-in bet, can be overwhelming. Many players do not really bother. They just rely on fuzzy thinking and do their best. The fact is, however, that these things become a lot easier with a bit of practice away from the tables, and the payoff is great. And you have to do it – there are no shortcuts (well, maybe a few).

Great, so hopefully at this point you have gotten some practice thinking about play in terms of ranges – your opponent's as well as your own. Hopefully you have become familiar with some of the thought processes involved in standard exploitative play in today's games. Effective hand reading is about recognizing patterns in your opponent's play to figure out what hands he plays certain ways, so it is an inherently opponent-specific process. However, we will see plenty more examples of hand reading in future chapters. Finally, hopefully you have some ideas about river starting ranges in particular, because we are soon on to river play! But first – a short detour.

6.5 Conceptualization

It is worth making an aside here on the important topic of proper conceptualization with regards to board texture and other strategically-relevant abstractions. A concept is an abstract idea generalized from particular instances. It is useful since, once you have the concept, you can reason about all those particular instances at once instead of having to consider each of them individually. For example, we have talked about identifying boards as strong for a player, and we have seen some strategic implications which apply to all of these cases.

Now, the terms "wet" and "dry" are also commonly used to describe board texture. People refer to boards as wet if they generally connect with lots hands in some way, either by making made hands or giving draws, and dry is the opposite of wet. So, wet means something like strong but also has some of the implications of volatile. Dry usually means something like weak and/or static. A minor problem with the use of these ideas is that they are often regarded as inherent properties of a particular flop, and we have seen that to be strategically-relevant, a description of board texture really must take into account the context of the players' ranges. But that is easily fixed. There is a bigger issue with these concepts which makes them of little use for strategizing.

You may have gathered from the preceding discussion that absolutely strong boards do tend to also be volatile insofar as they are the ones that "hit a lot of hands", and weak boards are often static. However, this is not always the case. For example, if a reasonably solid player defends his BB, then the flop A♣-K♥-9♦ is clearly quite static and strong for him. The 8♠-6♠-2♣ is relatively weak and volatile for the same BB. And so players who try to devise strategies for play on these boards using the wet and dry concepts have a problem. The correlations between strong and volatile and between weak and static are *built-in* to wet and dry, making it hard to reason effectively about these spots in those terms. The use of such concepts leads to poor results because they were not defined in relation to the relevant essentials of the situation.

This ham-fisted grouping together of ideas which should be kept separate is a logical fallacy known as package-dealing. Another example of this fallacy often arises in American politics. In politics, the essential involved is the success of government in protecting the rights of the people. A fundamental distinction often made is between conservative politics which involves the use of government power to limit peoples' social choices while leaving their economic lives relatively free, and that of liberal politics which is just the reverse. In both cases, rights-protecting has been grouped with rights-violating, and the resulting concepts are not useful. As with the concepts wet and dry, the problem is not that the terms are not specific enough. It is that they group together particulars with fundamentally contradictory attributes. So, reasoning about those concepts leads to results that do not actually make sense when you go back and try to apply your conclusions to particular instances.

To better understand the origin and use of valid concepts, let us consider a beginning poker player who has just for the first time been told the rules of HUNL. A flush beats a straight beats three of a kind which is better than two pair and a pair. Players act in turn and, when it is your turn, you can bet, check, call or fold. And so on. Our beginner sits down to play his first hand. He probably limps, and then a flop comes, and he has to bet or check. On what information can he rely to make this decision? He knows nothing. He sees his cards and the board cards and can probably name his absolute hand strength, but that is about it. Without any conceptual framework to guide his actions, he is at a loss for how to act.

Nevertheless, our hero does his best, plays for a while, and fairly soon, he will probably have identified his first poker concepts that extract some of the essentials of his situation on the flop. He will likely have noticed that flushes and straights tend to win at showdown, as do 3-of-a-kind and 2-pair hands to a lesser extent, pairs are OK sometimes, and worse hands usually lose. With this experience he will probably unconsciously arrive at his first inductive generalizations, "hands likely to win", "hands unlikely to win", and maybe even also "hands which sometimes win", each of which is a grouping of particular hands based directly on his experience.

He now has some tools to work with. The next time he sees a flop, he can look at his hole cards, look at the board cards, and rather than having nothing to go on, there are now three strategically distinct situations possible: he can find himself holding a good hand, a mediocre one, or a bad one. He can choose to act differently based on the situation. Clearly, his poker mind is still a very blunt instrument. When placed to a bet-or-check decision, there are only three situations he can be in, and so his strategizing in this spot will just amount to deciding which of the two actions he should take in each of the three situations. This is not a sufficiently rich conceptual framework to make the subtle distinctions necessary to compete with experienced players. This will have to change for him to improve his play.

To be the best player you can, think critically about the differences between A-high and K-high flops (and Q-high, and J-high, etc.) versus each of your opponents. Think about the difference between flops where the top two cards are adjacent and those where there is a 1-gap between the ranks (or a 2-gap or a 3-gap, etc.) Consider two-tone flops and think critically about the difference between the case when the top two cards are of a suit and the bottom two cards are of a suit. Remember to keep in mind the particular ranges involved – none of these ideas will be useful without that context.

The volatility and strength concepts themselves are ripe for refinement in a couple of different ways. Consider first volatility: how likely hand values are to change. We could be more specific about the nature of this change. First, to what degree are hands likely to improve? After a flop such as A♥-7♠-3♣, most hands from a wide range which are improved by a turn card will be given something like second or third pair. On other boards, hands which improve on the turn are much more likely to improve to top pair or better. This is an aspect of a board's texture which can have significant strategic impact.

Second, the primary draws on some boards are *open*, that is, it is in some sense obvious when they come in. For example, suppose a flop contains two of a suit and many of the weakest hands in Villain's range are flush draws. Then, on a 3-flush turn, it is clear that he has many value hands, while on a blank, Villain's betting range may be much more bluff-heavy. This is the case even if his overall distribution was seemingly well balanced at the end of flop play. On the other hand, on boards such as K♣-7♦-3♠, 7♥-3♠-2♦, or 10♥-9♦-4♣, most possible draws are *closed*. These are draws to top pair, two pair, sets or even straights – many turn cards will improve some of these but not others. Villain's turn distribution will often be a lot easier to play against on the first sort of board than on the second. The degree to which a board lends itself to open or closed draws is an important aspect of its texture.

Now consider strength: how good a new card is for a player's range. Clearly it could help to be more specific. If a card was strong for Villain's range, did it help all of his range a little bit or just part of his range a lot? Did it improve primarily what was the bottom of his range so that his distribution is now bounded below? Did it improve primarily his middling hands, thus leaving him with a polarized distribution? We have discussed many of these issues above in the context of particular boards and situations without giving the ideas names. However, if you think you will benefit from giving words to these things then go ahead and do it. This is likely to be especially helpful for multi-tablers who benefit more from the ability to make quick decisions rather than particularly accurate ones.

In general, try to extract general strategically-relevant concepts. If they prove useful, make up some new words for them. But avoid overzealous generalizations. Words like "wet" group together observations that can in fact suggest contradictory courses of action. Trying to strategize with these will simply muddle your thought processes and stunt your growth as a poker player. As a check, you should always be referencing any big ideas you come up with to particular situations. Do the math in as detailed a way as you know how and check that the result matches your high-level thought process. How you think about the game will determine how you play.

6.6 You Should Now...

♠ Understand how early-street strategizing depends on later-street play

♠ Understand the concepts of strength and volatility, how they depend on ranges, and how they are strategically useful

♠ Understand how new cards affect players' distributions

♠ Be familiar with some aspects of standard play including common approaches such as range-splitting on static boards and multi-street bluffing on volatile ones

♠ Have begun to develop the habit of range-oriented thinking: the keeping in mind of both players' ranges at every point in a hand

Chapter 7

River Play

Sometimes you'll miss a bet, sure, but it's OK to miss a bet. Poker is an art form, of course, but sometimes you have to sacrifice art in favor of making a profit. – Mike Caro

In some sense, the river is the simplest of the streets. There are no more cards to come. Hand values are fixed – there are no more draws to worry about. It is just your distribution versus that of your opponent. As we will see, this makes river play particularly amenable to analysis. Given the stack and pot sizes and assumptions about the players' ranges at the beginning of the street, we can find equilibrium and exploitative strategies which will often be intuitive and simple enough to apply in real-time at the table.

However, in terms of estimating the players' starting ranges, the river is the most complex street. For comparison, think about the others. The range of hands with which the players start preflop play is well known, of course, since it is just all hands. All preflop situations are the same in the sense that there are no board cards yet, so players get lots of clean data from which to estimate their opponents' getting-to-the-flop ranges. Thus, a player's flop starting distribution is usually also easy to estimate.

This situation changes on later streets, and it becomes significantly harder to figure out players' ranges. First of all, hands get to the later streets less often so there is less data to work with. Furthermore, postflop play depends heavily on the board and on prior-street actions, and there are many different combinations of such factors. It is necessary but often challenging to draw conclusions about a player's hand distribution in one later-street spot from samples of his ranges in past hands.

Because of these challenges, many players are the weakest on the river. They do not have a good understanding of what their opponents are doing, and thus they have little way to figure out how they should respond. Combined with the fact that the biggest bets tend to go in on the final street, river play is probably the easiest place to find an edge against moderately-skilled opponents in today's games. These factors also make many river situations good candidates for the use of pseudo-optimal strategies.

Our goal in this chapter is to analyze play in a variety of different river situations. Much of the discussion will be quite general as opposed to narrowly focused on a particular spot. However, in order to keep the discussion in context and understand how these ideas might be applied to real play, we will start out by considering a few hand examples. These have been chosen to represent a wide variety of river situations. We will set up the examples now and return to them to look at the players' strategies in each spot towards the end of the chapter.

7.1 River Starting Distributions and Hand Examples

With few practical exceptions, river strategy is based on the players' starting distributions and the stack and pot sizes only. The details of early-street play are only relevant insofar as they affect those things. That said, we will take advantage of this opportunity to put in a little hand-reading practice to show how we arrive at the river starting ranges. This will help us to see how different types of equity distributions can arise in the course of real play. For hand-reading purposes, we assume the players are generally thinking and competent, perhaps such as those that can be found playing mid-stakes games online.

For each of these example hands, we will go through the early-street play to make an estimate of the hands with which each player might arrive at the river. Then we will discuss the equity distributions induced by the players' river starting ranges. Keep in mind that the BB's equity distribution on the river is essentially just the complement of the SB's and can be visualized by flipping the graph as discussed in Section 5.3.

As always, it is good to think about how certain points might change if these hands were played by players with other tendencies. In particular, for each hand example and position, try to imagine your own range for getting to the river this way against an unknown opponent in your games or against a particular opponent with whom you have a lot of experience. You should try to do this very precisely. Understanding one's own ranges is a very important skill which is neglected by many players.

7.1.1 Example 1

Effective stacks: 25 BB
Preflop:
SB raises to 2BB, BB calls 1BB
Flop: 9♥-2♠-9♦ (4BB)
BB checks, SB bets 2BB, BB calls
Turn: A♠ (8BB)
BB checks, SB bets 4BB, BB calls
River: 6♥ (16BB)

This flop is very absolutely weak for both players. In particular, there are 1,326 hand combinations in the deck and 198 of them contain at least one 9. However, after the 9♦-2♠-9♥ flop, there are 1,176 possible holdings left in the deck, only 95 of which contain a 9. The SB will thus hold a 9 about 8 percent of the time if he is playing any-two-cards preflop. How likely is the BB to have hit the 9? Besides that, no draws are possible and many deuces and pocket pairs may be discounted from the players' ranges since they would have played differently preflop.

Since neither player has an absolutely strong holding very often, the SB is prone to c-betting with most of his hands to try to take down the pot. After the flop action, his range still contains almost anything while the BB is either slow-playing a strong hand, has weak showdown value (a high card or the rare deuce), or has an even weaker hand which will often try to win without a showdown on a later street. Many aggressive players, however, do not slow-play here often since a raise can look very bluffy and induce action.

The A♠ turn is interesting. If the starting stacks were a bit deeper, A-high would make up a lot of BB's range to call preflop and check-call the flop. As it is, most aces will be 3-bet preflop. As for the SB, he may or may not c-bet A-high on this flop. Without further information, however, the A is generally a strong card for the SB, but of course he still has a lot of pure bluffs in his range as well. After calling again on the turn, the BB's range is still composed of bluff-catchers and the occasional slow-play. The SB can have continued to bet most hands two-pair or better for value, and he is probably frequently bluffing as well.

Thus, at the beginning of river play, we can give the BB a lot of K-high, the rare high-card hand that called the flop and turned a spade draw, and the occasional slow-played nine. We give the SB some deuces, all better made hands, and many pure bluffs. The SB's equity distribution is shown in Figure 7.2a. It has a simple structure. A fair fraction of his hands have no equity at all and the rest are quite well off. This will often be the case on the river when one player has taken a very aggressive line and the other responded passively. The aggressive player has either a particularly good hand or a particularly bad one, and his opponent's holding is a mediocre one which was not strong enough to raise or weak enough to fold.

7.1.2 Example 2

Effective stacks: 50 BB
Preflop:
SB raises to 2BB, BB calls 1BB

Flop: Q♠-9♠-6♥ (4BB)
BB checks, SB bets 2BB, BB calls
Turn: 2♥ (8BB)
BB checks, SB bets 6BB, BB calls
River: 2♣ (20BB)

Let us assume that the SB gets to the river in this hand with most two-heart and two-spade hands (some may not have bet twice) as well as J-10, K-J, 10-8, 8-7 and any made-hand pair of queens or better. Slow-plays on his part will be rare due to the drawy nature of the board, but it may also be perceived as a relatively poor spot to make many pure bluffs since the offsuit deuce on the turn is unlikely to scare many hands that called the flop bet. The BB can also have missed flush and straight draws, although they may be discounted since he would have played them more aggressively sometimes and may have folded two hearts on the flop. Additionally, weaker queens and many nines are in his range for getting to the river. We will suppose he can slow-play earlier streets occasionally, as well, and gets to the river with

9♣9♦, 9♣9♡, KJs, K♡T♡, K♠T♠, K♠6♠, K♠5♠, K♠4♠, K♠3♠, K♠2♠, QTs-Q9s, JTs, J♠8♠, J♠7♠, T8s, 87s, KJo, QTo-Q7o, JTo, T8o, 95s, 97s, 98s, T9s, J9s, 97o, 98o, T9o, J9o

The players' equity distributions are shown in Figure 7.2b. The SB is somewhat polar here, having taken an aggressive line. However, as compared to the previous example, much more of the SB's range has at least a little showdown value, and the BB's range is not nearly as narrowly defined. Of course, these two observations are connected. Since we assumed the BB played a number of draws passively, some of the SB's bluffs actually end up with the best hand on the river. In fact, some players in the BB will check-call the flop in this hand with many unpaired holdings which have some way to improve and otherwise plan on bluff-leading the river. This tendency incentivizes the SB to continue betting on the turn with many more high-card "bluffs" (such as K-J) than he might otherwise.

7.1.3 Example 3

Effective stacks: 100 BB
Preflop:
SB raises to 3BB, BB calls 2BB
Flop: K♣-Q♠-8♥ (6BB)
BB checks, SB bets 4BB, BB calls
Turn: 5♥ (14BB)
BB checks, SB checks
River: 5♣ (14BB)

This flop is fairly static and strong for the BB. The SB might often stab once with air hands to try to fold out two cards below the Q, but he is unlikely to barrel since one call from the BB often represents a K or Q, high paired hands that will be unwilling to fold on later streets. He may have barrelled the turn with some draws, but these all missed on the river. Either way, the SB can therefore make it to the river this way with almost all the unpaired holdings. He also probably plays almost all rivered 3-of-a-kind hands this way, but these make up a small part of his overall range. Finally, the SB can have some queens and eights, although these could have played differently on earlier streets, and the occasional king, although these will often have bet on the turn.

The BB, on the other hand, probably has all the queens and eights that are in his preflop range, weaker kings that did not check-raise the flop, and, say, A-10, J-10, and J-9s. For this hand's discussion, we will assume that this is all the BB gets to the river with this way. It is probably about right for many players.

However, it is worth noting how play could differ in this spot. In particular, from the discussion so far, this BB range is almost certainly too tight. Notice that he always has something when he gets to the river – even his missed straight draws are high cards that are ahead of a significant part of the SB's range. Anticipating this, we assumed earlier that the SB was going to play much of his range by betting once and mostly giving up if called. This is a great spot to apply the equilibration exercise. Versus a SB with the described strategy, the BB can profit by calling the flop c-bet regardless of his hand and leading the river if he does not face a turn bet. This move is known as the *out-of-position float*, and we will call this line the out-of-position float line regardless of the BB's holding. As the SB, it is important to know if your opponent is capable of frequently making such a move. If he is, then (continuing the equilibration exercise) it may become more profitable to decline the option to c-bet the flop with air, to check back on the turn with more hands that can call a river bet, and/or to call the river bet with more hands than you would otherwise.

All that said, the SB's equity distribution with the given ranges is shown in Figure 7.2c. As we noted, the BB's distribution is relatively quite strong here, and about half of the SB's range has little-to-no equity.

7.1.4 Example 4

Effective stacks: 50 BB
Preflop:
SB raises to 2BB, BB calls 1BB
Flop: K♣-7♦-6♥ (4BB)
BB checks, SB checks
Turn: J♥ (4BB)
BB checks, SB checks
River: 3♠ (4BB)

The holdings players get to the river with in hands without any postflop action are especially player-dependent. On a board like this one, however, which is not usually strong enough for either player to scare the other off betting, solid, aggressive SBs will generally have a hand that they want to get to showdown with such as A-high or bottom pair. The BB could have a similar hand. He could also have a no-showdown-value hand that decided not to bluff. This can occur if he assumes the SB had to have "something" to have checked back the flop in the first place. He could also have a real hand that checked twice with the intention of check-calling or check-raising on the earlier streets. Certainly, your opponent's SB flop checking and BB turn leading versus missed c-bet tendencies are very important pieces of information to gather.

For the sake of this example, however, we will assume that the SB has various A-high hands and pocket pairs below the 6 and that the BB gets to the river this way with all of his preflop range except one-pair kings and jacks which he would have been likely to lead the turn for value but are not really strong enough to shoot for the check-raise. Of course, those one-pair hands are more or less the same as the nuts versus the SB's range, so excluding them will not make too much of a difference in our river analysis. The BB's turn strategy in this sort of spot is interesting and will get a lot of attention when we consider turn play. We will assume that the BB's preflop play eliminates AJ+, K-Q, and pairs 66+ from his range.

With our assumptions, the players' equity distributions are shown in Figure 7.2d. By virtue of the fact that the SB's range is so narrowly defined, almost any particular hand in the BB's range is either better than all of the SB's hands or is worse than all of the SB's hands. This is the reverse of the situation in several of the previous examples where the SB held a polar distribution and the BB held a bluff-catcher. The SB's few nut-type holdings are rivered three-of-a-kind.

We will now look at some board run-outs that lead to more complicated river distributions.

7.1.5 Example 5

Effective stacks: 160 BB
Preflop:
SB raises to 2BB, BB calls 1BB
Flop: 10♦-4♦-3♣ (4BB)
BB checks, SB bets 3BB, BB raises to 9BB, SB calls

Turn: J♦ (22BB)
BB bets 13BB, SB calls
River: A♣ (48BB)

This example comes from a fun hand which was played between two good and particularly aggressive high-stakes players. There is a lot of money to go in postflop since it was a minraised pot with moderately deep effective starting stacks.

Let us consider the BB's distribution first. His flop check-raise range likely includes 3-3, 4-4, and A-10 for value. It is possible but unlikely that he has some two-pair hands that were not folded preflop. It is also possible that he plays this way with worse tens since this is an aggressive match. He can have several straight draws and many flush draws as well. Additionally, this is a volatile board texture so the BB has a lot of hands with a bit of equity while many of his opponent's hands will be devalued on later streets. For this reason, the BB is also prone to check-raising this flop with hands like A♦-5♠, K♦-J♥, or Q-Jo which can improve or continue to profitably bluff on a variety of turn cards.

On this particular turn, he likely continues to bet with almost all of his flop check-raising range. Of course, he often has a flush which will want to bet for value. His bluffing hands which did not improve to a flush can represent having done so and may have picked up a flush draw besides. His 3-3 and 4-4 are generally still worth a value bet as well, and he may bet again with the A-10 just to avoid the awkward situation of checking and defining his range as exactly scared one-pair hands. In particular, his weak-looking turn-bet sizing suggests that this could be the case, but the player is strong enough to be aware of this issue, so it would be dangerous to make too many assumptions. We will assume he gets to the river this way with the whole of his flop check-raising range.

Now consider the SB's ranges. He starts the flop play with a very wide range which, unlike his opponent's, does contain all of the flopped two-pair hands. He bets the flop with most of his preflop range and gets raised. It is his flat call of the raise which first really starts to narrow his range of likely holdings. The same considerations that could motivate the BB to check-raise semi-bluff this flop could also lead the SB to bluff 3-bet with some frequency. Additionally, to take advantage of this dynamic and to get value from draws, the SB will often want to 3-bet the flop with his good made hands. Often on this sort of flop, some of the SB's A- and K-high flush draws will 3-bet the flop as well. While getting a flush draw all-in on the flop versus a made hand is moderately costly, giving oneself the opportunity to get it in versus worse draws (which you have crushed) can be worth the risk. However, the large stack-to-pot ratio (i.e. the deep effective stacks) here may make this less likely. Anyhow, the SB's flop flat-call eliminates some strong made hands and some strong draws from his range. His flatting range, of course, also includes many weaker made hands, weaker draws, and perhaps a few more speculative hands.

On the turn, the SB faces a bet. Any made hand weaker than a 10 (and without a diamond), will probably give up and fold. However, he is unlikely to raise with any of his range. The BB can easily have a flush and is prone to continue betting his bluffs on the river to represent it, so there is little reason for the SB to raise the turn with his strong hands. Thus, the overall effect of the turn call on the SB's range is to just trim off its weakest parts.

In the final analysis, we will assume the BB starts the river play with

$$33, 44, \text{ATs}, \text{KTs}, 65\text{s}, \text{ATo}, 65\text{o}, \text{K}\diamondsuit\text{J}\clubsuit+,$$
$$\text{A}\diamondsuit2\diamondsuit\text{-A}\diamondsuit8\diamondsuit, \text{K}\diamondsuit3\diamondsuit, \text{Q}\diamondsuit5\diamondsuit\text{-Q}\diamondsuit9\diamondsuit, 9\diamondsuit6\diamondsuit+,$$
$$8\diamondsuit6\diamondsuit+, 7\diamondsuit5\diamondsuit+, 6\diamondsuit3\diamondsuit, 5\diamondsuit3\diamondsuit, \text{K}\diamondsuit\text{J}\heartsuit+, \text{K}\diamondsuit\text{J}\spadesuit+$$

and the SB with

$$33, \text{AA}, \text{ATs}, \text{KTs}, \text{QTs}, \text{JTs}, \text{T2s}, \text{T3s}, \text{T5s}+, \text{ATo}, \text{KTo}, \text{QTo}, \text{JTo}, \text{T5o}+,$$
$$\text{A}\diamondsuit4\clubsuit, \text{A}\diamondsuit7\diamondsuit, \text{K}\diamondsuit7\diamondsuit, \text{K}\diamondsuit8\diamondsuit, \text{Q}\diamondsuit2\diamondsuit\text{-Q}\diamondsuit5\diamondsuit, \text{Q}\diamondsuit7\diamondsuit, \text{J}\diamondsuit2\diamondsuit\text{-J}\diamondsuit7\diamondsuit, 9\diamondsuit3\diamondsuit, 9\diamondsuit5\diamondsuit,$$
$$9\diamondsuit8\diamondsuit, 8\diamondsuit3\diamondsuit, 8\diamondsuit5\diamondsuit, 8\diamondsuit7\diamondsuit, 7\diamondsuit3\diamondsuit+, 6\diamondsuit3\diamondsuit+, 5\diamondsuit3\diamondsuit, \text{A}\diamondsuit3\heartsuit,$$
$$\text{A}\diamondsuit4\heartsuit, \text{A}\diamondsuit3\spadesuit, \text{A}\diamondsuit4\spadesuit, 8\diamondsuit8\clubsuit, 8\diamondsuit8\spadesuit, 8\heartsuit8\diamondsuit, 9\diamondsuit9\clubsuit, 9\diamondsuit9\spadesuit, 9\heartsuit9\diamondsuit$$

The players' equity distributions are shown in Figure 7.3a. Although all of the SB's hands have a non-negligible amount of equity, the BB's range is clearly stronger. However, in contrast to some of the earlier examples, the SB's range itself does overlap significantly with that of his opponent. That is, both players get to the river with many hands which may or may not be best. This is in contrast to some of the previous examples where one of the players held a distribution which was reasonably polar. In such a case, the polar player could be relatively certain if his hand was best or not.

7.1.6 Example 6

Effective stacks: 30 BB
Preflop:
SB raises to 2BB, BB calls
Flop: J♥-10♣-2♥ (4BB)
BB checks, SB bets 1.75BB, BB calls
Turn: 8♠ (7.5BB)
BB checks, SB bets 3.25BB, BB calls
River: 10♦ (14BB)

The BB's flop call in this hand usually indicates a jack, ten, or draw since most deuces and pocket pairs play differently preflop. The 8♠ on the turn improves many of these to pair plus straight draw or two pair. So, it is hard to see how the BB will fold to the turn bet very often, and thus the SB is probably rarely bluffing on the turn. In some similar situations, that could make it a good spot for the SB to bet the turn as a bluff with the intention of following up on a lot of river cards since various weak pair-plus-draw hands will end up as just weak pairs. However, that move is less promising in this particular spot for a couple of reasons. The jack and ten are relatively high cards, and so the BB's pairs are less likely to be devalued on the river. An overcard (which is perceived as good to bluff) is less likely to come on the river, and if it does, it will coordinate with many holdings in the BB's range. Secondly, the stack sizes on the turn are such that the BB might check-raise all-in a lot, and getting put all-in is fairly disastrous for the SB's semi-bluffs.

In general, the range with which the SB gets to the river this way depends a lot on his view of the BB's tendencies, and here we assume that he does, in fact, barrel the turn with some semi-bluffs and combo-draws. His range for getting to the river is made up of the hands shown in Figure 7.1. The figure is more compact than a complete listing of this range since it includes a wide sampling of hand combinations. In fact, this range was adapted from the solution to a game with the same flop in this hand but which included the play on the turn as well as the river. Anyhow, there is a box for each suited and unsuited hand, and each one is filled in corresponding to how much of the hand is contained in the range. Unfortunately this representation does not distinguish between hands that differ only by suit, but that is the price we pay for conciseness. Although it may not always be the case when looking at this sort of plot, every individual combination is either 100% in or out of the range. So, for example, all of the suited hands which look to have about 25% occupancy in fact have exactly 25% occupancy, and, as you might guess, these are primarily the heart flush draws. Similarly, the BB's river starting range is shown in Figure 7.1.

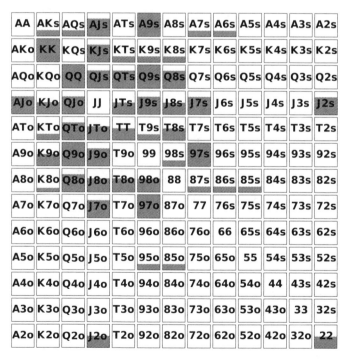

(a)

AA	AKs	AQs	AJs	ATs	A9s	A8s	A7s	A6s	A5s	A4s	A3s	A2s
AKo	KK	KQs	KJs	KTs	K9s	K8s	K7s	K6s	K5s	K4s	K3s	K2s
AQo	KQo	QQ	QJs	QTs	Q9s	Q8s	Q7s	Q6s	Q5s	Q4s	Q3s	Q2s
AJo	KJo	QJo	JJ	JTs	J9s	J8s	J7s	J6s	J5s	J4s	J3s	J2s
ATo	KTo	QTo	JTo	TT	T9s	T8s	T7s	T6s	T5s	T4s	T3s	T2s
A9o	K9o	Q9o	J9o	T9o	99	98s	97s	96s	95s	94s	93s	92s
A8o	K8o	Q8o	J8o	T8o	98o	88	87s	86s	85s	84s	83s	82s
A7o	K7o	Q7o	J7o	T7o	97o	87o	77	76s	75s	74s	73s	72s
A6o	K6o	Q6o	J6o	T6o	96o	86o	76o	66	65s	64s	63s	62s
A5o	K5o	Q5o	J5o	T5o	95o	85o	75o	65o	55	54s	53s	52s
A4o	K4o	Q4o	J4o	T4o	94o	84o	74o	64o	54o	44	43s	42s
A3o	K3o	Q3o	J3o	T3o	93o	83o	73o	63o	53o	43o	33	32s
A2o	K2o	Q2o	J2o	T2o	92o	82o	72o	62o	52o	42o	32o	22

(b)

Figure 7.1: SB and BB river starting ranges, respectively, in Example 6.

In this case, the players' equity distributions at the beginning of river play
are shown in Figure 7.3b. The BB's range is capped here, and so the SB has
a chunk of relatively nutted hands. Again, this sort of thing can often happen when the one player is betting and the other is check-calling down
without many slow-plays in his range. Beyond that, however, by virtue of
the fact that the SB was barrelling the turn with many combo-draw type
hands, the players' river ranges in this hand overlap greatly.

7.1.7 Example 7

Effective stacks: 26 BB
Preflop:
SB calls 0.5BB, BB checks

Flop: 9♦-5♥-2♥ (2BB)
BB checks, SB bets 1BB, BB calls
Turn: 6♦ (4BB)
BB checks, SB checks
River: 5♦ (4BB)

This is another hand in which the players' river starting ranges will be quite player-dependent. In particular, starting with the preflop play, SB limping ranges vary widely from player to player. Many do not even have a limping range at this effective stack depth. Then, postflop in the BB, some players will just check-fold frequently with bare two-overcard and the many other weak drawing hands. Others see it as a good semi-bluffing opportunity since they have outs to good hands, it is hard for the SB to have a hand that can stand a lot of heat, and they do not want to take the weak-looking check-call line with a weak hand. Other BBs, however, are comfortable just check-calling with these holdings. Whether or not an opponent in the big blind is comfortable check-calling with weak draws or always plays them raise-or-fold is an important opponent tendency of which to take note. As we noted in a previous example, BBs may be much more likely to call weakly on the flop if the SB is not prone to betting again on the turn. Additionally, many BBs will tend to check-raise their stronger draws on this board since almost all of them have some potential outs to go along with the primary draw whether that be a pair, a gutshot, or one or two overcards. Other BBs are capable of getting to later streets with more missed or made draws.

For the sake of the river play discussion, we will assume the BB raises most of his best hands and checks back the weaker ones when facing the limp preflop. He then check-calls the flop with any flopped single-pair hand, some A-high, and about half the possible combinations of each possible draw. Perhaps he raises the flop with the other half. Postflop, many players rarely "bet out of turn". That is, they will not lead the turn very often after check-calling on the flop. So, without any more information about the BB, it is reasonable to assume that his range for getting to the river is just the whole range of hands with which he check-calls the flop.

As for the SB, he can limp and stab the flop with a very wide range, most of which he will check back on the turn since the 6♦ connects strongly with much of the BB's perceived flop check-calling range and is not a particularly scary card for the rest of it. Thus, the SB's river starting range is quite wide, and it is probably easiest to list the hands that are not in it. These include big cards and most pocket pairs which would have played differently preflop and on the turn, as well as made hands on the turn nines or better. Additionally, we will suppose that on average, he checks back the turn with about half of his possible draws.

With these assumptions, the players' equity distributions on the river are shown in Figure 7.3c. The SB's range is much weaker than his opponent's. In particular, much of the SB's range has little to no equity. The SB gets to the river this way with a lot of air, but it is quite hard for the BB to do so after calling on the flop, since the turn improved many of the draws. This is another spot, however, where we have assumed that the BB is only continuing versus the flop bet when he has "something". You might guess that the BB is generally going to get the best of these river situations by virtue of his stronger range. And you would be correct. However, that does not mean his overall strategy for the hand was superior since he had to fold a lot of hands on the flop in order to end up with such a relatively strong range on the river. Additionally, the board in this hand ran out more or less perfectly for the BB. This sort of river situation will not arise after the 9♦-5♥-2♥ flop nearly as often as after the K♣-Q♠-8♥.

7.1.8 Example 8

Effective stacks: 100 BB
Preflop:
SB raises to 3BB, BB calls
Flop: 10♠-7♣-2♥ (6BB)
BB checks, SB bets 4BB, BB calls
Turn: 9♠ (14BB)
BB checks, SB bets 11BB, BB calls
River: 6♠ (36BB)

We will suppose that the SB double-barrels here with any made hand T or better (except 7-2 and 9-2 which he folds preflop), and any Q-J, Q-8, and spades that also have a straight draw or two overcards. We will assume that the BB calls preflop and then check-calls twice with 10-6s, 10-8, Q-10, 10-8, J-10, J-9, 9-8, 9-7, 8-7, and any 1-pair 7♠-X♠ and 2♠-X♠ in his preflop range, sevens with at least a 5 kicker and deuces with at least a K kicker. Then, the players' equity distributions are shown in Figure 7.3d.

We now have a collection of hand examples that sample a variety of the different types of river distributions and stack sizes that can arise. Of course, there are many more river situations than we can treat individually, and the idea is to develop the basic principles to solve new problems. With this in mind, we will now work through the solutions to some more abstract situations. We will start with a few relatively simple spots where the structure of players' distributions makes it easy to find solutions. We will then move on to treat more complex starting ranges.

As we go over these situations, keep our hand examples in mind and try to use the solutions we generate to determine proper play in these hands against various types of opponents. We will come back to each of them at the end of the chapter.

River starting distributions (Example 1)

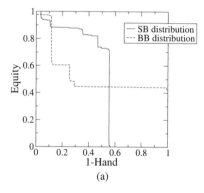

(a)

River starting distributions (Example 2)

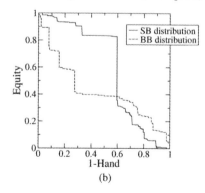

(b)

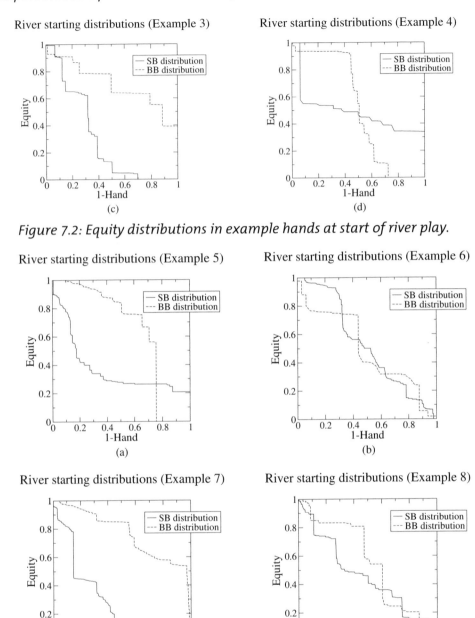

Figure 7.2: Equity distributions in example hands at start of river play.

Figure 7.3: Equity distributions in example hands at start of river play.

7.2 Simple Asymmetric Situations

We will now consider equilibrium and exploitative river play in some common situations made amenable to analysis by the simplicity of the players' distributions. Try to build intuition for the structure of river play here.

7.2.1 All of Hero's Range is Stronger than Villain's

By the arrival of the river in most hands, the relatively flat preflop starting distributions have changed drastically. In the very simplest case, one player's range is much stronger than his opponent's. For example, consider a hand where the player in the SB is prone to double-barreling very frequently both for value and as a bluff. He raises preflop, c-bets on the flop, and gets called. Both players check the turn. The board runs out 10♦-7♥-2♣-A♣-8♦. In this case, the SB's range at the beginning of the river consists primarily of hands with weak showdown value (deuces, 33-66, and maybe some weak sevens) as well as plenty of complete air that decided not to continue bluffing on the turn. The BB, on the other hand, since he called preflop and on the flop, probably holds either a 10, a decent 7, a flopped A-high that turned top pair, or a flopped straight draw which was necessarily improved by the 8 either to a pair or to a straight. So, in this situation, all of the BB's range is stronger than all of the SB's. The equity distribution of the weak-ranged player here is just a horizontal line – his equity is essentially 0 for all of his hands.

In this extreme case that all of Hero's range beats all of Villains's, GTO play should be clear. There are actually many strategies which have the same value for both players. Essentially, Villain will never put any more money in the pot, and Hero will never fold. Given this, Villain will never bet, but it does not really matter if Hero does either, or, if he does, with what sizing, since he should never get called. Notice that the players' positions actually do not matter here. We get the same result whether the strong-ranged player is in the SB or the BB.

In practice, of course, Hero should try for a bet. If he is in the SB, he has to bet when checked to. If he is in the BB his decision depends on whether Villain is more likely to incorrectly call or bet or to bluff when checked to. At equilibrium, however, Villain never puts any money in the pot, Hero never folds, and Hero wins whatever is in the pot on the river every time.

This point about the value of the game should resonate with something we saw in our analysis of preflop-only situations. The river spot where Hero always has the best hand is perhaps the best possible situation for him. It results, at equilibrium, in his always winning what is in the pot on the river – no more and no less. We saw earlier the total profit from playing a hand should never be below –1 BB for the BB or –0.5 BB for the SB. In general, at the equilibrium, neither player should expect to win more than is in the pot, at any point, on average. There is an easy strategy which his opponent can play to enforce this limit: never put any money in the pot, i.e., always check and fold. Thus, if we are ever in a spot where we can bet our entire range and capture the whole pot all the time, then doing so is at least as good as any other strategy versus a GTO opponent, and we should probably do so in practice.

By the way, this idea has been expressed in an intuitively-pleasing way by saying that all the action preflop is motivated by the fight for the blinds. If there were no blinds, there would never be any reason to put any money in the pot with anything other than the nuts. Similarly, on the river, all the action can be thought of as a struggle to capture as much of the pot as possible, and a player's EV should never be more than the whole pot, nor lower than if he just gave up on the river. Of course, in the situation where Hero's hand is always stronger than Villain's, just giving up is Villain's GTO play.

7.2.2 Almost all of Hero's Range is Stronger than Villain's

Now, let us make the situation slightly more interesting and realistic. Suppose that Hero does get to the river with just a few hands that do not beat the SB's weak pairs. In the example hand above, perhaps Hero makes it to the river with K♦-J♦, or perhaps the A or 8, both of which improved the weaker parts of the BB's flop check-calling range, did not come. So, most of Hero's range beats all of Villain's, but some does not. We will assume furthermore, for the sake of the discussion, that Villain always has some sort of showdown value. If we are to continue with the previous example, perhaps we think that Villain would have bluffed all of his air on the A turn. So Villain's equity distribution is again just a horizontal line, but now the equity of all his hands is somewhat above 0. In particular, the equity of each of his holdings in this spot is equal to the fraction of Hero's range which is air. We will often refer to hands such as Villain's as *bluff-catchers* since that is about all they are good for – catching bluffs. We will also call hands with little to no equity such as Hero's bluffing range in this case *air*.

What do the equilibrium strategies look like here? The first thing to notice is that Villain will still never bet himself, despite having the best hand occasionally. Since Hero's range is polar, Hero knows whether or not he has the best hand and can just call when he has it and fold when he does not. Betting serves no purpose for Villain. Because of this, positions are unimportant, just as before.

What about Hero? His range has gotten weaker. Is there any strategy he can adopt that will nevertheless allow him to continue to win the entire pot on average? Indeed, it should be intuitive that if he bets sufficiently large on the river with all of his hands, Villain will never be able to call. For, even though Villain will have the best hand occasionally, this will not be the case often enough to make it a profitable call. A call would always lose money on average relative to just folding. So, Villain will always fold to the bet, and Hero will again win the whole pot. In this case, Hero's bluff hands win him just as much money as his value hands. In fact, there is no advantage for him in having the best hand 100% of the time at the equilibrium. As long as he can put in a bet, having it *almost* all of the time is just as good.

As for Villain, any equity had by his bluff-catchers in this case is essentially wasted. To put this in perspective, it is easily possible for Villain to get to the river with a range of hands, every one of which has 40% equity hot-and-cold, and yet his best play is to fold and give up the pot all the time. At the root of the situation is information. Hero knows whether or not he has the best hand. Villain does not. It is fair to say that the polar distribution is easier and more profitable to play than the bluff-catching one.

This raises an issue that will have a significant influence on early-street strategizing. Recall Example 3 at the beginning of the chapter. During the analysis, we noted that the BB arrived on the river with a particularly strong range, and thus he was almost certainly playing too tight on the earlier streets. Now we can start to see why. He could have included a little more air in his getting-to-the-river range, and then, as we just saw, he might be able to play those air hands just as profitably as his real hands! This would, of course, be a better way to play those hands than folding them on the flop.

There are a couple of caveats to this sort of reasoning. First, of course, the turn and river cards are unknown during flop play, so the BB can not engineer his river distribution exactly. He must play to achieve the best result on average over all the possible future cards. Second, it is important not to get confused when thinking about this sort of balance-related issue. There is a tendency to think of the value hands in Hero's range here "protecting" the bluffs in the sense that having the value hands lets him profitably make the bluffs also. This is more or less true. However, players extrapolate to conclusions such as "the bluff hands are not being played profitably in and of themselves, but having the bluffs makes the value hands more profitable, giving us a better expectation overall." This sort of reasoning is incorrect. We are considering equilibrium play, and at equilibrium, every individual hand is being played as profitably as possible. In this case, it is just that Hero's few air hands can be played most profitably by bluffing because Villain will fold by virtue of the fact that we also have many value hands in our river betting range.

Now, what can we say about Hero's bet size? If he bets small enough with his entire range, then Villain can call since he wins sometimes and the relative payoff compared to the amount he has to risk is large. In this case, Hero wins less than the full pot on average. If Hero bets huge, however, then Villain can not call, and Hero wins the entire pot, thus achieving his maximal expectation. So betting huge is a fine play for Hero in this simple case. He can do no better. In real situations, however, perhaps there is is some danger of Villain having slow-played a good hand (this is a common response to huge river bets after all) or perhaps there is not actually that much money in the remaining stacks.

It is thus useful to find the minimum size bet Hero can make to attain an EV of the whole pot. If Hero bets huge, his EV is the whole pot since his opponent always folds. If he bets tiny with his whole range, his EV is somewhat less since Villain profitably calls with his bluff-catchers. There is only one sizing in-between for which Hero can bet his whole range and Villain is indifferent to calling and folding with his bluff-catchers:

$$EV_{SB}(call) = EV_{SB}(fold).$$

If Hero bets with this sizing, his EV at this point is still the whole pot (even if he sometimes gets called), but if he goes any smaller, Villain always calls and Hero loses EV.

So what is this size? It depends on the fraction of Hero's betting range which is beat by Villain's bluff-catchers. Call this fraction F. So, F is the fraction of Hero's range which is something like K♦-J♦ in our motivating example, and the remainder – $(1-F)$ of his hands – is good sevens or better. Notice that F is also the equity of Villain's bluff-catchers versus Hero's whole river starting range. It is the fraction of Hero's range which is beat by a bluff-catcher.

Now, let P be the size of the pot and S the effective remaining stacks at the beginning of river play. If Hero makes a bet of size B, then our opponent has the following total EV indifference equation.

$$EV_{Villain}(fold) = EV_{Villain}(call)$$
$$S = (S - B) + F(2B + P)$$

If the SB folds, he simply ends the hand with a stack of S. If he calls, he always has $S-B$ remaining plus another $(2B+P)$ when he wins the pot which happens F of the time. This equation is satisfied if $B=PF/(1-2F)$.

For example, if $F=10\%$ of Hero's betting range is a bluff, then the minimum bet size which wins him the whole pot is $B=12.5\%$ of the pot. This is quite a small bet, but that is all it takes when so much of Hero's range is stronger than Villain's.

What happens as F gets larger? That is, Villain's range is still capped at bluff-catchers, but Hero's range contains more air. Hero will have to bet larger to discourage Villain from calling. If $F=30\%$, we find an equilibrium river bet size of 75% of the pot. For $F=40\%$, we get a river bet size of 200% of the pot – twice the pot – quite an over-bet, but that is what it takes to achieve our maximal EV in this spot. At $F=48\%$, the equilibrium bet size is 12 times the pot! Notice what is happening as the fraction of bluffs in Hero's range approaches 50 percent. The bet size needed to keep Villain indifferent to calling is blowing up. In fact, in a mathematical sense, as F becomes nearly 50%, the bet size goes to infinity. This should make sense intuitively – if our opponent actually has the best hand at least half the time when facing a bet, then he can call profitably no matter how large we bet.

Of course, as the required bet size becomes larger, making large over-bets may become a less attractive plan in practice. First, there may not be enough chips behind to make these bets, and second, errors in your estimation of the hand distributions become more costly. For example, it becomes more problematic if Villain does happen to show up with a slow-played monster. However, this analysis certainly goes to show that restricting one's bets to the "standard" sizings between 1/2 and 1 pot-sized bet can be non-ideal.

So, we have found the GTO river strategies in the easily-analyzed case that at least 50 percent of one player's range beats all of the other player's range. Assuming that there is sufficient money behind, the strong-ranged player can win the whole pot by betting large enough that his opponent always folds. This is an example of a situation where there are many different equilibrium strategies for Hero – he can bet with any sizing larger than the minimum which we identified. These different strategies are referred to generally as *co-optimal*. They will all have the same value if Villain is playing his equilibrium strategy. If he is not, however, some may be more or less profitable than others.

We will now consider how this situation changes in the case that there is not enough money behind or when Hero's range is more than half bluffs.

7.2.3 Hero's Range is Almost all Stronger than Villain's but there is Little Money Behind

Now consider the case that there is not sufficient money left behind for Hero to make the minimally-sized bet that we found in the previous section. Villain, with a range of all bluff-catchers, is still not going to bet, but what should the Hero do? At least two options might seem reasonable. He can:

Option 1
Continue betting his entire range as large as he can (i.e. all-in), or

Option 2
Bet with all of his value hands and some bluffs but give up with some air in order to decrease his bluffing frequency to the point that he can make his opponent indifferent between calling and folding to a bet.

Which of these is most profitable?

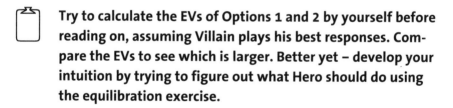 **Try to calculate the EVs of Options 1 and 2 by yourself before reading on, assuming Villain plays his best responses. Compare the EVs to see which is larger. Better yet – develop your intuition by trying to figure out what Hero should do using the equilibration exercise.**

We can see which option is preferable by working through the equilibration exercise. Suppose that Hero was shoving his whole range. Then, as we saw, Villain would be calling with all of his bluff-catchers. But then Hero could improve his expectation by ceasing to bet with with his air hands. But then the Villain can improve by folding to the bets with his bluff-catchers. But then it becomes best for Hero to start bluffing again. And so on.

Whenever Hero is betting with all his bluffs, Villain's counterstrategy makes him want to stop bluffing, but whenever he is never bluffing, Villain's counterstrategy makes him want to start bluffing. So, at the equilibrium, he will be playing a mixed strategy with these hands, sometimes bluffing and sometimes not bluffing. As for Villain, whenever he is always folding his bluff-catchers, Hero's counterstrategy makes him want to start calling, but whenever he is always calling, he is incentivized to fold. At the equilibrium, he will sometimes fold and sometimes call. Thus, the players' equilibrium strategies are as follows. Hero bets with all of his value hands, and then he adds bluffs to his betting range just up to the point where Villain's best play is no longer to fold. That is, he includes enough bluffs in his betting range that Villain is indifferent between calling and folding. In practice, this means that the fraction of Hero's betting range which is bluffs (which is equal to Villain's equity facing a bet) equals Villain's pot odds when facing a bet. Villain, on the other hand, calls with the precise frequency to make Hero's air hands indifferent between bluffing and giving up.

7.2.4 Hero is Polar but has Mostly Air

We have focused so far on the case where at least half of one player's range beats all of his opponent's hands. We will now relax this assumption slightly and look at a related and more common situation. Again, suppose Villain has a range composed of bluff-catchers, and Hero has a polarized range consisting of some hands that beat all of the bluff-catchers and some hands that lose to all of them. We can refer to these two parts of Hero's range as nuts and air since that is what they effectively are versus Villain's range. The difference, however, between this situation and the previous one is that we will assume that most of Hero's range is air and that he has relatively few nut hands. After all, it's hard to make the nuts heads-up! So, in our notation, the fraction F of Hero's range which is air satisfies $F > 0.5$.

As above, Villain will never want to bet since there is no value in it. Since his range is clearly divided into nuts and air, Hero can easily just choose to only put money in when he has the best of it. So, given these river starting distributions, position again does not matter. Hero will always get the chance to bet first (since he will always be checked to if he is in the SB), and his opponent will call or fold when facing a bet. What is the GTO river strategy here?

Since Hero's range is mostly air, there is no bet he can make with his entire range to force Villain to always fold. So, as in the previous case, the equilibrium will occur when Hero gives up with some of his air and bluffs just enough to make Villain indifferent between calling and folding. This bears much similarity to the reasoning in Section 7.2.3, so we will proceed quickly. Again, suppose the pot size is P, there are stacks of S behind at the beginning of the river play, and Hero bets with size B. Then, if Villain is indifferent between calling and folding, we have

$$\mathrm{EV}_{\mathrm{Villain}}(\mathrm{fold}) = \mathrm{EV}_{\mathrm{Villain}}(\mathrm{call})$$
$$S = (S - B) + A(2B + P)$$

where A is the fraction of Hero's betting range which is bluffs. Thus, this GTO bluff fraction is $A=B/(2B+P)$. This frequency, of course, gives Villain odds on a call such that he is exactly breaking even by calling with a bluff-catcher relative to folding it.

For example, if Hero is betting the size of pot, then $A=1/3$ of his betting range is a bluff at equilibrium. If 20% of his range is the nuts, he can achieve this if he bets 10% of his total range as bluffs. Since 80% of his range is air, this is equivalent to betting his air once out of every 8 opportunities. Then, he will be betting with 30% of his hands in total. If he doubles his bet size to twice the size of the pot, then $A=2/5$ of his betting range is bluffs at equilibrium. If he bets 10 times pot, then $A=10/21$ of his betting range is bluffs. It should make sense that, no matter how large his bet size, A never quite reaches $1/2$, but the larger he bets, the more bluffs he can have at equilibrium.

Now, what is Villain's calling frequency? Just as Villain's indifference equation let us solve for Hero's strategy, an indifference on Hero's part will allow us to solve for Villain's strategy. In particular, if Villain is calling with an unexploitable frequency, Hero will be indifferent between bluffing and giving up with his air. Let C be the frequency with which Villain calls a bet. Then, we have

$$\text{EV}_{\text{Hero}}(\text{give up with air}) = \text{EV}_{\text{Hero}}(\text{bluff air})$$
$$S = (S - B) + (1 - C)(B + P)$$

since, after bluffing, Hero always has at least$(S-B)$, and he gets another $(B+P)$ the $(1-C)$ of the time that Villain folds. So, we find that Villain's GTO calling frequency is $C=P/(B+P)$.

There is a lesson here about poker strategy that many players find unintuitive. Consider the case that Villain's bluff-catchers all have 99 percent equity. That is, 1 percent of Hero's range beats the bluff-catchers, and the rest does not. It is fair to say that Villain's range is relatively strong. However, despite having a very strong range and the best hand almost always, his GTO strategy does not involve betting. It is to check down and if he faces, say, a pot-sized bet, to fold half the time. Many players are uncomfortable taking such a "weak" line with many strong hands, but this is somewhat misguided. This situation is not a terrible one for Villain – his expectation at the equilibrium is still nearly the whole pot, the best he can expect, and his expectation will only grow if Hero bluffs too frequently.

The more important lesson here regards the construction of betting ranges. Intuitively, it is that a betting range on the river needs to include some weaker hands so that Villain will call with some holdings that make bets with higher-equity holdings profitable. Conversely, the betting range needs some value hands so that Villain will fold sometimes and bluffing is not throwing away money. As we will see repeatedly in more complicated examples, it is not the strength of a hand that determines whether it should be bet. Rather, it is Villain's response to the betting range as a whole that will determine the merits of betting with a particular hand.

Finally, we can see that, as far as the bet sizing here is concerned, bigger is better. Feel free to try as an exercise to find the EV of betting an arbitrary size and prove to yourself that it increases with the bet size. We, however, will just give some intuitive reasoning that will hopefully be more instructive.

First, notice that Hero's EV when he bets, averaged over his nuts and his air, is the whole pot, no more and no less. (He expects more with his value hands and less with his bluffs.) This is easy to see. Since Villain is indifferent to folding, the players' EVs are the same on average as if he just always folds, i.e., Hero wins the whole pot. On the other hand, when Hero gives up with a bluffing hand, he loses the whole pot. So to maximize his EV, he simply wants to size bets so that he can be betting as much as possible. That is, since he always bets his nuts, he wants to size bets so that he can be bluffing as much as possible. We saw above that the bigger Hero's bet sizing, the bigger his equilibrium bluffing fraction. So, his best bet size is as big as possible, i.e. all-in.

To drill this point home, let us consider a situation where Hero is playing a strategy which involves playing with two different river bet sizes. Suppose he is betting all-in with half his nut hands and half that size with the other half. Then, for Villain to be indifferent to calling each bet, Hero can bluff some frequency with the all-in sizing and some smaller frequency with the half-all-in sizing. His average expectation with his betting range (regardless of the size) is just what is in the pot on the river, and with his not-betting range his expectation is to lose the pot. But notice that this is fewer total bluffs than if he had just bet all-in with his whole betting range and is thus less profitable.

7.2.5 Our Bluff-catching Player also Holds some Slow-plays

We will make one final elaboration on this series of situations to make the solutions a bit more applicable to real river situations. You may have gathered that holding a range of all bluff-catchers is often a poor situation in which to find oneself. Here, we give Villain a tool to fight back. In addition to his bluff-catchers, we will assume Villain also has some amount of slow-played or trapping hands. In particular, assume a fraction T of his hands are traps, and the rest are bluff-catchers. Hero still has some value hands and some pure air. His air loses to everything. His value hands beat all of Villain's bluff-catchers but lose to all of his traps. Figure 7.4 represents the players' distributions. Hero's value hands have a bit less than 100% equity, and the rest have 0%. In addition to the standard equity distribution, we can represent the relative strengths of the various parts of both players' ranges on a single line, since the players have non-overlapping ranges. The weakest and some fairly strong hands belong to Hero, while various middling and a small number of nut holdings belong to Villain.

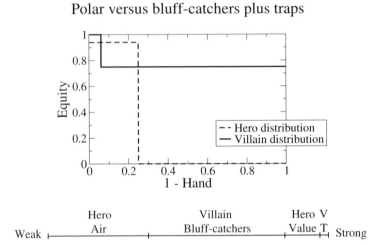

Figure 7.4: Representation of players' ranges and equity distributions.

We also tweak decision tree a bit here. Previously, Hero's best sizing was all-in whenever he bet. However, it is not clear that that will be best in this game since Hero faces a trade-off. Betting larger is best versus Villain's bluff-catchers for the same reasons as in the previous situations, but his bigger bets run the risk of losing more when Villain shows up with a slow-play. The particular details of the stack sizes and hand distributions will determine whether or not the all-in bet is unexploitable. So, we will allow Hero to make non-all-in bets of size B. In this case, Villain will have the chance to raise all-in as well as to call or fold. The decision tree for this situation is shown in Figure 7.5. As usual, there is P in the pot at the beginning of river play.

As in the preceding, this game plays out more or less the same regardless of the players' positions. Hero always effectively acts first. This is not quite as obvious as it was earlier, however, since Villain does have some good hands that could potentially lead for value from the BB. As we have seen, this would involve Villain betting these value hands as well as some of his bluff-catchers which are actually being used as bluffs. Then, Hero's value hands would effectively be bluff-catchers.

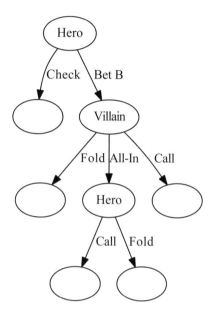

Figure 7.5: Decision tree for polar versus bluff-catchers and traps.

It turns out that this does not help Villain overall. Since Villain has so few nut hands, he can not make all that many bluffs, and he then has to check all the rest of his weak bluff-catchers to Hero. Hero can take advantage of this situation, especially by over-betting, as we saw before. In this case, it becomes more advantageous for Villain to go back to checking with his slow-plays on the river rather than leading out with them. All of this is to say that, by virtue of the fact that he has very few trapping hands, Villain finds it best to keep them combined with his bluff-catching range in checking the river, and Hero effectively gets to act first in the hand, no matter if he is actually in the BB or the SB.

There is, however, an important challenge here for our Hero. He can never have the nuts. If stacks are deep enough he will not ever want to bet all-in since running into a slow-play would be too costly. Furthermore, in some cases, he might not even want to make the smaller bet for fear of being raised off his hand. How deep must stacks be so that this starts to happen? The spots where Hero starts checking back value hands occur when the EV of betting them equals the EV of checking. If checking necessarily gets him to showdown (i.e. he is in position), then the value of checking a value hand is $S+P(1-T)$. By setting this equal to the EV of betting with a particular sizing (which we will find shortly), you can find criteria for this degenerate case. It turns out that, if slow-plays make up a small fraction of Villain's range, these conditions are only not satisfied for very deep stacks. Checking back value hands will almost never be as good as betting B if, for example, B is less than the size of the pot and T is less than 10 percent of Villain's range. If checking means check-folding (possibly the case if Hero is out of position), then the value of checking falls even more, and checking value hands is an even less attractive option. So, we will not worry about checking back value hands here – it really only comes up in situations which violate the spirit of the situation.

Now, to solve this game, we really just need to worry about the most profitable way to bet our value hands. Then we can just bet enough bluffs to balance. Consider first the value of betting S, all-in. This is essentially the same problem as before with a small twist. As before, Villain will call just enough to keep Hero breaking even on his bluffs. From the relevant indifference equation, we find that Villain's necessary not-folding frequency is $P/(S+P)$. His not-folding range will contain all of his traps (a fraction T of his total hands) and then enough bluff-catchers to make up the difference, i.e. bluff-catchers totalling a fraction $(P/(S+P))-T$ of his range. In this way, we can see here exactly how the value of the spot for Villain is improved by adding some value hands to his distribution. He is still calling Hero's shove with the same frequency, but now, some of his hands are actually happy to call as opposed to previously when he was always indifferent.

We can now break down the situation to find Hero's EV when he shoves with a value hand. T of the time, he runs into the nuts and ends up with 0 chips. $(P/(S+P))-T$ of the time he gets called by a bluff-catcher and ends up with a stack of $(2S+P)$. The rest of the time he bets, Villain folds, and he ends up with $(S+P)$. On average,

$$\text{EV}_{\text{Hero}}(\text{shove}) = (\frac{P}{S+P} - T)(S+P+S) + (1 - \frac{P}{S+P})(S+P)$$

Now consider Hero's non-all-in bet option. Villain still has a total not-folding frequency of $P/(B+P)$ from the same arguments as before. (If he continues in the hand versus a bet any more than that, Hero stops bluffing completely. If he continues any less, Hero can profitably bluff with his entire range). Additionally, however, Villain will go all-in with his trapping hands. Furthermore, at equilibrium, he will also turn enough of his "bluff-catcher" hands into bluffs to make Hero indifferent to calling with his "value" hands which are now effectively bluff-catchers. This indifference (which holds for Hero's "value" hands) lets us solve for Villain's bluff-shoving frequency.

$$\text{EV}_{\text{Hero}}(\text{fold to jam}) = \text{EV}_{\text{Hero}}(\text{call jam})$$
$$S - B = (F_B)(P + 2S) + (1 - F_B)(0)$$

where F_B is the fraction of Villain's shoving range which is bluffs. We have

$$F_B = \frac{S - B}{2S + P}$$

So, the fraction, X, of Villain's entire river starting range which is bluff-shoving when facing Hero's small bet satisfies

$$\frac{X}{X + T} = \frac{S - B}{2S + P}$$

so that

$$X = \frac{T(S - B)}{B + P + S}$$

Villain's total jamming frequency is $(T+X)$, the slow-plays plus the bluff-shoves. Whenever Villain jams, Hero has total EV $(S-B)$, whether he calls or folds: that is clearly how much he has if he folds, and Villain has chosen his bluff frequency to make Hero indifferent between folding and calling. Then, $P/(P+B) - (T+X)$ of the time (i.e. his total not-folding frequency minus his jamming frequency), Villain just calls with a bluff-catcher, so Hero wins and ends up with a stack of $(S+P+B)$. The remainder of the time, Villain folds to the bet, and Hero ends up with $(S+P)$.

Overall, when Hero bets B with a value hand, he has expected value

$$EV_{\text{Hero}}(\text{bet } B) = F_J(S - B) + (F_{BC})(S + P + B) + (1 - F_J - F_{BC})(S + P)$$

where Villain's jamming frequency is

$$F_J = T((1+(S-B)/(S+P+B))$$

and his bluff-catching frequency is

$$F_{BC} = P/(B+P)-F_J.$$

This section's final task is to check which of Hero's bet sizing options is preferable. With small effective stacks, the threat of occasionally running into the nuts is not particularly important, but with deep stacks, it can be quite costly, and Hero should definitely bet smaller than all-in. To find the stack depth where betting some particular size B becomes better than using bet size S, we could just set

$$EV_{\text{Hero}}(\text{shove})=EV_{\text{Hero}}(\text{bet } B)$$

and solve for the stack size.

However, we can do a little better and just find the single most profitable bet size for Hero which may or may not be all-in. Now, the following computation leverages a little calculus. There are a couple of points in this book which do, since the ends justify the means. If it's a subject you are a bit rusty in – don't panic! Skipping to the result in these sections is fine.

To find the bet size which maximizes $EV_{Hero}(betB)$, we simply take that quantity's derivative with respect to B and set it equal to 0. Solving the resulting equation for the bet sizing gives us its optimal value. If we call this GTO bet size B^*, then we have

(7.2)
$$B^* = \frac{1 + S - T - 4S(1 + S)T + \sqrt{(S + 2S^2)^2 T}}{(1 + 2S)^2T - 1}$$

where we have set $P=1$ to obtain the bet size in terms of the size of the pot. If this value lies out the range of possible bet sizes [0,S], it indicates that there is no optimal value on that interval, and Hero should shove.

Optimal Hero bet sizing

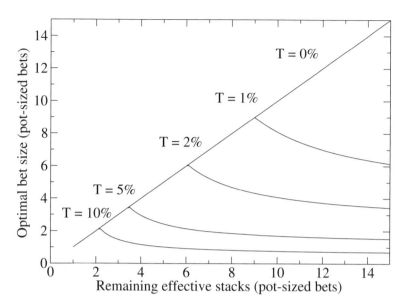

Figure 7.6: GTO bet sizing B* for Hero with respect to remaining effective stacks. Both quantities are in units of the pot size.

In Figure 7.6, we have plotted B^* versus S for several different choices for the composition of Villain's range. We can see that when $T=0$, Villain holds no slow-plays and the equilibrium bet size is always all-in. When Villain has a non-zero amount of slow-played hands, Hero's GTO strategy involves betting all-in up to some critical stack depth where he starts making non-all-in bets. The more traps Villain has in his range, the lower this critical stack size is. Notice that the bet sizes can still be fairly large over-bets even when Villain has a non-negligible number of slow-plays in his range.

7.2.6 Summary of Simple River Situations

We have covered a variety of river spots which center around Hero's distribution being more or less polar with respect to his opponent's range. We saw that he generally bets all of his value hands, and, if there is no danger of running into a trap, he bets as big as possible. In this case, if he has at least half value hands and there is enough money behind, he can bet big enough to always win the pot. If he has fewer strong holdings or there is not enough money behind to make the required bet, he has to give up with some bluffs at equilibrium. Additionally, when Villain can have some slow-plays, Hero's GTO bet size is no longer necessarily all-in. We will conclude this series with some comments about when these situations come up in real play, some discussion of exploitative play, and a review of some of the big ideas we saw.

First, when does a player get to the river with a relatively polar distribution? On static boards, it often occurs when he bets the flop and turn and his opponent responds passively. Because hand values are not changing much, the bettor's primary motivation for betting is to make better hands fold or to get worse hands to call. Middling strength hands are hard pressed to accomplish either of these things, so a bettor's range is generally made up of particularly strong and particularly weak hands. The caller, on the other hand, having not folded nor raised, tends to have more modest holdings, worth showing down but not raising. So, the bettor's distribution is relatively polar. Depending on how bluffy and aggressive the betting player is here, the value part of his polar range could be quite large, i.e. possibly larger than 50% of his range.

These situations can arise in more subtle ways in smaller pots as well. Suppose the SB raises preflop, c-bets a fairly nondescript flop, and the BB check-calls. The turn checks through, and the BB also checks the river. With many board run-offs and BB tendencies, the BB will have *something* here since he called the flop and did not bluff-lead the river, but not too much of anything since he did not lead the river for value either. Depending on the board, we will often be able to narrow a lot of players' ranges to something like exactly bottom flopped pair here with a high frequency. (Take a moment now to think of a few boards where the turn and river cards are below or above the various flop cards, and determine what your own ranges are in the BB's spot versus an unknown opponent in your games.) The SB, on the other hand, can likely have a lot of different holdings here, and due to how narrowly defined the BB's hand is, the SB's range is effectively polar. In contrast to the previous situation, however, the value portion of this SB range is often rather small.

On volatile boards, players often put in multiple bets with a wider variety of hands. However, with certain assumptions about players' tendencies, these situations can also come up, especially when draws either come in or miss in a way which leaves little middle ground for one player's distribution. We will see this in a couple of our examples at the end of the chapter. The big point here, as always, is to think hard about your range and that of your opponent at every decision point in a hand.

Now, to see another important way to apply what we have learned here, we need to look at exactly what happened in the final situation we considered. The river play started out with Hero betting (for value or as a bluff) and Villain mostly bluff-catching. But occasionally Villain raised, and then the players' roles were reversed. Suddenly, Villain played a polar distribution, and Hero was forced to bluff-catch with those hands which he was previously betting for value. Thus, in this section of the river play, we effectively found ourselves in one of the simpler situations which we had encountered previously. Which of the earlier solutions applies depends on the stack sizes, but notice that it is always the case here that Villain's shoving range consists of more than 50 percent value hands (or else Hero would always call, thus motivating Villain to shove fewer bluffs). Essentially, the players switched roles and both of their total ranges are smaller, but we can still directly apply the solutions to the simpler situation to analyze this spot.

It turns out that analysis of this sort of situation is one of the most useful applications of these simple-distribution solutions for real river play. As we will see in the examples, players get to the river with all sorts of ranges, and, especially when skilled players are involved in the hand, these ranges can often contain a variety of types of hands. However, when a (good) player puts in a raise on the river, it is necessarily because raising is more profitable than (or at least as profitable as) calling or folding. And this is only the case for particularly weak or particularly strong hands, by virtue of the fact that hand values are completely static on the river. So raising the river has a very polarizing effect on the raiser's range, making our results useful. In general, it is very important to be able to identify river situations where players' ranges fall into these categories and to be able to implement effective counterstrategies at the table. Put in some practice, and you will develop the intuition necessary.

We have also seen some big ideas which, together, foreshadow some of the important properties of unexploitable play on earlier streets. First, we argued that a player with a range composed primarily of bluff-catcher type hands will never want to bet himself. He will always essentially play check-and-guess. We have also seen that, in many situations, a player who has been leading the betting in a hand will tend to have a polar range while his opponent's distribution is composed of more middling holdings. In combination, these two observations explain a common pattern found in NLHE play. Many people are generally in the habit of "checking to the raiser". They do not lead out with a bet on one street if they flat-called a bet on the previous one. That is, they rarely check-call the flop and then lead the turn or check-call turn and then lead the river. This makes sense because they generally have a bluff-catcher-heavy range after making the earlier-street flat call. And, even if a small fraction of the player's range is strong because of the new card or a slow-play, these hands generally have reason to keep playing the same way as the weaker ones in the player's range.

We will see, however, this tendency is not always ideal, especially on cards that drastically affect the equity distributions or on volatile boards in general. Sometimes we might check-call the turn in the BB, representing a bluff-catcher-heavy range, but then a card comes that is particularly strong for us. That is, it improves a significant part of our range. We can then consider leading the turn with some of those strong hands as well as some bluffs since the nature of our distribution has changed. In fact, this often occurs on almost all turns after a draw-heavy flop. On turns where draws get there, part of our range is improved to very strong, and part is devalued and can thus be used as a bluff. Even more commonly, when draws miss, flopped made hands increase in relative strength and can lead the turn for value while the missed draws are devalued and can be used to semi-bluff. One good example of a hand in which a significant portion of the BB's flop check-calling range might want to lead the turn and/or the river is Example 6 at the beginning of the chapter. We are getting a bit ahead of ourselves, but the theoretical underpinnings of these plays can be seen in the river situations just covered.

In any case, the tendency to "check to the bettor" leads to three common river situations with respect to the earlier-street play. Either the SB put the last bet in on the turn, has a fairly polar range, and is checked to on the river. Or the BB put in the last bet on the turn, has the polar range, and is prone to leading with a bet on the river. Thirdly, if no bets went in on the turn, the situation is more complicated. This, of course, resonates with our earlier explanation of the reason why position is actually unimportant on the river in these polar-versus-bluff-catcher situations. The play proceeds essentially the same way and the values achieved are the same regardless of position.

We did mention, however, that in the more complicated situation where Villain had an increasing number of traps, Hero began to check back the river with some of his "value" hands. In this case, the option to check back and get immediately to showdown rather than be faced with his own bluff-catching decision was valuable for SB. However, when Hero begins checking back "value" hands, Villain might start leading the river with some of his nut hands, and the situation can no longer really be said to be a polar-versus-bluff-catcher spot anyhow, even approximately. In general, position will have more value in river situations with more complex structures.

Exploitative play in these spots is easy on the surface. If Villain with his bluff-catchers does lead out on the river, it is easy to play perfectly against him. He is more or less exploiting himself. Other exploitative adjustments are fairly obvious to a player who has understood the discussion so far. If Villain is calling a bit too much, Hero can maximize his EV by cutting his bluffing frequency down to zero. Conversely, if Villain calls too little, Hero can profitably bluff 100 percent of the time. From Villain's perspective, if Hero is not bluffing enough, Villain can check and fold 100 percent of the time. If Hero is bluffing too much, Villain should check and call with his bluff-catchers always. Notice that these exploitative strategies are binary. At equilibrium, a player might take two different lines with the same hand, but if his opponent deviates from the equilibrium just slightly in either direction, one of his options becomes better than the other and is best taken 100% of the time.

Now, these adjustments can be easy to state abstractly but tricky to implement at the table without more study. The fact is, almost all players are quite exploitable in many river spots. It is not just because they have over-arching tendencies to be either bluffy or not bluffy. That could certainly be the case with any given opponent, and we should certainly watch out for that since it is so basic. More importantly, however, players get to the river with such a wide variety of distributions that any general strategy that does not account for the details of a spot ends up being unbalanced very frequently.

For example, suppose we have a hand in which many draws miss. Then, in an extreme case, the polar player's range might be only 10% value hands and 90% bluffs. If his river bet is the size of the pot, then a third of his betting range should be bluffs, so 5% of the range with which he gets to the river consists of air hands which should be turned into bluffs. This means that every time he gets to the spot with any of his air hands, he bets it as a bluff 5/90=5.6%of the time, at equilibrium. On the other hand, if Hero arrives at the river with 40 percent nuts and 60 percent air and is making a pot-sized bet, he should bet each bluff hand 33% of the time. In practice, it is hard for people to estimate those frequencies and then to randomize appropriately in any particular hand. If you know that you are "supposed to" bet in a spot 5.6% of the time, what do you do? You might just not bet ever or, if you do bet sometimes, it is very easy to do it too frequently. The solution here is, of course, careful consideration of players' ranges (and especially an awareness of your own ranges), and practice or a predetermined plan for randomizing play with particular holdings or for choosing the hands which are best to bluff with. And, of course, it is often best not to stress too much about perfectly randomizing but instead to focus on playing exploitatively. We will say more about the practical solutions to these issues in this volume's epilogue.

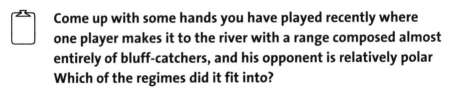 **Come up with some hands you have played recently where one player makes it to the river with a range composed almost entirely of bluff-catchers, and his opponent is relatively polar Which of the regimes did it fit into?**

Finally, it is important to always keep in mind where the money comes from in poker. In particular, in order to evaluate various turn options, we need to know the value of getting to the river with particular hands and distributions. We saw that the best a player could do on average in equilibrium was to win the money already in the pot at the start of river play, and indeed Hero achieved this by simply always having the best hand or even just usually having the best hand. In this second case, his distribution worked together to increase his EV as compared to what it would have been if the players had just showed down at the beginning of river play. Conversely, the worst-case scenario at equilibrium is to lose the whole pot on the river.

To begin developing a feel for the values of other river situations, we can look directly at the fraction of the pot P we expect to capture with each part of our range in some of these simple river spots. In Figures 7.7 and 7.8, we present some of these plots for the most general river situation covered so far, whose decision tree is shown in Figure 7.5. We plot the fraction of P that a player expects to win at equilibrium for a sample of different values of F, the fraction of the polar player's range which is air, T, the fraction of the bluff-catching player's range which is traps, and S, the effective stacks behind.

To make a plot like this, we essentially just need to know how much of each type of hand a player has and the value of each type. Keep in mind that a hand has a particular value at equilibrium, regardless of whether or not the player is playing it in more than one way. So, Hero obtains a certain value with his value hands which he always bets with size B^*. His bluffs are indifferent between betting and check-folding, so his total expected stack size is just S with these hands whether he bets or checks. For Villain, with his slow-plays, he has value

$$(S+P)(\text{Hero check frequency}) + (S+P+B)(\text{Hero bet–fold frequency}) + (2S+P)(\text{Hero bet–call frequency}).$$

Finally, with his bluff-catchers, Villain is indifferent to folding when Hero bets, so these have value

$$(\text{Hero bet frequency})(S) + (\text{Hero check frequency})(S+P).$$

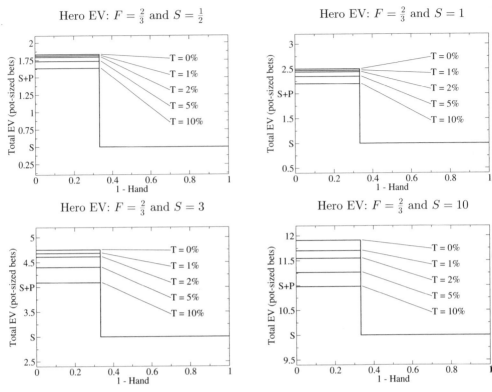

Figure 7.7: Hero EV distributions

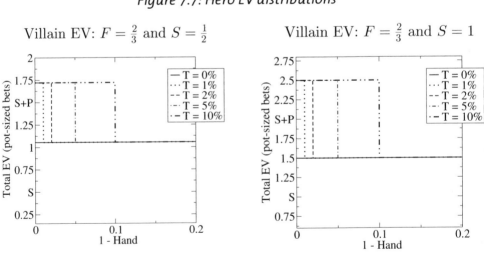

Villain EV: $F = \frac{2}{3}$ and $S = 3$

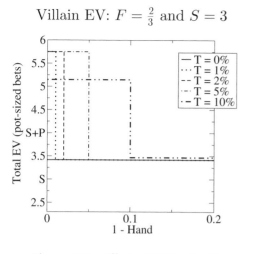

Villain EV: $F = \frac{2}{3}$ and $S = 10$

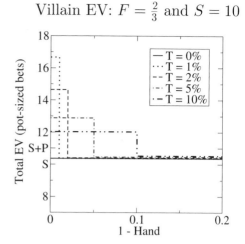

Figure 7.8: Villain EV distributions

These plots can be thought of as *EV distributions*. They are similar to equity distributions but instead of showing the equity of various parts of a player's range, they show the EV. In the situation on which we are focusing, Hero is polar with bluffs making up *F*=2/3 of his range, and a fraction *T* of Villain's range is slow-played nut hands while the rest is bluff-catchers. *T* varies between 0 and 10 percent, and we consider effective remaining stack sizes of 0.5, 1, 3, and 10. These stack sizes and the EVs themselves are given in terms of the pot size at the beginning of river play. On the horizontal axis is the fraction of the player's range, and on the vertical axis is the total stack EV in multiples of the size of the pot.

First consider Hero's EVs in Figure 7.7. In each case, his air hands have a value of *S* regardless of Villain's trapping frequency. His value hands generally expect a stack of somewhat more than (*S+P*), but this decreases significantly as Villain begins to slow-play. Notice that the slow-plays are much more effective at reducing Hero's expectation in the deeper-stacked situations.

Now consider Villain's EV distributions. We have not shown the player's whole range of hands in these since it is just a straight line all the way to the right, and the interesting stuff happens with Villain's trapping hands. Indeed a few fun trends show up here. First, all of his bluff-catchers do better than *S*. In the shorter-stacked cases, Villain's bluff-catchers have the same value regardless of his trapping frequency. The slow-plays only increase Villain's overall average expectation by making money themselves. However, in the deeper-stacked cases, Hero's equilibrium bet size becomes less than all-in when Villain slow-plays. In particular, the higher the value of T, the smaller Hero's bet size becomes. This means that Hero must bluff less and thus check and lose more, and Villain's bluff-catchers make more money by getting to showdown more often. In this way, having slow-plays in his range has helped Villain's weak hands make more money too.

Similar reasoning explains the trend seen with the value of Villain's traps. At short stacks, they all have the same value for all the different values of T. Hero shoves with all of his betting range in these cases, and his bluffing frequency does not depend on T (remember, it is just what is necessary to keep Villain's bluff-catchers indifferent between calling and folding), so Villain is facing the same range when he calls a shove, and all of his traps have the same value. However, at deeper stacks, Hero bets smaller when Villain has more traps in his range, and he bets with a lower frequency as well, since the smaller bet size means he can not bluff as often. So, the more traps Villain has, the lower their value.

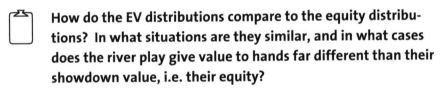 **How do the EV distributions compare to the equity distributions? In what situations are they similar, and in what cases does the river play give value to hands far different than their showdown value, i.e. their equity?**

We will now consider some more complicated spots where the players' ranges do not necessarily divide nicely into non-overlapping sections. Before we continue, go back through the example hands at the beginning of the chapter. Which can essentially be solved by reference to the simple situations we have covered so far? Which could be if we had made some different assumptions about the players' early-street tendencies and thus the river starting distributions? Think outside the box.

7.3 General Asymmetric Starting Distributions

So far, we have focused on situations where we are able to partition the players' ranges into disjoint sets of hands. Simple distributions led to simple play. Hero's bet size was just all-in in most cases. The bluff-catching player never bet out which made position unimportant. However, in many real cases, both players' ranges contain some nut hands, some air hands, and various amounts of everything in between. In this section, we will analyze some river games where the players hold arbitrary starting distributions.

Before we get started, we can gain a little insight into how these games might go by recalling our experience with preflop-only situations. River play actually has a lot in common with preflop-only games. Why is this? Well, think about the situation: two players can hold, potentially, many different types of hands, and they play out a full street's worth of betting, raising, etc, but there is no calling to see future cards. There is either a fold or a showdown where players capture their equities immediately after the street's play is complete.

There are of course a few important differences between the situations. Players will often call to see a showdown on the river without getting all the money in, whereas in preflop-only games, the hands only ended in a fold or an all-in and call. This property of preflop-only games led to play which was loose and aggressive to the point of being unrealistic at most stack depths. However, action in the preflop-only games could be thought of as a battle for the 1.5 BB in the pot, and, similarly, river play is essentially motivated by a battle for whatever is in the pot at the beginning of the street. A second, and relatively minor, difference between the situations arises from a certain oddity of preflop play – the SB has to make a larger bet to contest the pot (by 0.5 BB) than the BB has to call.

The more important difference, however, between preflop-only and river play is in the players' equity distributions. First of all, in contrast to the preflop case, the starting distributions are not symmetric. As we have seen, it is very common for players' ranges to differ on the river, and this affects play significantly. Also, even when players both have wide and relatively symmetric distributions, the distributions on the river are still qualitatively different than preflop. They are much less flat. Hand equities preflop range mostly in the 25 to 80 percent range and are somewhat evenly distributed between the two extremes (see Figure 5.3). On the other hand, on the river, the nuts have near 100 percent equity, and many air hands will have close to 0. Depending on the board and early street play, there could be more or less anything in between.

In any case, this situation will lead to relatively tight and conservative play as compared to the preflop situation. If a player's bluff gets called on the river, he generally loses all the money he put in the pot. Bluffs gone bad preflop and on volatile boards in general are not nearly as costly since the bluffer still wins a significant fraction of the time. This is why, preflop 6 BB deep, over-bet shoving several times the pot with most of one's preflop starting range is fairly standard while it would be a poor strategy with a similar stack-to-pot ratio on the river. Might that be a good approach to play on particularly volatile flops?

Anyway, in this section we will work with the equity distributions themselves, and focus on the parts of a player's range he plays in various ways. It is finally time to apply our discussion of river equity distributions from section 5.3! Recall that we can essentially line up all hands from the nuts (beats everything) to the nut low (beats nothing) and that there is a strict ordering of everything in between since the board is final and there are no draws. (And we will continue to neglect card removal effects in most cases.) Please review that section if you have forgotten the relationship between the SB and BB river equity distributions.

We will consider first the case where a player is deciding between betting and checking on the river.

7.3.1 BB Bet-or-check on the River

Hero is in the BB deciding whether to bet or check. If he checks, it is to check-fold and, if he bets, the SB can either call or fold. This is a very simple situation – the decision tree is analogous to that of the shove/fold game preflop. We will cover it quickly since most of the methodology should be very familiar, but the parts that are new are especially important.

First, let us look at the form of the solutions. The SB, when facing a bet, will either call or fold each of his hands, depending on which choice is more profitable. Since calling with a better hand is always at least as profitable as calling with a worse hand, we can basically describe the SB's strategy by reference to a single cutoff holding, call it h_c. The SB calls with all hands better than h_c and folds all worse. For the BB, since his options are to bet or to check and lose, he will also have a particular hand, call it h_b, such that he bets all hands better and gives up with all hands worse. Since he has no chance to see a showdown if he checks, there is no reason for the BB to ever bet with a worse hand than he checks.

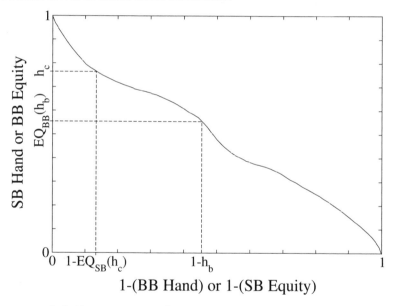

Figure 7.9: Solution structure for asymmetric BB bet-or-check game.

So we have essentially divided each of the players' ranges into two sections. Hero has betting and checking sections, and Villain has calling and folding sections. We will refer to this sort of parameterization as the *structure* of the solutions. Identifying the structure of the solutions to various situations can often be done logically and is at least as important as precisely identifying the threshold hands themselves (h_c and h_b in this case) for developing a solid strategy.

The structure of the players' strategies is shown in Figure 7.9. The figure shows the players' equity distributions from the BB's point of view. The distribution itself is arbitrary. What is important are the two axes and the connection between them.

The first thing to notice here is that we have essentially labeled the hands themselves from 0 to 1, where 0 is the worst hand in the range and 1 is the best. So, the hand 0.7 is the 70th percentile hand, etc. This natural assigning of numerical values to the hands will make it easier to talk about the solutions. For example, if we find that h_c=0.7, then we mean that 0.7 is the SB's weakest calling hand. In other words, he is calling with the top 30% of his range and folding the rest.

With that in mind, the BB hand h_b is shown on the horizontal axis in the figure, and we can read its equity versus the SB's range right off the graph. This equity is labeled $EQ_{BB}(h_b)$. Now, since we are on the river, $EQ_{BB}(h_b)$ is just the fraction of the SB's hands that it is beating. So the number $EQ_{BB}(h_b)$ is the numerical value of the particular hand combination h_b if it were part of the SB's range. Thus the numeric value of a BB hand, h, tells us its strength percentile with respect to the BB's range, and $EQ_{BB}(h)$ tells us the same hand's place if it were part of the SB's range. Thus, in general the vertical axis can also be thought of not only as giving the equity of the BB's hands but also as describing the value of SB holdings.

In this spirit, we have indicated the hand h_c on the vertical axis, and if we follow it down to the horizontal axis, we can see what fraction of the BB's range it beats. But of course, the fraction of the BB's range it beats is just the SB's equity on the river with that hand. For this reason, we have labeled the horizontal axis both "1-BB hand" and "1-SB equity" and labelled the vertical axis "SB hand" as well as "BB equity". The "1-" just accounts for the fact that equity distributions are drawn with hands on the horizontal axis decreasing in strength from left to right as opposed to the reverse. This was done for historical reasons – this is how equity distributions are drawn, but there is no deep meaning behind it.

Now, the SB will never call a bet when he has no chance of winning the pot, that is, with a hand worse than all of the BB's betting range. Thus, in our numerical notation, we know that $h_c > EQ_{BB}(h_b)$ and, equivalently, that $EQ_{SB}(h_c) > h_b$. This order was taken into account in the drawing of Figure 7.9.

We have made the implicit assumption that there is some hand for any number between 0 and 1. This is close enough since there are lots of different hands even though there are not infinitely many in reality. So, Hero's strongest checking hand is essentially the same hand as his weakest betting one. Since he is playing this hand in both ways at the equilibrium, he must be indifferent between the options.

Our approach to finding the GTO strategies in this sequence of games will rely on the indifferences associated with the cutoff hands that describe the solutions' structures. In general, there is one indifference equation associated with each of the players' threshold hands. Thus, finding the GTO strategies in this game is straightforward. Let P be the size of the pot, and suppose both players have S left behind at the beginning of the river play. Let B be the BB's bet size. With his cutoff hand h_b, the BB is indifferent between his check-folding and betting options. We work in terms of total stack sizes at end of hand, as usual. Then, we have for Hero's betting cut-off h_b:

$$EV_{BB}(\text{check-fold } h_b) = EV_{BB}(\text{bet B with } h_b)$$

$$S = (\text{SB fold freq})(S+P) + (\text{SB call freq})((S-B) + (P+2B)(EQ_{BB}(h_b \text{ vs a call})))$$

where $EQ_{BB}(h_b$ vs a call) is the BB's equity with h_b versus the SB's calling range, that is, the chance he wins the hand when he gets called. This is simply 0 since, as mentioned previously, the SB always has a better hand than h_b when he calls. Additionally, the SB's folding frequency is h_c, and his calling frequency is $1-h_c$, as this is the definition of h_c. So,

$$S = h_c(S+P) + (1 - h_c)(S - B)$$

and we find

$$h_c = B/(B+P)$$

Now for the other indifference – with his cut-off hand h_c, the SB is indifferent between calling and folding to a bet.

$$\text{EV}_{\text{SB}}(\text{fold}) = \text{EV}_{\text{SB}}(\text{call})$$
$$S = (S - B) + (\text{chance SB wins with } h_c)(2B + P)$$

since he always has (*S−B*) after calling the bet, and he gets another (*2B+P*) when he wins.

Now, evaluating the chance that the SB wins and loses if he calls with h_c is an important skill for understanding the rest of this chapter. It is easiest to do by looking at the horizontal axis of Figure 7.9. The BB bets with all the hands between $(1 - h_b)$ and 0. When he has one of those between $(1 - \text{EQ}_{\text{SB}}(h_c))$ and $(1 - h_b)$, the SB's h_c hand wins. The rest of the time, it loses. So, the total fraction of hands the BB bets is $(1 - h_b)$, and the total fraction of hands that he bets that are beat by h_c is $(1 - h_b) - (1 - \text{EQ}_{\text{SB}}(h_c))$. So when the SB calls a bet, we have

$$(\text{chance SB wins with } h_c) = [(1 - h_b) - (1 - \text{EQ}_{\text{SB}}(h_c))] / (1 - h_b)$$

We have found this essentially just by dividing the lengths of the appropriate line segments from the horizontal axis of the graph. Plugging in, our last equation now becomes

$$S - B + \frac{(1 - h_b) - (1 - \text{EQ}_{\text{SB}}(h_c))}{1 - h_b}(2B + P) = S$$

or

$$h_b = \frac{\text{EQ}_{\text{SB}}(h_c)(P + 2B) - B}{B + P}$$

We now have the complete solution to this game so long as the indifference equations can be satisfied. Notice that the stack size *S* drops out of both equations, and we find that the strategies depend only on the pot and bet sizes. This of course makes sense – as long as we can make our bet of size *B*, the total amount of money behind never comes into play.

Let us take a quick example. Suppose the pot size, the effective stacks behind, and the bet size are all the same. In other words, the BB is making a pot sized bet all-in, and *P=S=B*. Then, the worst hand that the SB calls a bet with is

$$h_c = B/(B+P) = 1/2$$

The SB is calling with 50 percent of his range. Notice that this result does not depend on the equity distributions at all. It came directly from stipulating that the BB be indifferent between betting and checking his cutoff hand at the equilibrium.

Now, we saw situations earlier where this indifference could not be met. The BB's range was too strong and so betting had higher value than checking for his entire range. This was the case, if you recall, in our first application of the equilibration exercise in Section 2.2.3 (see the equity distribution in Figure 5.7). However, this will not usually be the case, and whenever it is not, the SB's GTO calling frequency in this game is 50 percent regardless of the starting distributions.

Intuitively, you might think that as the BB's range gets a bit stronger, the SB should call a bit less often, but this is not what we see. It is always valuable to build intuition for situations like this by going through the equilibration exercise. The reason for our observation is as follows. As soon as the SB starts calling even slightly less than that equilibrium amount, the BB finds it best to start betting with 100 percent of his bluffing hands since it will be more profitable than check-folding. Then, it will once again be profitable for the SB to start calling more. Unless, of course, the BB's range is so strong that he can bet his whole range and the SB still does not want to call with his 51st percentile hand, and we have the case where the indifference breaks down. So as the BB's range becomes stronger, the SB keeps calling with the same hands (which do lose more money but not as much as if he folded more) until it all of a sudden becomes so strong that he does start calling less, and that is the same point at which the BB starts bluffing 100 percent of the time.

Continuing with our example, we can also find the BB's GTO strategy. With *P=B=S* we have

$$h_b = 1/2(3EQ_{SB}(h_c)-1)$$

The BB's strategy does depend on the equity distributions. Now, in the case of *symmetric distributions*, when the players have the same ranges,

$EQ(h)=h$ for all hands h for both players. (Do you see why? If not, refer back to Figure 5.8 and the surrounding discussion.) If we continue with our example with this assumption for simplicity, we have

$$\mathrm{EQ_{SB}}(h_c) = h_c = 1/2$$

and we get the BB's cutoff hand $h_b=1/4$. So, in this case, BB is betting 3/4 of all his hands, 2/3 of which beat h_c. Since the SB is getting 2-to-1 on his money for a call, this is just right to keep him indifferent with his cutoff hand. The 1/3 of hands which lose to h_c are essentially pure bluffs since they never win when called.

Asymmetric distributions

In general, starting distributions are not symmetric, and the BB's weakest betting hand h_b depends on the equity of the SB's weakest calling hand. Let us continue with the $P=S=B$ stack and bet sizings. Notice that when $EQ_{SB}(h_c)$ = 1/3, we can plug into the formula to find $h_b=0$. In other words, the SB's cutoff hand is so weak that the BB has to bet with 100 percent of his range to make SB indifferent between calling and folding with h_c. If the SB's h_c is any weaker than this, the indifference breaks down – the BB bets his whole range, and the SB calls with those hands that have odds, less than 50% of his hands in total. When the SB's range is stronger, however, the BB has to tighten up. For example, if the 50th percentile hand in the SB's range actually has 2/3 equity versus the BB's entire river starting range, then the BB has to tighten up to just bet half of his hands and check with the other half.

Finally, if $EQ_{SB}(h_c)$ = 0.96 (i.e., almost all his hands are the near-nuts), then h_c = 0.94, i.e the BB only bets the top 6 percent of his range. To be clear, what is going on here with the indifference is this: $EQ_{SB}(h_c)$ = 0.96 means that 4% of BB's range actually beats h_b. So, the BB is betting with that 4 percent, and then he is betting with another 2 percent of hands so that h_c is indifferent between calling and folding.

Notice in this last case that the SB is folding hands to a pot-sized bet which have 95% equity versus the BB's river starting range! This is his most profitable strategy since the BB is betting so rarely at equilibrium. So, at equilibrium, the SB will still win the pot almost always, as you would expect. But indeed, he will win more than that, on average, by playing his equilibrium strategy versus a BB who is bluffing too much, so folding strong hands so often is, of course, not exploitable. However, the SB's maximally exploitative strategy could certainly involve loosening up his calling requirements significantly were the BB betting too often.

Of course, restricting ourselves to the BB bet-or-check decision tree may be unrealistic when the SB's average hand is so strong. Unlike the case where he had all bluff-catchers, here he does have a whole distribution of different strength hands, and, as we will see, he certainly may have reason to bet with some of it as a bluff and for value.

Another interesting property of these results is that they do not depend on the detailed structure of the distributions. Unless there is breakdown of the indifference equations, the only property of the distributions that affects the equilibrium strategies is $EQ_{SB}(h_c)$, the equity of the SB's cutoff hand versus the BB's entire range. In the case of the pot-sized bet, the BB's betting frequency depends only on the equity of the middle of the SB's range. It did not matter if the upper 40 percent of the range is all very strong or if it is just slightly stronger than h_c. The reason for this is that the SB is simply calling just enough to keep the BB from doing better than break-even with his bluffs, and the BB is then bluffing as much as he can get away with without motivating the SB to call with more hands. The BB's bluffs do not care if the top part of the SB range is extremely strong or simply able to beat a bluff, since they lose either way when called. It is just the overall calling frequency which is of interest to the BB's bluffing hands.

Again, in GTO play, it is often the bulk frequencies with which you take particular actions which are especially important. In real play, people tend to focus on the strength of individual holdings. This is partly because it is pretty easy at the table to figure out your particular hand, while it may be harder to figure out and break down its spot within your entire range. However, this second skill is very important for proper strategizing.

Come up with (or choose from the selection of examples at the beginning of the chapter) a specific river spot where Hero's distribution contains a significant chunk of very strong hands (perhaps it comprises 30% of his range) and nothing else stronger than a bluff-catcher. Do you find that your opponents find this a good spot to bluff, or are they scared off the opportunity by the strength of your value holdings? If so, this may be a good spot to make an exploitative fold with all of your bluff-catchers facing a bet. Now switch spots with Villain. Suppose he is a good player and thinks about his own distribution. Might he overestimate his not-folding frequency when facing a bet, and thus be exploitably prone to fold with all his bluff-catchers, by virtue of the fact that the hands he does not fold are particularly strong?

Now, we can do a little more to build some intuition for how strategies change with other player distributions. This will be useful in approaching real hand situations. First, consider the GTO solutions for the symmetric distributions case which we have already found. The BB is betting with some hands and check-folding others, and the SB is calling some hands and folding others. Now, suppose we change Hero's distribution slightly.

If Villain's strategy stays the same, then, despite the fact that Hero's overall distribution has changed, his maximally exploitative strategy is to just keep playing each of his holdings as he was before. This is because he was already playing every individual hand as profitably as possible versus the SB's ranges. That is, the numerical rankings of Hero's holdings have changed since we changed the BB's starting distribution, but each of his particular hand combinations should be played the same as before. We can reference his holdings in this case by how much equity they have versus Villain's range which has not changed. So, if he was previously betting all hands with at least M_B equity, then his best response to a SB who did not change his strategy is to just keep betting all hands with at least M_B equity.

Now, if the SB's old strategy also still happens to be his most profitable one despite the perturbation to Hero's distribution, then we still have an equilibrium. If not, we have to think about how the SB will adjust à la the equilibration exercise. This will become clear as we look at some examples.

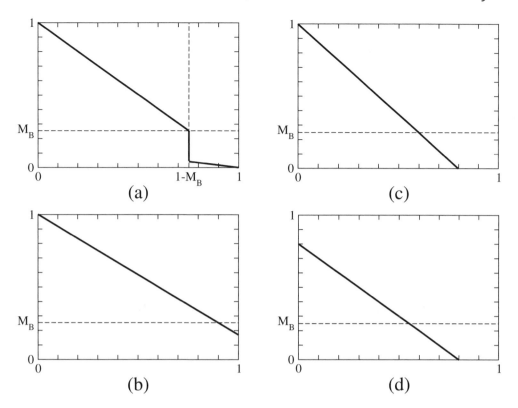

Figure 7.10: Alternate BB equity distributions for the river bet-or-check situation. As usual, the vertical axis stands for both the BB's equity and the SB's numerical hand value. The horizontal axis can be thought of as one minus the BB's hand value or one minus the SB's equity.

Consider first the BB distribution in Figure 7.10 (a). We have labelled M_B, the minimum equity the BB needs to bet in the symmetric distributions case. As compared to the symmetric case, we have simply decreased the equity of the hands with which the BB was giving up. In this case, the equilibrium strategy pair does not change. If both players keep playing each of their holdings the same as before, then the BB has no incentive to deviate since each of his hands was already being played most profitably, and the SB has no incentive to deviate since the situation at his one decision point – after the BB bets – is identical to before. In fact, any modification of the details of the BB's check-folding range (i.e. the part of the distribution to the right of $1-M_B$) that does not change any of it into a betting hand (i.e.

does not give it equity above M_B) has no effect on the equilibrium. In some sense, any equity that those hands had was wasted anyway, since they were just check-folded and given no chance of seeing a showdown.

Next, consider the BB distribution in Figure 7.10b. We have essentially just chopped off the weakest part of the BB's range, and in effect, a larger fraction of his total range is in the betting category. In this case, if the BB keeps betting all hands with equity above M_B and checking the others, he is playing most profitably versus the SB. On the other hand, after the BB bets (although he bets more often), the situation for the SB is essentially the same as it was before – all of his holdings have the same equity versus the betting range as they did previously. Similar reasoning also gives us the GTO strategies in the case of the distribution in Figure 7.10c where we have evenly decreased the total number of betting hands in the BB's range.

Lastly, we have the BB distribution shown in Figure 7.10d. We have shifted his whole distribution downward, effectively removing some proportion of his strongest holdings. In this case, the GTO play of the players' holdings does change. For, suppose that the BB keeps betting with all hands with equity at least M_B. His betting range is overall weaker than before, and the SB's cut-off hand which was previously indifferent between calling and folding now becomes a clear call. The SB is indifferent between calling and folding with some weaker holdings, i.e., he starts calling more often. Do you think that, in response, the BB starts betting more to get value from those weaker hands, less since his bluffs are getting called more, or the same as before?

> **Work out new equilibrium corresponding to equity distribution in Figure 7.10d.**

7.3.2 SB Bet-or-check on the River

Now consider a variation of the previous situation. Hero is again deciding whether to bet or check back on the river, but he is now in the SB. If he bets, the BB can call or fold. This situation is different than the previous one in one important respect. In this case, checking means going to showdown and perhaps sometimes winning, whereas before, it meant giving up and losing the pot. Let us see how this changes things.

Firstly, the strategies of the caller (the BB in this case) will look about the same as before. There is still no reason to ever call with a worse hand while folding a better one. So, if distributions are such that he is indeed calling with some hands and folding some others, there will be a threshold hand, h_c such that all better hands will be calls and worse hands will be folds. He is indifferent between calling and folding with the particular hand h_c.

The solutions for the bettor, however, will have a different structure than before. Remember from the previous section that the weakest part of the BB's betting range never won when called. Betting with those hands was essentially just necessary to keep the caller bluff-catching appropriately. So, the bettor could have just as well used some of his very worst hands to bluff with instead of his hands which were decent but still not getting called by worse. He had no motivation to do so, however, since checking with these hands meant simply wasting them since they never got to showdown. The present situation is different in that checking on the river does get the SB's hands to showdown. Thus, his holdings which are decent but always lose when they bet and get called can be played more profitably by checking back, and very poor hands which do not win much at showdown can be used to bluff.

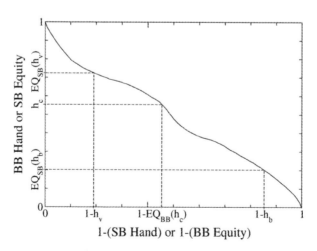

Figure 7.11: Solution structure for asymmetric SB bet-or-check game.

The structures of the players' strategies in this case are shown in Figure 7.11. The SB bets hands between 0 and h_b as bluffs and those between h_v and 1 for value. He checks back with everything in between. So, there are two cutoff hands which describe the SB's play. Along with the cutoff describing the BB's strategy, we have a total of 3 indifference equations in this game.

Derivation of these equations is similar to those in the preceding section. We first assume that $h_v > h_c > h_b$. The first of those inequalities comes from the fact that the bottom of Hero's value-betting hands must beat Villain's calling cutoff or else some of Hero's value-betting hands never win when called. That is, they are being used as bluffs, and he should be checking these back and using weaker hands to bluff instead. The second inequality comes from the fact that the top of Hero's bluffing range can not ever win when called. If it did, then that would mean Hero was bluffing with some hands strong enough that Villain calls every single time he has a better hand. In other words, these bets completely fail as bluffs, and Hero should be checking back with these hands instead.

With this, we can write down the indifference equations and compute the necessary probabilities by just reading the relevant lengths off the figure. It would be instructive to work these out yourself before proceeding. If you can honestly do this, then you probably understand the principles involved well enough, and the hurried reader can safely just take my word for the rest of the indifference equations in this chapter without feeling too bad about it.

At h_b:

$$\mathrm{EV_{SB}(bet\ } h_b) = \mathrm{EV_{SB}(check\ } h_b)$$

$$(S - B) + h_c(B + P) = S + P \cdot \mathrm{EQ_{SB}}(h_b)$$

At h_c:

$$\mathrm{EV_{BB}(fold\ } h_c) = \mathrm{EV_{BB}(call\ } h_c)$$

$$S = (S - B) + (2B + P) \left(\frac{h_b}{h_b + 1 - h_v} \right)$$

At h_v:

$$\text{EV}_{\text{SB}}(\text{bet } h_v) = \text{EV}_{\text{SB}}(\text{check } h_v)$$

(7.3)
$$h_c(S + P) + (1 - h_c)\left[(S - B) + (2B + P)\left(\frac{\text{EQ}_{\text{SB}}(h_v) - h_c}{1 - h_c}\right)\right] = S + P \cdot \text{EQ}_{\text{SB}}(h_v)$$

Solving these requires explicit inclusion of the SB's equity function EQ_{SB}. This is straightforward with a computer algebra program, but the results depend on the choice of equity distributions and are generally messy enough that we will not reproduce them here. We can, however, take a quick look at the symmetric distribution situation when $P=S=B$, as in the previous section. In this case, $h_b=1/9$, $h_c=5/9$ and $h_v=7/9$. The SB is betting only 1/3 of his range in total, and the BB is calling with 4/9 of his. It is not surprising that Hero does not bet as frequently as in the analogous spot in the BB. Checking is a lot more attractive when he can realize his showdown value.

Asymmetric distributions

The symmetric solutions are interesting. However, the relative strengths of players' distributions does make a big difference in the strategies. If

$$\text{EQ}_{\text{SB}}(h_v) = 0.9h_v \text{ (i.e. the SB's range is moderately weak)}$$

we find that he value-bets only 10% of his range, he bluffs with 5%, and the BB calls 47% of the time. If

$$\text{EQ}_{\text{SB}}(h_v) = 1.1h_v \text{ (i.e. the SB's range is moderately strong)}$$

we have that he value-bets 31% of his range and bluffs with 16%, while the BB calls 42% of the time. We will not focus on these numbers too much now – we will see such effects in a more meaningful way in the context of hand examples towards the end of the chapter.

One instructive way to think about this situation, however, is to focus on $\text{EQ}_{\text{SB}}(h_v)$ – the equity of Hero's worst value-betting hand versus the BB's entire range. The weakest value-betting hand in a spot is something many players seem to have good intuition about. Once we know this, we can immediately find Villain's calling cutoff through Equation 7.3. Either of the other indifference equations may then be used to infer our bluffing range. Basically, we will be bluffing just enough to make all of Villain's hands in between our weakest value-bet and our strongest bluff indifferent to calling and folding. So, assuming the indifference equations can be satisfied, specifying h_v is enough to find the other frequencies in both players' strategies. Many other details of the equity distributions affect the value of the game for each player, but have little effect on the equilibrium. The maintenance of certain frequencies is often at least as important as the play of particular hands in GTO strategies.

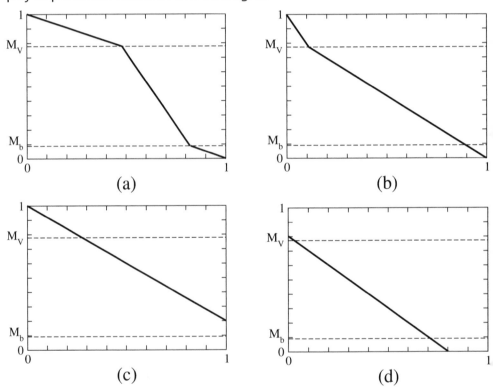

Figure 7.12: Alternate SB equity distributions for the river bet-or-check situation.

As in the BB bet-or-check game, we can consider some perturbations to Hero's equity distribution and investigate the result on the equilibrium strategies. These results will be particularly useful in navigating real-world bet-or-check decisions from the SB on the river. We will look at the distributions shown in Figure 7.12. In the figure, we have labeled M_v, the equity of the weakest hand that Hero was value-betting in the symmetric case, and M_b, the equity of the strongest hand he was using to bluff.

To start out, consider Figure 7.12a. We have essentially just removed some checking hands from Hero's distribution while maintaining the same ratio between the proportion of hands he was using to bluff and value-bet. As you can probably quickly see by this point, this change to the equity distributions does not change the GTO play of any of the players' holdings. By continuing to bet all his hands with more than M_v or less than M_b equity and checking the rest, the SB is still playing most profitably. As for the BB, all his hands have the same equity versus the SB's betting range as before, so he is still playing maximally exploitatively as well. So, the minimum equity needed to value-bet is the same here despite asymmetric distributions. This is essentially the situation where Hero is polar, but not artificially so as in Section 7.2.

Now, take a look at Figure 7.12b wherein we have removed some of Hero's value hands. Take a moment – can you guess the equilibrium? Did you guess that Hero keeps betting all the same value holdings and just bluffs less to get the right ratio of bluffs while Villain's strategy is unchanged? That is good intuition which is essentially right if we are in the simple case that Hero's value hands are all nuts and his bluffs are pure air. However, things are actually a bit more complicated here since Hero's bluffs have some showdown value.

Let us see why this strategy pair would be unstable by considering each of the three indifference relationships. First, consider Villain's situation. He needs to be indifferent between calling and folding his cutoff hand when Hero bets. And indeed he is – we specified Hero's strategy by saying that he would bet the same value hands and then just enough bluffs to keep Villain breaking even with a call with his cutoff hand. Now consider Hero's ranges. The EVs of his weakest value betting hand and his strongest checking hand need to be equal. This is also true since these are the same hands as before and Villain is playing the same as before versus the bet.

Lastly, consider Hero's bluffing hands. Is it clear why he is not indifferent between betting and checking with his new cutoff hand? The cutoff was reduced in strength to obtain the right bluff frequency. However, all those hands that he was bluffing with but is no longer are still profitable bluffs because Villain is still playing the old strategy versus a bet! Thus, this situation is unstable, and it all starts with Hero's bluffing range. Let us apply the equilibration exercise to see how things will shake out. First, Hero wants to start bluffing more because it is profitable to do so. Then, Villain can weaken his standards for calling the bet. And then, as a result, Hero will be incentivized to both widen his value-betting range and tighten his bluffing one.

For comparison, recall that in the symmetric case where $P=S=B$, we had Hero value-betting with 22.2% of his range, bluffing with 11.1%, and Villain calling 55.6% of the time. If we keep the same sizings but essentially halve the number of Hero's value hands by taking the distribution in Figure 7.12b with the "kink" at $(1-h)=1/9$, we find $h_b=0.0635$, $h_c=0.5278$ and $h_v=0.8730$. Essentially, by reducing the number of value-betting hands in Hero's range, we have kept him from betting with a lot of hands he was previously able to turn into bluffs. However, he is less happy to check back his weakest checking hand than he was previously. So, he bluffs a bit more than half his previous frequency and compensates by value-betting some weaker hands than he did previously as well.

For our next case, take a look at Figure 7.12c. Here we have removed some of the hands Hero was previously using to bluff. The equilibrium play here may be somewhat surprising. Hero actually keeps value-betting and bluffing with exactly the same frequencies as in the symmetric case. Since his overall range has gotten stronger, this means that he has higher standards for value-betting – he is checking back some holdings he used to bet for value. At the same time, some of his weaker hands which used to be shown down are now used as bluffs. Villain, on the other hand, is calling less, which should be intuitive since Hero's overall betting range is stronger.

Why does it work out this way? Well, we can compare the situation with each cutoff hand to that in the symmetric case to see that it is reasonable that the indifferences are maintained with the same betting frequencies, despite the fact that the cutoff hands themselves have increased in strength. First, at the SB's strongest bluffing hand h_b, the EV of bluffing has increased since Villain is folding more, but the EV of checking back has increased as well since the hand has more pure showdown equity, and the indifference is maintained. At the weakest value-betting hand, again the EV of betting has increased since it is a stronger hand (although this may not be immediately obvious since Villain is calling less frequently), but the EV of checking back has also increased. In fact, even in the case that Hero's range is very strong – say, his very weakest hand has 75% equity versus Villain's range – he still value bets just the top 2/9 and bluffs the bottom 1/9 at equilibrium when $P=S=B$. It is just that Villain's calling frequency gets smaller, down to about 11.1% in this case. This would be an exploitably tight calling range if Hero had a lot of air in his range to use as bluffs. However, since the hands he has to use to bluff have a lot of showdown value as well, Villain must do much less bluff-catching to keep these hands indifferent to checking behind.

Lastly, consider Figure 7.12d. In this case, Hero's whole distribution has been shifted downward. In effect, his range is actually capped below the nuts and the bottom part of his range is pure air. It is easy to see what happens here in most cases. Of course, if the degree of weakening is very small, we have nearly the symmetric distributions case. But as we lower the distribution line, Hero's range gets weaker, and he can value-bet less often. He also bluffs less often, and in particular, his strongest bluffing hand soon falls into the 0-equity region. This strongest bluffing hand will be indifferent between bluffing and checking, and we know that its value of checking is to just lose the pot 100% of the time. So, the EV of bluffing must also be to end up with just his stack on average. In other words, in the $P=S=B$ case, Villain must be calling exactly 1/2 of the time. This keeps Hero exactly breaking even with his bluffs.

This sort of result frequently occurs in situations where the SB has enough 0-equity air in his range that his strongest bluffing hand falls into this category. We can use this to find the equilibrium strategies quickly. Because the bettor's strongest bluffing hand has 0 equity, his opponent's calling frequency will be just P/(P+B), 1/2 in the P=B case, to keep these hands indifferent to bluffing. Once we know the BB's calling range, we can find those hands which Hero can profitably bet for value, relative to checking back. Given that, we can find the precise number of his 0-equity hands that Hero needs to bluff with at equilibrium.

This is in contrast to the case where some of Hero's bluffing hands have some showdown value as well. When we bluff with hands with showdown value, Villain has to call less to keep us indifferent to checking back, since, of course, checking back has more value. In this case, since Villain is calling less, our value-betting range has to tighten up as well. So we see that having stronger bluffing hands means that our equilibrium value-betting range must get tighter as well, and conversely, a weaker air range leads to a wider value-betting range. This sort of reasoning is very useful for evaluating play in real spots, but keep in mind that you can find all these answers and more by reference to the indifference equations in Section 7.3.2.

Bet sizing

The more complicated structure of the equity distributions in these situations does have another interesting effect. We saw earlier that the best bet sizing with a polar range is all-in. Even when some slow-plays were involved, there was a single GTO bet sizing with all of Hero's betting hands. But what about in general? Now that our Hero has many different "types" of hands with many different equities, can he profit by using more than one bet sizing at equilibrium? Oh yeah!

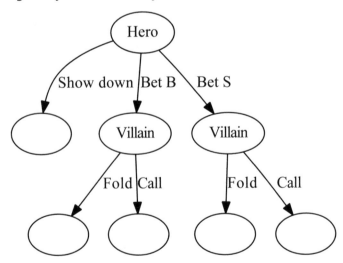

Figure 7.13: Hero's equilibrium strategy can contain multiple bet sizings when the players' starting distributions are non-trivial.

We will add the bare minimum of complexity to the current game in order to see this. Consider the decision tree shown in Figure 7.13. The SB can check back and go to showdown, bet his whole stack S, or bet a size B which is less than all-in. Facing a bet, the BB can call or fold. There are 3 decision points in this game. The first is the SB's. We partition his starting distribution into 5 parts: hands with which he checks back and those with which he value-bets and bluffs for each of the two bet sizings. In particular, with hands from 0 to h_{bb} he bluffs with sizing B. With hands from h_{bb} to h_{bs} he bluffs with sizing S. He checks back with hands from h_{bs} to h_{vb}, which is the weakest hand with which he value-bets with size B. Finally, he value-bets with size S all hands from h_{vs} up to 1. The structure of each of BB's ranges is more or less the same as before except that he has a separate calling cutoff facing each bet size. He calls bets of size B with hands as weak as h_{cb}, and he calls bets of size S with hands as weak as h_{cs}.

Structure of SB bet-or-check solutions with two sizings

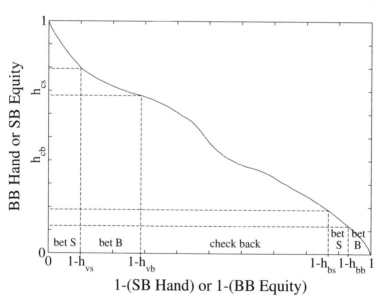

Figure 7.14: Structure of the equilibrium strategies for the decision tree in Figure 7.13. The locations indicated for the cutoff hand values are taken from the symmetric distribution case when B is a half-pot-sized bet and S is twice the size of the pot.

These structures are shown in Figure 7.14. Now, these structures do impose some constraints on the form of the solutions we will obtain, and, unlike the previous situations, the correctness of the structure of the SB's ranges given here might not be intuitively obvious. For one thing, there actually is no good reason for choosing the *B*-bluffing range to be composed of hands weaker than the *S*-bluffing range. That does not really matter. Since none of those bluffing hands will ever win at showdown, it is just the sizes of those regions that will be important. The choice to put all of the SB's *S*-value betting hands stronger than any of this *B*-value betting hands will receive a little more justification in the discussion after we find some solutions.

We have an indifference relationship at each of the various cut-off hands. Figure 7.14 might be a bit misleading with respect to the BB's ranges, since we represented his play at both of his decision points on one number line. At each of the points, he is, of course, indifferent between calling and folding with the respective threshold hand when facing a bet of the appropriate size.

We have, at h_{cb}:

$$\text{EV}_{\text{BB}}(\text{call } B \text{ with } h_{cb}) = \text{EV}_{\text{BB}}(\text{fold } h_{cb})$$

$$(S - B) + (2B + P)\frac{h_{bb}}{h_{bb} + h_{vs} - h_{vb}} = S$$

At h_{cs}:

$$\text{EV}_{\text{BB}}(\text{call } S \text{ with } h_{cs}) = \text{EV}_{\text{BB}}(\text{fold } h_{cs})$$

$$(2S + P)\frac{h_{bs} - h_{bb}}{h_{bs} - h_{bb} + 1 - h_{vs}} = S$$

At h_{bb}:

$$\text{EV}_{\text{SB}}(\text{bet } B \text{ with } h_{bb}) = \text{EV}_{\text{SB}}(\text{bet } S \text{ with } h_{bb})$$

$$(S - B) + (B + P)h_{cb} = (S + P)h_{cs}$$

At h_{bs}:

$$\text{EV}_{\text{SB}}(\text{bet } S \text{ with } h_{bs}) = \text{EV}_{\text{SB}}(\text{check } h_{bs})$$

$$(S + P)h_{cs} = S + P \cdot \text{EQ}_{\text{SB}}(h_{bs})$$

At h_{vb}:

$$\mathrm{EV_{SB}}(\text{bet } B \text{ with } h_{vb}) = \mathrm{EV_{SB}}(\text{check } h_{vb})$$

$$h_{cb}(S+P) + (1-h_{cb})\left[\left(\frac{\mathrm{EQ_{SB}}(h_{vb}) - h_{cb}}{1 - h_{cb}}\right)(S+P+B) + \left(1 - \frac{\mathrm{EQ_{SB}}(h_{vb}) - h_{cb}}{1 - h_{cb}}\right)(S-B)\right]$$
$$= S + P \cdot \mathrm{EQ_{SB}}(h_{vb})$$

And at h_{bb}:

$$\mathrm{EV_{SB}}(\text{bet } B \text{ with } h_{vs}) = \mathrm{EV_{SB}}(\text{bet } S \text{ with } h_{vs})$$

$$h_{cb}(S+P) + (1-h_{cb})\left[\left(\frac{\mathrm{EQ_{SB}}(h_{vs}) - h_{cb}}{1 - h_{cb}}\right)(S+P+B) + \left(1 - \frac{\mathrm{EQ_{SB}}(h_{vs}) - h_{cb}}{1 - h_{cb}}\right)(S-B)\right]$$
$$= h_{cs}(S+P) + (1-h_{cs})\left[\left(\frac{\mathrm{EQ_{SB}}(h_{vs}) - h_{cs}}{1 - h_{cs}}\right)(S+P+S) + \left(1 - \frac{\mathrm{EQ_{SB}}(h_{vs}) - h_{cs}}{1 - h_{cs}}\right)(S-S)\right]$$

As in the game with the single bet size, an explicit form of the equity distribution must be assumed to obtain solutions to these equations. We will just take some examples here from the case of symmetric distributions to obtain the interesting result. In this case, if $S=3P$ and $B=3/4P$ (i.e. we are choosing between a standardly-sized bet or an over-bet shove) we find, approximately, a bluff-B frequency of 0.08, a bluff-S frequency of 0.045, a value-bet-B frequency of 0.187, and a value-bet-S frequency of 0.062. The SB checks back the remaining 62 percent of hands. For comparison, if $S=P$ and $B=1/5P$ (i.e. we are making an under-bet or a pot-sized shove) we find a bluff-B frequency of 0.03, a bluff-S frequency of 0.082, a value-bet-B frequency of 0.183, and a value-bet-S frequency which, coincidentally, is also 0.183. In this case, the SB only checks back with 51 percent of his range.

In both cases, both value ranges are balanced by bluffs so that the caller is breaking even with calls at his cutoffs. We can see in both games and by comparing them that Hero can value-bet weaker hands with smaller bets since he risks less, and in this case, Villain has to call with a wider range to keep him from profiting with his bluffs. Anyhow, in both cases, if we limit our options as such, we find significant betting regions with both sizings. This is because Hero can gain more value from the larger sizing with his big hands but can also get value with his weaker hands as long as he bets smaller.

In fact, suppose we played a version of the SB bet-or-check game and allowed the SB to use any sizing. It turns out that Hero would bet with a whole spectrum of sizings at equilibrium if he were given the options to do so. In this case, the GTO play is for Hero to bet bigger the stronger his hand and to balance each bet size with the appropriate amount of bluffs. Intuitively, this lets him get as much value as possible from his stronger hands for essentially the same reasons a bet size of all-in was best in the extreme polar-versus-bluff-catchers case. Here, however, we can also go smaller with weaker hands to capture a bit more value.

This betting of value hands according to their strength and balancing them each with bluffs is a pleasingly simple result. However, it is unrealistic. By betting a certain size corresponding to the strength of the value part of our betting range and balancing with some bluffs, we have essentially protected ourselves from being exploited by an opponent who is either calling or folding. However, we have not accounted for the possibility of a river raise. By employing this strategy, we would give away that our range is capped. That is, we signal our maximum hand strength through our bet sizing. Villain can take advantage of this knowledge through river raises. If we consider a game where the BB has the option to shove over the SB's river bet, the GTO ranges for the SB's different bet sizings no longer break down nicely according to hand strength. Hero still uses multiple sizings, and he tends to go larger with his better hands, but the betting regions are to some degree all mixed up so that Hero can always have some strong hands to play versus a raise. Additionally, the SB can not value-bet nearly so much in total when the BB can threaten a raise.

This sort of reasoning makes it clear that the bet-or-check solutions are not perfectly applicable at the table except in a few situations. In particular, if you are choosing between checking and betting all-in from the SB, you can apply these solutions directly. Additionally, these games approximate reality fairly well if you are playing an opponent who does not bluff-raise rivers. This is actually a fairly common tendency, at least in pots where a river bluff-raise is a large fraction of effective stacks. Some players are just too scared or tight to make a bluff-raise in a big pot. Others can make big bluffs on the river with air but tend to only consider their call and fold options when they hold a hand that could be good. In this case, if the hand played out such that Villain almost certainly has at least a pair, you can assuming that Villain is not bluff-raising nearly enough.

When you are not scared of a bluff-raise, you can keep value-betting with hands which would not be profitable bets if Villain were playing better. In this case, Villain actually does not get any extra value from his raising range because you can fold those weaker value bets to his raise. This is the same result as if Villain just called with his strong hands in the first place, i.e. it is the same as if he were playing simply fold-or-call versus the bet, which is the situation we considered in this section. Thus, it turns out that these solutions are actually useful versus many players. By the way, from this reasoning, we can see that Villain essentially needs to be capable of bluff-raises to actually profit from his value-raising range. But we are getting ahead of ourselves.

Before we get into situations involving river raises, let us consider Hero's bet sizing in the basic SB bet-or-check game assuming he uses one sizing with his entire betting range. Sticking to one sizing may not be his most profitable strategy, but it avoids the issues associated with giving away too much information. Our results will still be somewhat unrealistic insofar as they do not account for the possibility of a raise. However, we can still quickly start to see the effect of holding different distributions on GTO bet sizing. The way to do this is to find the value of the game for Hero as a function of his bet sizings and then to find the particular bet sizing B that maximizes this quantity.

First, take the case of symmetric distributions. It turns out that the most profitable single bet size versus a BB who responds well in the context of the SB bet-or-check game is the size of the pot, P. This is a larger bet than is standard in most games, and we have arrived at it not for some semi-artificial case where one player has a ton of hands that beat all of his opponent's range, but in quite the opposite situation where they hold the same ranges. The threat of a re-raise will decrease his sizing somewhat, but again some people just are not prone to bluff-raise rivers, especially facing a full pot-sized bet.

The decrease in value of the game for Hero due to deviating from the equilibrium sizing is not huge but not negligible either. If he goes about 25%

too large or too small in the symmetric case, the game decreases in value for him by about 0.01 BB (i.e. by 1 BB per 100 hands). If he only bets 1/2 the pot, however, he loses value at the equilibrium of about 5 BB per 100 hands. This is on par with the win rate that many good players will expect to have versus most opponents. Bet sizing is very important in NLHE, and losses stemming from habitual use of poor bet sizes will add up over time.

Now, how does the SB's bet sizing change in the case of the asymmetric distributions in Figure 7.12? The GTO sizing for the distribution in Figure 7.12a is the same as in the symmetric distributions case. We already argued that this perturbation of the symmetric distribution did not change the equilibrium play of any hands, and indeed, this includes the bet sizing. The reason the equilibrium did not change stemmed from the fact that the distribution of hands that Hero actually bet with did not change. So, when the distribution of Hero's betting range is the same as the symmetric case, the best sizing is pot.

Now consider the distribution in Figure 7.12c. If Hero holds this distribution, his betting range is actually stronger than it was in the symmetric case. The distribution is a straight line fixed at $EQ_{SB}(1)=1$, so we can describe the degree of strengthening of Hero's range by just specifying the equity of his weakest hand. (As drawn in the figure, it looks to be about $EQ_{SB}(0)=0.2$). So, how does his GTO bet sizing change with respect to this parameter? If his weakest hand has 10% equity, the sizing is around $1.1P$. If it has 20% equity, it increases to about $1.3P$. Lastly, if his weakest hand has 30% equity, Hero's best sizing with his whole range is around $1.6P$. So, as we may have expected, Hero should generally go bigger when he holds a stronger range.

Now consider the distribution in Figure 7.12d. If Hero holds this distribution, his betting range is weaker than in the symmetric case as we have shifted the whole curve down by some amount. If that amount is 10% (i.e. his strongest hand has 90% equity and 10% of his range is pure air) then his equilibrium bet sizing is $0.55P$. If that amount is 20%, his sizing becomes about $0.22P$. Note that our perturbation of the symmetric distribution was qualitatively different between the cases of Figures 7.12c and 7.12d. In the first case, we just tilted the distribution in a way that had relatively little effect on Hero's value hands. This is not so when we shift the whole distribution as in the second case. Certainly we could imagine river spots where Hero's distribution was modeled by shifting the whole symmetric curve up (as in the reverse of 7.12d) leading to a situation where the GTO sizing was a very large over-bet as well as situations which are qualitatively the reverse of 7.12c which decrease the unexpoitable bet sizing in a more subtle way than we have just seen.

7.3.3 River Raises

Now that we are all warmed up, let us take a look at a river situation with a wider range of strategic options. Consider the decision tree shown in Figure 7.15. The BB acts first, and he can bet or check. If he checks, he can fold, call, or raise facing a bet. If he bets, the SB can fold, call or raise. This decision tree can be used to model many river situations. We will solve this game under various conditions and see how to break down our ranges into different lines. Let's get right to it.

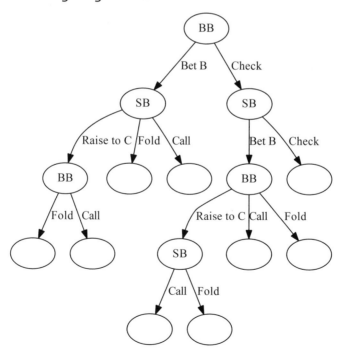

Figure 7.15: Complex river decision tree.

The structure of the solutions is shown in Figure 7.16. We can essentially think of the BB as having to partition his range once, at the tree's first decision point. The SB, however, divides his range differently depending on whether he is facing a check or a bet by the BB. We therefore represent the structure of the solutions of this game in two separate equity distribution plots. They are both from the perspective of the BB, but one indicates how the SB partitions his range facing a bet and the other, facing a check.

Distribution Structure after BB Check

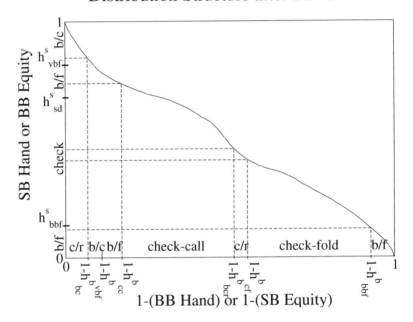

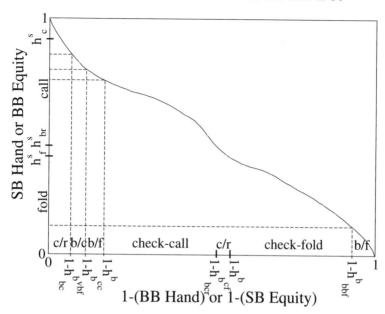

Figure 7.16: Structure of solutions in river situation. Cutoff hands are located to represent the solution with symmetric distributions, a bet size of 3/4P, and raises to 3P. Labels between the cutoff hands on each axis show the action taken with each group of hands.

The notation for the structure of the solutions is as follows. We proceed from the weakest to the strongest hands. The BB *bluff bet-folds* hands from 0 to h^b_{bbf}. He *check-folds* hands up to h^b_{cf}. He *bluff check-raises* hands from h^b_{cf} to h^b_{cr}. After that, he *check-calls* hands up to h^b_{cc}, *bet-folds for value* up to h^b_{vbf}, and *bet-calls* up to h^b_{bc}. From h^b_{bc} to 1, the BB *check-raises for value*.

Facing a check, the SB *bluff bet-folds* hands from 0 to h^s_{bbf}. From there to h^s_{sd}, he *checks and goes to showdown*. From h^s_{sd} to h^s_{vbf}, he *value bet-folds*. With hands from h^s_{vbf} to 1, he *bet-calls*. When facing a bet, the SB can fold, call, or raise. He *folds* his worst hands, from 0 to h^s_f. He *bluff raises* hands from h^s_f to h^s_{br}. He *calls* with hands from h^s_{br} to h^s_c. Finally, he *value raises* hands from h^s_c to 1.

The volume of notation is unfortunate, but getting it down will help you to really understand what follows. (You need not memorize it of course – just refer to Figure 7.16 when necessary.) Happily, however, the dozen indifference equations necessary for solving this game have been relegated to an online appendix since they are bulky enough to interrupt the flow of the text. That said, working them out yourself can be rewarded by many insights into the structure of river strategies. Additionally, this game was solved in the special case of symmetric distributions in the article "Uniform(0,1) Two-Person Poker Models" by Ferguson et al. These games are sometimes referred to as [0,1] games since players are both dealt hands with static values between 0 and 1, and the word 'uniform' refers to the symmetric distributions case.

In our analysis here, we will focus on the solutions to the symmetric case. These have plenty to teach us. We will address some of the extra complexity introduced by asymmetric distributions in the context of the hand examples at the end of the chapter. That said, as in all the previous [0,1] games, we have written the equations for the more general asymmetric case. These are available on this book's website in a format amenable to experimentation with a computer algebra system.

Let us now skip to some results. If we assume symmetric distributions and take some values for the bet size B and raise size C, we can solve this game. The important information is not really the threshold hands themselves, but the hands and total frequencies with which the players take each of their possible actions. The easiest way to visualize this information is on a number line. We will look at the results for some examples to get a feel for how the game works out and then break down what is actually going on.

Consider the three cases

(a) $B=0.25P, C=1.25P$

(b) $B=2/3P, C=3P$, and

(c) $B=P, C=5P$

These are more or less standard choices for a bet and raise size at different effective stacks. Equilibrium strategies in each of these cases are drawn to scale in Figure 7.17. Take a look at these solutions. Here are some things to think about as you begin to familiarize yourself with the structure of optimal river play:

♠ Which hands can the BB hold after he leads the river? Given this, does the structure of the SB's response seem reasonable?

♠ Which hands can the BB hold after he checks on the river? Does the SB's strategy when facing a check resemble the solutions to the SB bet-or-check game we have seen previously?

♠ How do the players' strategies change with the different bet and raise sizings?

Devise a situation where the players arrive at the river with very similar ranges (or choose one from the selection of examples at the beginning of the chapter). Find the specific hand corresponding to each threshold in the solutions by reading off Figure 7.16. For example, we can see that h^s_{vbf} falls around 0.82. Thus, find the 82nd percentile hand in the SB's river starting range. When facing a check, the SB is bet-calling every hand better than this, given the bet and raise sizings we assumed.

$$B = \tfrac{1}{4}P \text{ and } C = \tfrac{5}{4}P$$

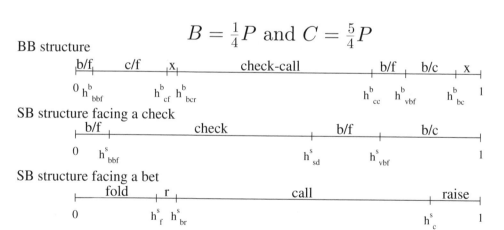

$$B = \tfrac{2}{3}P \text{ and } C = 3P$$

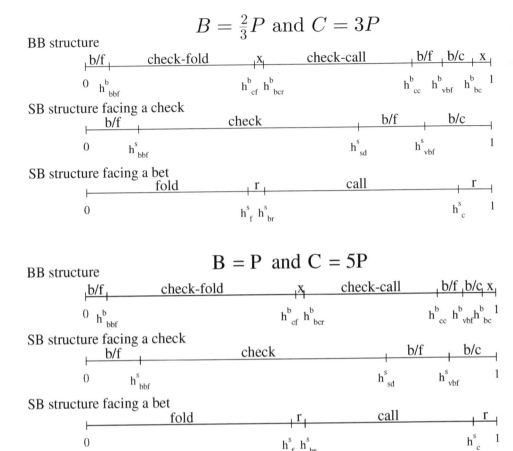

Figure 7.17: Structure of the GTO strategies for the symmetric distribution river situation with several different stack and bet sizes. The BB's check-raising hand regions are indicated with an 'x'.

Let us start at the top of the tree and consider the situation from the BB's perspective. Notice from the solutions that, in general, the BB usually checks. He bets relatively rarely, despite the fact that the players have the same ranges. If you want some intuition, it is more or less correct to think of his value-betting hands as ones that do best by putting one bet in and his bluff-betting hands as ones that have to bet because they never win at showdown. Everything else just checks, whether it wants to go to showdown and is happy check-calling but not strong enough to value bet, it wants to go to showdown but has to check-fold, or wants the opportunity to get two bets in and is thus hoping to check-raise.

Of course, the bottom line is that the BB is just playing each holding as profitably as possible versus the SB's strategy. Take, for example, the BB's play with his hand of value 1, that is, the absolute nuts. Why is it better to check-raise than to lead out on the river? We can break the situation down based on how often each option gets one bet in and how often it gets two bets in. Leading out gets the one bet in $(h^s_c-h^s_{br})$ of the time and two bets in $(1-h^s_c+h^s_{br}-h^s_f)$ of the time, that is, whenever Villain calls or raises, respectively. Checking gets the one bet in $(h^s_{vbf}-(h^s_{sd}-h^s_{bbf}))$ of the time and two bets in $(1-h^s_{vbf})$ of the time, that is, whenever Villain bet-folds or bet-calls facing a check. You can see on the figure that for each of the example sizings, Villain bet-calls more facing a check than he raises a lead, but he flat-calls a lead more than he bets when checked to. In fact, these two effects cancel out, and bet-calling and check-raising the nuts actually have exactly equal EVs here! However, with our weaker value hands, it is better to take the line which is more likely to get one bet in and does so versus a wider range of hands.

It is beneficial to go through each sort of hand in this way and ask two questions. First, why is the GTO play more profitable than any of the other choices given Villain's strategy? Second, what exploitable tendencies on the part of our opponent might make another option best? We can answer this second question for the BB's nut hand. We have seen that his decision is essentially a trade-off between the option which allows him to get two bets in the pot as much as possible and the option that lets him put in one bet most frequently. With his strongest hand, the chance to get two bets in outweighs the other considerations. However, suppose Villain did not bluff often enough on the river when checked to nor even value-bet as much as he should. These properties of the SB's play versus a check would make a check-raise attempt with a nut hand less profitable and a lead relatively better. What properties of his play versus a lead would make a lead have more value than it does at equilibrium? Well, consider each of the SB's possible actions versus a lead and decide how the action's frequency could change to benefit a lead with the nuts. His folding hands could fold less, and he could call, bluff-raise, and value-raise more. All of these tendencies would lean the maximally exploitative play towards a bet with the nuts.

Now, what about the BB's check-calling hands? In fact, he has two types of check-calling hands as you can see by lining up and comparing the structures of the players' strategies in Figure 7.17. He has check-calling hands that only beat bluffs, and he has check-calling hands that actually beat some of the SB's value bet-folding holdings. The ones that beat only bluffs are all actually indifferent between check-calling and check-folding. Indeed, so are many of his check-folding hands, since all the hands in the BB's range between h^s_{bbf} and h^s_{sd} (that is, hands between the SB's strongest bluff and weakest value bet) have the same equity versus the SB's polarized betting range. However, as in many other spots we have seen, having the frequency right leads to the most profitable play at the equilibrium. When the SB is playing poorly however, the BB's maximally exploitative strategy can change a lot. If the SB is not bluffing enough, check-fold becomes better than check-call for all of those hands. Conversely, if he is bluffing too much, check-call becomes best for all of them.

The other type of BB check-calling hand actually beats some of Villain's value bets. These are actually fairly strong hands. You can see from the figure that, if these hands were to lead the river with a bet, they would in fact get called by worse more often than they would get called by better. However, Villain's raising option decreases the profitability of leading, and they can get a bet in versus a worse hand quite frequently with a check-call as well. Thus, check-calling these is best versus an unexploitable opponent. However, when facing an opponent who is likely to play the river too loosely or passively, these hands can become more profitably played with a bet.

Now, identifying opponent tendencies and changing your ranges to capitalize on them is what poker is all about. However, when designing strategies to exploit players' weaknesses by deviating from equilibrium, it is always important to keep in the back of your mind how you open yourself up for exploitation and to be aware of whether or not your opponent is taking advantage of the opportunity.

To drill this important point home, let us consider an example of a real hand in which we might want to make the adjustment we just mentioned and see how it opens us up to Villain's counter-adjustment. Suppose you are on the river, and the board has run out 2♦-3♦-4♠-A♦-7♦. You are in the BB and bet a hand with the J♦ on the turn. The SB called, you rivered your flush, and now you have a decision. Villain can certainly have the K♦ or Q♦, but he can have a lot of weaker flushes too, and it is almost impossible for him to have gotten here without at least some sort of hand, pair or better. At equilibrium, depending on the exact distributions, your J♦ hand could very well be a check-call. However, you think that Villain is a weak player too fixated on absolute rather than relative hand strength, and he will be prone to check back and show down various 1-pair type hands even though he should use them to bluff since they are the weakest hands he can possibly have. At the same time, he will over-value medium flushes here and call with them more than he should. So, with hands such as the J♦, depending on the details, it might be most profitable to go ahead and lead out with a bet rather than to make the unexploitable check-call. At the same time, your weaker check-call hands which beat none of a SB's equilibrium value-betting range and are indifferent between check-call and check-fold at the equilibrium become clear check-folds since Villain is not bluffing frequently enough.

Great – that is an exploitative river strategy we can be proud of. However, it opens us up to counter-exploitation in at least a couple of different ways. First, consider our new river checking range. We changed our weaker check-calling hands to check-folds, and our stronger check-calling hands to bet-folds. So now, when we check, we are almost always check-folding! If Villain knew this, he could just bet with his entire range when checked to and profit greatly. At this point, of course, it would become once again more profitable for us to play many hands with a check-call since Villain is betting so much when checked to. Thus, play would return towards the equilibrium. Consider secondly our betting range. With our adjustment, we increased our bet-folding frequency but not that of bet-calling. (In fact, working off the assumption that Villain is too passive, it would be reasonable to have decreased the size of our bet-calling range.) Therefore, after we bet, we are folding to a raise much more frequently than before, and this is exploitable.

After a BB bet

Now, look at the game from the SB's perspective. Take first the case when the BB bets. From the symmetric distributions assumption, the BB basically starts the street with an even distribution of all hands. However, after he bets, the distribution that the SB is facing is no longer the same straight line!

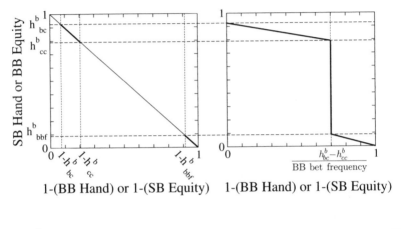

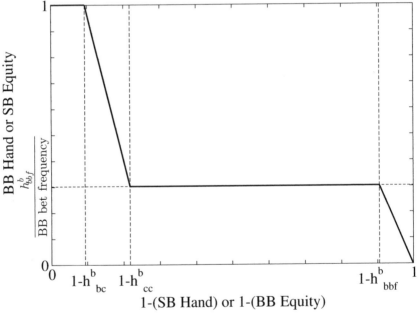

Figure 7.18: Distributions after a BB bet.

Figure 7.18 shows the effect of the bet on the BB's distribution. On the left we have the original symmetric distributions, and we have emphasized the part with which the BB leads the river. After betting, these are the only hands in his range, but they have the same equity since the SB's range has not changed. So we can plot his new equity distribution by essentially stretching those hands out on the graph, and this is shown on the right hand side of the same figure. We can then invert it to find the SB's distribution when he arrives at his first decision point after the BB bets. This is shown in the large pane of the figure.

We can see that after betting, the BB is somewhat polar with a clearly defined chunk of value hands and a region of bluffs with little to no equity. Additionally, his range is capped – he has no nut hands after betting. This can be problematic as stacks get deeper, and, indeed, in this case, we see his leading range shrink and become stronger. Anyhow, all of the SB's hands which fall between the bottom of the BB's value-betting range and the top of his bluffing range have the same equity facing a bet. (They have the same EV, too. Do you see why? What is this EV?) So, when the BB leads polar, it effectively turns many of the SB's hands into bluff-catchers. In addition to these hands, the SB holds a region of hands which are the effective nuts and some transition hands in between.

We essentially already solved the situation where Hero has a more or less polar range and Villain has bluff-catchers plus a few nut-type holdings. It was a rather simple problem, and now we see it arise here in a sub-tree of a more complex situation. Previously, we assumed that the bluff-catching player's few nut holdings were the result of slow-playing. Here, however, we see that the BB's choice of his betting range essentially allows him to specify how many "traps" the SB has when facing a bet. Whereas before we just assumed the players started on the river with distributions of that form, here they arise as a result of the BB's betting strategy. Again, our earlier asymmetric situations were chosen because the results are simple enough to internalize while still being applicable to real situations at the table, and the lessons we learned about play in those spots with asymmetric ranges can be applied in the subtrees of more complex games.

The SB's response is familiar. He raises with his strongest hands – his nuts as well as some near-nut holdings. He folds a significant portion of his worst hands which include some bluff-catchers and everything worse. He bluff-raises with some hands slightly stronger than that. Finally, he calls with everything which is stronger than his bluff-raises but weaker than his value-raises.

What hands does the SB use to bluff-raise? In the analogous simple asymmetric case, all of the SB's non-trapping hands were equivalent bluff-catchers, so he had to raise with some of these to reach his desired bluffing frequency. Here, however, he has a variety of weaker hands he could conceivably use instead. It is important to notice that his bluffs in this spot are not taken from the very bottom of his range, but instead come from the strongest of his folding hands. If the BB is playing well, it will not matter since neither choice of bluff will ever win when it is called (nor does the choice matter when the SB folds). However, there is still no reason to fold a better hand while raising with a worse one, and if the BB ever makes an incorrect call, the SB could do better by using a stronger hand in his bluffing range rather than a weaker one. As we will see, this is in contrast to the SB's strategy after the BB checks the river. In that case, the SB can take advantage of the opportunity to show down with his intermediate-strength hands and should use his very weakest holdings to bluff.

What hands are good enough for the SB to raise for value? It turns out

$$h^s_c = 1/2(h^b_{vbf} + h^b_{bc})$$

That is, the SB's weakest value-raising hand falls right in the middle of the BB's bet-calling range. In other words, the SB prefers to value-raise here with those hands that get called by worse more often than they get called by better – an intuitively pleasing result. Since we know the BB only has two choices when facing a raise – call or fold – it is easy to identify the tradeoffs facing a SB hand which is close between calling and value-raising. We consider all the worse and all the better hands with which Villain would call a raise. If the first group is bigger than the second, we raise, else we call. This is easy to say in theory and easy to imagine doing in practice at the tables. We will do a more in-depth analysis of the tradeoffs surrounding other close decisions shortly, and we will find that things are not always this simple.

After a bet and a raise

Now, what happens if the BB bets and the SB raises? The BB has a call or fold decision. As always with a call or fold decision, the structure of his response will be to just fold all hands worse than some particular threshold hand and to call with all better. Refer again to Figure 7.17 to compare the hands the BB is betting and those the SB is raising. The SB is raising his near-nuts and some bluffs that come from the middle of his river starting distribution. So, the BB has some amount of 0-equity air between 0 and h^b_{bbf}, some hands between h^b_{cc} and h^s_c that can only beat the SB's bluffs, and a few better hands that are actually ahead of some of the SB's value raising range. However, he really has no nut or near-nut holdings. The distributions themselves are shown in Figure 7.19.

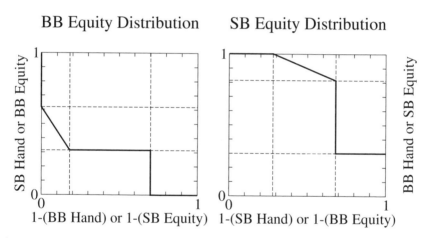

BB Equity Distribution   SB Equity Distribution

Figure 7.19: River distributions after BB bets and SB raises.

The BB's 0-equity holdings have to fold, of course, but much of the BB's value-betting range has now been turned into bluff-catchers. As you might expect, these are made indifferent between calling and folding at the equilibrium. The hands that are ahead of just a little of the SB's value range have more EV when calling than do the pure bluff-catchers, so EV(call) for these is clearly greater than EV(fold), and so they always call. This is an important fact to note. If Villain raises a polar range which is well balanced in that it effectively turns all your holdings between his value and bluffs into indifferent bluff-catchers, then a hand ahead of any of his value range is a clear call.

So, the BB's GTO response here is pretty clear. He calls with all hands that are clearly better than bluff-catchers, and then he calls with enough of his bluff-catchers so that his total not-folding frequency keeps the SB from bluff-raising too much in the first place. Notice that, the higher the amount of "value-calling" hands in the BB's range, the less he has to bluff-catch to remain unexploitable.

As far as the BB's exploitative adjustments in this spot go, the bottom line is that he should simply call here with just the set of hands that have the correct odds. It is just that, at the equilibrium, many of his hands are given the exact odds that make them indifferent between calling and folding. However, if Villain deviates from equilibrium, most of the BB's holdings become either clear calls or clear folds.

After a check

Now, let us look at play after the BB takes his other option at his first decision point. When the BB checks, he has a wide variety of hands: his whole starting distribution except for some near-air and a relatively small chunk of value hands. The BB's distribution after the BB check and its complement, the SB's distribution, are shown in Figure 7.20. This is similar to the SB bet-or-check game. As in that game, the SB will take the opportunity to show down his middling holdings and to value-bet and bluff with a polar range.

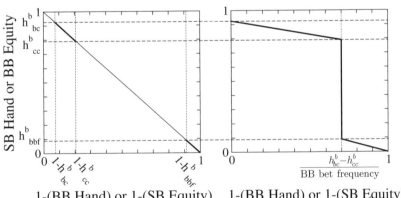

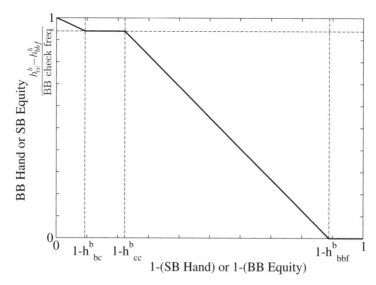

Figure 7.20: Distributions after a BB check.

An important difference with this situation is that the bettor has to contend with the possibility of a raise. We can see the effect that the threat of a raise has on his betting range by comparison to the results of Section 7.3.2. If $P=S=B$, in the bet-or-check game, he bets 1/3 of the time and checks back the other 2/3. In the new case, if he is facing the possibility of a raise to $C=4P$ (i.e. a pot-sized raise) after making a pot-sized bet, he bets when checked to 40% of the time. This is more than in the symmetric SB bet-or-check game! This is primarily by virtue of the fact that the BB's range no longer includes a big chunk of value hands.

Additionally, the pot-sized raise on the part of the BB leads to the lowest SB bet frequency. Smaller raise sizings do less to discourage the bet since they are smaller, and a larger sizing means that the BB can not raise as often, and so also does less to discourage the SB's bet. For example, if the raise size is to $2P$ (a minraise), the SB's betting frequency is about 42%, and it is about the same if the raise is to $10P$. The fact is that the BB is not actually check-raising the river all that often (about 9%, 7%, and 4% in the $C=2P$, $C=4P$, and $C=10P$ cases, respectively). So, the difference in distributions has a much bigger effect on the SB's betting frequency than the threat of being raised. Again, the relatively intuitive results of the simple SB bet-or-check game are quite applicable in real play, despite neglecting the possibility of a raise.

Now consider the exploitative adjustments the SB can make if the BB plays poorly after checking. If we looked at the SB's EV (not EQ!) distribution at equilibrium, we would see more or less a strictly decreasing function (i.e, one which was decreasing without any long flat regions). This is because after the BB checks, the SB has the option to showdown. The showdown EV of each of his hands is different (with the exception of those holdings with which the BB would have led the river), and he only takes another line with a particular holding if that choice is more profitable than just showing down. This contrasts with his equilibrium EV distribution after the BB bets in which case a huge amount of his hands (the folding hands and the calling hands that only beat bluffs) have the same EV.

This property of his EV distribution has consequences for the SB's exploitative strategizing. In particular, there are no binary adjustments with respect to the BB's bluff-catching frequencies in this case. If the BB is incorrectly check-calling a bit too much, it means that the SB should shrink his bluff betting range some, but his maximally exploitative strategy is not necessarily to eliminate it altogether. Although bluffing is less profitable since BB is calling more, checking back is also less and less profitable for weaker bluffing threshold hands which win less at showdown. Similarly, if the BB is incorrectly check-calling too little, the SB should increase his bluffing frequency, but he should not necessarily bluff with his entire range because it still might be better to just show down many hands.

In some sense, it is the option to showdown that lets the SB effectively realize the equity of all his holdings. As we have seen, Hero can do well by betting a polarized range. Essentially, betting with bluffs improves the EV of our value hands, and betting value hands keeps Villain folding enough that we break even with our bluffs. Being able to show down mediocre hands and immediately capture their value leaves the SB free to bet with all his strong hands, and thus, many bluffs as well. The BB's situation is not so nice. He has to check on the river with many of his strong hands for what are essentially balance reasons. So, the SB's ability to just show down medium-strength hands lets him take full advantage of a polarized betting range, and this is a large part of what constitutes the SB's positional advantage on the river.

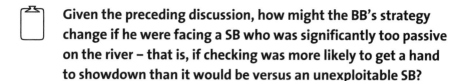

Given the preceding discussion, how might the BB's strategy change if he were facing a SB who was significantly too passive on the river – that is, if checking was more likely to get a hand to showdown than it would be versus an unexploitable SB?

After a check and a SB bet

Finally, let us consider the situation for the BB after he checks and the SB bets. What do the distributions look like here?

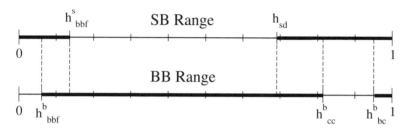

Figure 7.21: How the SB's betting and the BB's checking ranges stack up.

The BB has wide variety of holdings. The SB has a somewhat tighter range clearly divided into value and bluff portions. Figure 7.21 shows how these two ranges stack up against each other. Making a plot like this one makes it easy to find the new equity distributions which arise after the players take actions which narrow their ranges. We consider each relevant threshold hand and find Hero's equity with it and its location in his range. We can then just plot each of these points and connect the dots.

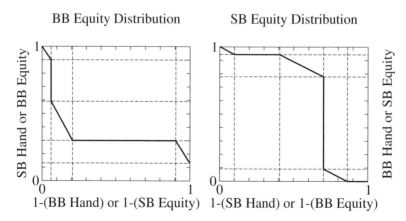

Figure 7.22: River distributions after BB checks and SB bets.

The players' distributions are shown in Figure 7.22. The SB has bet fairly po-lar, as described. Thus, the BB's distribution, despite containing a very wide variety of hands, has been largely turned into bluff-catchers with a few near-nut slow-plays. He also has a region of holdings which beat some of the SB's value bets and a region which loses to some of the SB's bluffs. This is again similar to one of the simple asymmetric situations we covered earlier.

The GTO structure of the BB's response to a bet after he checks is essen-tially the same as the SB's after the BB leads the river. He folds his worst hands, bluff-raises with some slightly better ones, raises his best holdings for value, and calls with everything else. In this case, the BB holds a well-defined set of slow-plays that he raises for value, and he turns some bluff-catchers into bluffs as well for balance. In addition to these raising hands, the BB has to call with enough bluff-catchers so that his total not-folding frequency deters the SB from bluffing too much.

It is worth taking a moment to bring the big picture into focus. As we have seen, when he is checked to, the SB can make money by betting some strong hands for value and at the same time some weak hands as bluffs. In the simplest cases, he knew exactly which of his hands were strong and which were bluffs, so his decision making was easy, but in general he has to play with a whole spectrum of relative hand strengths. So, he has to choose the weakest hand he can value-bet, and with that hand there are tradeoffs. He must weigh things such as getting called by worse hands as against running into better ones. We will talk more about how to navigate these tradeoffs shortly.

Notice that bet sizing is intimately connected to the choice of weakest value-betting hand. Running into better is not as costly with smaller bet sizings, but you can lose some value with stronger hands when your oppo-nent calls a small bet but would have paid off a larger one. We will see that the intuitive solution to this problem – tending to bet smaller with weaker value hands in order to lose less when behind and get called by a wider range – does show up in unexploitable play.

After the BB check-raises the river, how do the players' distri-butions look, and what is each player's GTO strategy?

Thin value betting

Players often find it intuitive that, facing a check on the river, the SB bets some especially strong hands for value, bets some especially weak ones as bluffs, and opts to just show down anything in between. Also, after our discussion thus far, it should be clear that the amount of bluffs that the SB can "get away with" is tied directly to the number of his value bets. This is because the SB's polar betting range turns much of the BB's range into bluff-catchers, and the GTO bluffing frequency is just chosen to keep Villain from finding an edge by either calling or folding all these hands.

 Pick out a few hands from the examples at the beginning of the chapter. For each of them, suppose you are the SB, and the BB checks to you on the river. Work through your river betting range as follows – What is your river starting distribution if, e.g., this hand was played against an unknown opponent? What is your standard bet sizing in this spot? What is the weakest hand you bet for value? Thus, what fraction of your total starting range are you value-betting? Given your sizing, what fraction of your betting range needs to be bluffs in order to make Villain's bluff-catchers indifferent between calling and folding? Thus, if you are bluffing with some amount of your weakest holdings, what is your strongest bluffing hand?

So we know that the SB is going to value-bet some hands, and after we know how many, that nails down his bluffing frequency and thus also his checking-back range. But the question remains – how many hands should he value bet? In other words, what is the weakest hand with which he can profitably bet for value? Conventional wisdom says to value-bet whenever you get called by worse more often than by better, and this is usually more or less correct. However, a closer look at things can help us to understand the situation a bit better.

The indifference in question is that between checking back and bet-folding. We have labeled the hand which is indifferent between these two actions h^s_{sd}. The EV of checking back is S+P x (equity of h^s_d versus BB's checking range). On the other hand, when we bet-fold, we end up with at least (S–B), another (B+P) when the BB folds, and another (2B+P) whenever he calls and we win. So the EV of bet-folding is (S−B)+(B+P)(BB fold to bet frequency)+(2B+P)(BB calls and we win frequency).

We could just take the difference of these two EVs to see which is bigger and find the conditions under which one action is better than the other. However, we can approach the comparison of the two options in a way which will do a little more towards building intuition which is useful at the tables. Suppose you are the SB with a hand h which is considering a value bet. That is, it is fairly near the borderline between bet-folding and checking back.

Consider each possible type of hand the BB can have, and compare how your two options do versus each of those types of hands. It is helpful to look at a figure like 7.17 to see what the BB's range looks like. We will consider the various hand regions that the BB checks on the river from weakest to strongest. First, the BB can have a check-folding hand. Since h is stronger than all of these, and the BB is not going to put any more money in the pot, it does not matter what we do with h. We win the pot either way, no more and no less. Next, Villain can have a bluff check-raising hand. This is disastrous for our bet-folding option. When the BB holds one of these hands, our bet-fold option gets us a total stack of S−B whereas we would have won the whole pot and ended up with S+P if we had checked. Next, the BB has some check-calling hands which are beat by h. Against these hands, we end up with (S+P) after a check but (S+P+B) after a bet. Finally, the BB can have a check-calling hand that beats us or a value check-raise. In both of these cases, we end up with (S−B) with a bet or S with a check.

Now, taking the difference in EVs with respect to the various Villain holdings, we find

$$
\begin{aligned}
\mathrm{EV_{SB}(bet\text{-}fold)} - \mathrm{EV_{SB}(check)} = {} & ((S-B)-(S+P))(\text{chance BB bluff raises}) \\
& + ((S+B+P)-(S+P))(\text{chance BB check-calls with worse}) \\
& + ((S-B)-S)(\text{chance BB check-calls with better}) \\
& + ((S-B)-S)(\text{chance BB value check-raises}) \\
= {} & (B)(\text{chance BB calls with worse}) \\
& - (B+P)(\text{chance BB bluff raises}) \\
& - (B)(\text{chance BB has a better hand})
\end{aligned}
$$

First of all, if Villain is never bluff raising, a bet-fold is clearly better than a check whenever Villain calls with a worse hand more often than he holds a better one (whether he calls or raises with it). In this case, the conventional wisdom is right. However, if Villain is capable of bluff check-raising, then we have to increase our standards for value-betting until the point where we get called by worse enough to make up for the times when we get bluff-raised off of the best hand. And since we lose more by getting bluff-raised than we gain by placing a successful value bet, a little bit of bluff-raising can discourage our value bets quite a bit.

Now, the situation is a bit different for a player in the BB who is considering a value bet. His weakest value bet-folding hand, h^b_{cc}, is facing the choice to check-call rather than to immediately show down. How does this change his decision? We will again go through all of Villain's possible holdings and look at the tradeoffs between bet-fold and check-call. Our job is a little trickier this time since we have to look at the solution structures at two of the SB's decision points at once, but this is made easier by just following from left to right on Figure 7.17.

First, the SB has hands that will bluff when checked to but fold when facing a bet. Versus these, our check-call option does better by an amount B. Then, the SB has a chunk of hands that will check back if given the chance or fold to a bet. Hero's play with a value hand does not matter against these since he wins exactly the whole pot either way. Then, the SB has a region of hands that will bluff-raise versus a bet but check back if given the chance. Against these, check-call does better by an amount B+P. There is then a region of hands that will call when facing a bet but check down if checked to. Versus these, bet-fold does better by B. Finally, whenever the SB has a better hand than this, one bet is going in no matter if the Hero check-calls or bet-folds, so his play against those hands is effectively unimportant for this decision.

In total, we have the difference in EVs between the options

$$
\begin{aligned}
\mathrm{EV_{BB}}(\text{bet-fold}) &- \mathrm{EV_{BB}}(\text{check-call}) \\
&= (B)(\text{chance SB calls a bet with a hand that would otherwise check back}) \\
&\quad - (B+P)(\text{chance SB bluff raises}) \\
&\quad - (B)(\text{chance SB bluffs when checked to})
\end{aligned}
$$

In this case, the decision between bet-folding and check-calling has nothing to do with how often Villain has a better hand. The reason for this is that if we do not value-bet, we are going to check-call, and so a bet goes in versus all of Villain's better hands regardless. If Villain never bluff-raises on the river, then the decision here rests on whether he has a higher frequency for bluffing when checked to or for calling a bet with a hand he would check back if given the chance. However, as before, a non-zero bluff-raising frequency can tilt things towards the passive option pretty quickly.

This is an important point that you should internalize. Assuming Villain is going to bet any better hand than ours when checked to, his frequency of having such a hand is irrelevant when we are considering a thin value bet-fold with a hand we would otherwise check-call. The more Villain is prone to bluff-raising, the more we should lean towards check-calling, but our decision rests primarily upon whether we are more likely to get a bet versus worse hands by betting or by checking, that is, whether Villain is likely to have a weak hand and call a lead or to have an even weaker hand and bluff with it. We will talk a bit more about bluff-catching shortly. Becoming familiar with the challenges facing your borderline value-betting hands in each position can be very helpful for your real-time decision making.

The trade-offs surrounding thin value bets from each position that we have outlined here turn out to be fairly robust. However, our reasoning has assumed that the structure of Villain's play follows the equilibrium for the case of symmetric starting distributions. What if it is not just his frequencies but the whole *structure* of Villain's solution which is wrong? For example, many players will just lead the river from the BB with all of their strong hands and reserve no nut holdings for check-raising, especially if they had the betting lead on the turn. Other opponents will do things which are indefensibly bad such as calling with a worse hand while folding a better one in the same spot. On the other hand, Villain's strategy might not be wrong – it may just be the case that some particular asymmetric distributions justify an alternate river strategy. How might these issues affect our play?

Come up with some alternate river strategy structures which make sense in the context of a specific hand and a particular opponent's tendencies, and repeat the analysis of this section to find the trade-offs governing a thin value-betting decision.

Bluff-catching

We have seen that when Hero faces a bet on the river, it is often the case that a lot of his range is turned into bluff-catchers, all of which are indifferent between calling and folding. The EVs of both actions are the same with all of these hands, and yet we call with some and fold others when we are playing unexploitably. It is important to note, however, that we actually achieve the same EV if we just call with all of them or fold all of them, as long as Villain does not deviate from GTO play. Hero's strategy in this sort of spot is called *flexible* – we can change our strategy a bit away from equilibrium and not lose any EV, as long as Villain does not adjust. Strategies which are not flexible are *brittle* – deviating from equilibrium loses us EV immediately. In most of these river spots, the bettor is indifferent between his two actions with his cutoff hand but prefers one action over the other with hands slightly to the left or right of it. That is, his strategy is brittle. (When is this not the case?)

Anyhow, we call attention to these spots, which come up all the time, because players tend to play them with strategies with suboptimal structures. If our strategy were brittle, then a small change in our beliefs about Villain would likely affect our strategy only slightly. However, when we hold a distribution containing many equivalent bluff-catchers, a small change in Villain's strategy can induce a huge change in ours. If Villain is bluffing slightly too often, then we call with a huge chunk of hands. If we believe he is bluffing just slightly too little, then we fold all of them. This can lead to very exploitable bulk tendencies – if a player figures that folding and calling have equal EV, and then always decides to call, then his two options are unlikely to have equal EV for long if his opponent is observant. But even if we are more careful, there is a lot of guesswork in this decision, and it is easy to mix up our play without great reasons. Over the long term, this can easily lead to folding some better hands and calling with some worse ones in what are essentially the same spots. This is exploitable and, furthermore, it will cause you to bleed money over time against many weak opponents who are not even consciously exploiting you.

In general, if you have a solid rational belief that one extreme strategy, such as always calling with any bluff-catcher in a spot, is best, then by all means go for it. However, with a less solid read, consider adjusting your strategy by just shifting your threshold hand slightly. That is, keep your whole range in mind, determine your weakest calling hand, and relax that requirement somewhat. But avoid making an extremely exploitable and exploitative adjustment without a good reason. If nothing else, showing down a low pair instead of Q-high after calling a bet could keep Villain from realizing you believe he is extremely exploitable in that spot and counter-adjusting.

Now, how do players usually approach exploitative call-or-fold decisions with their bluff-catchers? Unless Villain is an extreme case – either particularly aggressive and bluffy or not – it is often difficult to say how often he might really be bluffing in a particular river spot. Thus, it is often helpful to break the question down into two parts. First – how likely is Villain to get to the river with a hand that feels it needs to bluff? This is likely the case if a lot of draws which were present on early streets missed, if Villain never faced a bet on an earlier street, or if Villain is just the type of player that tends to call bets very loosely on early streets. Second, when Villain does get to the river with an air-type hand, how likely is he to turn it into a bluff? This is primarily a question of the player's general tendencies, although it can be much deeper and more situationally-dependent if Villain is a smart, thinking player. Together, the answers to these two questions can give us an idea as to whether or not Villain is bluffing more or less than his unexploitable frequency. If he gets to the river with a lot of air, he only needs to decide to bluff with each of these weak holdings occasionally to achieve a large bluffing frequency in total. On the other hand, if it is hard for Villain to get to the river without a made hand in the first place, then he may not be bluffing very much in total even if he bets all of his air 100% of the time.

Now, when players face opponents who do not have obviously exploitable bluffing tendencies, they often focus on the second issue more than the first when deciding whether calling down with a bluff-catcher is appropriate. This approach can be very successful, particularly since many opponents will choose to bluff without giving much thought to their entire distributions. However, it is a somewhat exploitable approach to bluff-catching. Against players with such a thought process, a bettor should decrease his bluffing frequency significantly in spots where he is perceived to hold a lot of air.

Related considerations can have a big impact on our check-call-versus-bet-fold decisions from the BB. We showed in the previous section that the tradeoff here is primarily between how often the SB will call a bet with a worse hand that would have checked back versus how often he will bluff when checked to. So, all of our recent discussion about estimating Villain's bluffing frequency is relevant. If it is high, we should tend towards the check-call, and if it is low, we should prefer a bet-fold with many hands.

If we think this approach is appropriate versus a certain SB, it is important to think hard about how his early-street play could affect his range. For example, his c-betting tendencies are often especially important here. Is he the type to c-bet all his air? If so, we can include or exclude many air hands from his range depending on whether or not he c-bet. Is he the type to mostly just check back with weak showdown value? Then we can assume his bluffing frequency will be a lot lower if he checked back the flop by virtue of having few air hands, and we should tend to lead the river for value against those holdings he is trying to get to showdown.

However, when Hero is in the SB, he can certainly take advantage of a BB with this approach. How? If the BB is checking all his thin value hands intending to check-call, it means you probably should not bluff much when checked to, of course. It also implies that his leading range is fairly bluff-heavy, or at least polar, depending on whether he will also check the river with his very strong hands. Perhaps light calls or some small raises are called for when facing a lead. On the other hand, suppose the BB is leading the river with all his value hands. How should we respond to a bet and to a check in that case?

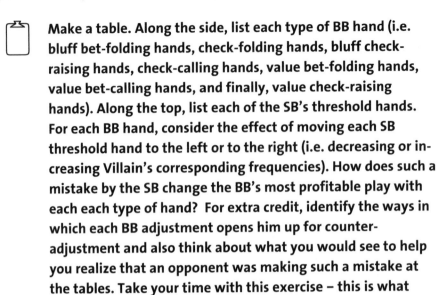

Make a table. Along the side, list each type of BB hand (i.e. bluff bet-folding hands, check-folding hands, bluff check-raising hands, check-calling hands, value bet-folding hands, value bet-calling hands, and finally, value check-raising hands). Along the top, list each of the SB's threshold hands. For each BB hand, consider the effect of moving each SB threshold hand to the left or to the right (i.e. decreasing or increasing Villain's corresponding frequencies). How does such a mistake by the SB change the BB's most profitable play with each each type of hand? For extra credit, identify the ways in which each BB adjustment opens him up for counter-adjustment and also think about what you would see to help you realize that an opponent was making such a mistake at the tables. Take your time with this exercise – this is what poker's all about.

Each one of these questions is quite simple to answer in itself, but going through all the possibilities in a structured way can help you organize the information in your head and make more accurate adjustments quickly at the table. (This is why we think it's best for you to go through it yourself instead of just publishing the table here.) By the way, focusing on moving the SB's cutoff hands rather than focusing on the hand groups themselves (and, say, thinking about making an individual region larger or smaller) forces you to keep in mind that the adjacent groups are connected. If Villain value-raises too much facing a bet, then that means he does not call enough, or else he calls enough and does not bluff-raise or fold enough. This is rather easy to say but takes some work to fully incorporate into your exploitative strategizing.

Block-betting

Suppose we add another branch to the decision tree corresponding to a new option for the BB at his first decision point. In addition to his check and bet *B* options, he can now choose to lead the river for an under-bet, that is, some small fraction of the size of the pot. We will call this sizing *L* for bLock, since *B* was already taken. Facing this action, the SB can call, fold, or raise to the normal bet size B. If the SB raises, the BB can call, fold, or re-raise to C (C comes after B). As before, the player facing a raise to C can just call or fold.

This sort of bet has sometimes been called a *blocking bet* since it can be used by a mediocre hand in order to try to get to showdown cheaply, that is, to "block" an opponent from making a larger bet. Now, taking this line exclusively with this sort of hand would be a very exploitable thing to do, and it is not obvious to many players that the play makes much sense with stronger or weaker hands. Thus, many players do not work this move into their games at all. However, the blocking bet certainly is a part of GTO river strategy, and including it in the decision tree often significantly improves the BB's expectation at equilibrium. Additionally, it can often be used very profitably in an exploitative manner, since many opponents are not accustomed to facing it and will thus respond poorly.

So how should we use it – how should we fit block-betting hands into the BB's strategy? First of all, as we mentioned earlier when looking at the bet sizings in the SB bet-or-check game, certain issues arise at decision points with multiple bet sizing options when there is a possibility of being raised. The bettor needs to play certain types of hands in more than one way for what we saw were essentially information-hiding reasons.

In particular, in the case of blocking at sufficiently deep stack sizes, if the SB is capable of over-bet shoving versus the small bet, the BB's equilibrium strategy will often involve block-betting a few near-nut hands for balance purposes. If, on the other hand, the SB can only make a smaller raise, then being able to show up with the nuts after blocking is not nearly as important for the BB. However, in practice, the BB's block-betting range will still overlap with his bet-B range. Often, the EVs of various options are close here, and card removal effects decide the play of many holdings. The bottom line is that, in practice, describing strategies as nice, well-defined action regions separated by indifferent threshold hands is no longer a great approximation when we want to use more than one bet sizing.

That said, equilibrium block-betting ranges are mostly composed of hands which are not particularly strong but figure to be best more often than not. Then, some stronger value hands and some bluffs are included for balance. We will now look at the tradeoffs involved to see when a hand is better played with a blocking bet than with any other of the BB's options.

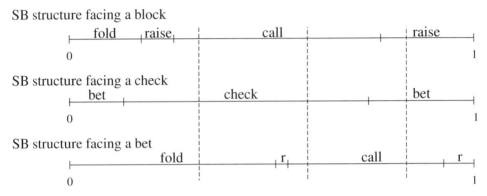

Figure 7.23: Structures of the SB's ranges in the river situation including a blocking bet option.

The structure of SB's ranges in response to each of the BB's actions is shown in Figure 7.23. These are drawn more or less to scale for the symmetric distributions case where $L=1/5P$, $B=P$, and $C=3P$. These structures should all be familiar to you by now. Versus a check, the SB bets a polarized range and checks back his middling hands. Facing a bet, the SB folds his worst hands, raises with his strongest ones as well as some bluffs which are just barely stronger than his strongest folding hands, and calls with everything in between. Of course, the relative sizes of his various regions are different when he faces the blocking bet and the pot-sized bet.

We have also marked on the figure the strengths of some possible block-betting hands. The weaker might be deciding between the block-fold and the check-fold lines, and the stronger could be deciding between block-call and check-call or block-call and bet-fold. What factors determine which is the best option for each hand? We will work through the tradeoffs for each decision similarly to our analysis of thin value-betting earlier. Again, we will consider the sections of the SB's ranges from left to right on the figure.

First, consider the decision between block-folding and check-folding. There are four portions of the SB's ranges such that when the SB holds a hand from one of them, the values of these two options are different. The value of block-betting over that of check-folding is as follows.

$$\text{EV}_{\text{BB}}(\text{block-fold}) - \text{EV}_{\text{BB}}(\text{check-fold})$$
$$= (+P)(\text{chance SB folds but would have bluffed})$$
$$+ (-L - P)(\text{chance SB bluff raises but would have checked})$$
$$+ (+L)(\text{chance SB calls with worse but would have checked})$$
$$+ (-L)(\text{chance SB has a better hand})$$

Each of these terms is moderately important. Those with the factors of L involve relatively small wins and losses since L is small, but they are the situations which occur frequently. So, the upside to block-folding here is in keeping Villain from playing his weakest hands profitably by bluffing and in getting a little bit of value out of some weaker hands that would just check to show down if given the chance. The losses are in inducing bluff-raises and in giving the extra L to stronger hands.

Now, consider the decision between block-betting and calling the raise to B and check-calling with the strongest of the hands marked on the figure. Again, there are four cases where the two options have different values. The value of block-calling over that of check-calling is as follows.

$$\text{EV}_{\text{BB}}(\text{block-call}) - \text{EV}_{\text{BB}}(\text{check-call})$$
$$= (-B)(\text{chance SB folds but would have bluffed})$$
$$+ (+B)(\text{chance SB bluff raises but would have checked})$$
$$+ (+L)(\text{chance SB calls with worse but would have checked})$$
$$+ (L - B)(\text{chance SB calls but would have bet})$$

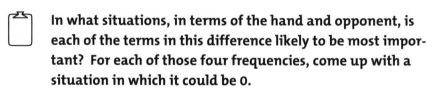 **In what situations, in terms of the hand and opponent, is each of the terms in this difference likely to be most important? For each of those four frequencies, come up with a situation in which it could be 0.**

Thirdly, consider a decision between block-calling and bet-folding with a relatively strong holding. Again there are four differences between the options, and the value of block-calling over that of bet-folding follows.

$\mathrm{EV_{BB}(block\text{-}call)} - \mathrm{EV_{BB}(bet\text{-}fold)}$
$$
\begin{aligned}
= \; & (+B)(\text{chance SB bluff-raises but would have folded}) \\
& + (+L)(\text{chance SB calls } L \text{ but would have folded to } B) \\
& + (+L + B + P)(\text{chance SB calls but would have bluff-raised}) \\
& + (L - B)(\text{chance SB calls } L \text{ but would have called } B)
\end{aligned}
$$

Here, block-betting wins by getting the SB to put money in the pot when he would not have otherwise and by avoiding the larger bluff-raise that we can not call. In only one of the four cases is bet-folding better: when the SB has a strong enough hand that he would have called the larger bet B but instead only calls L. Of course, this assumes that our initial normal bet sizing is the same as the amount Villain raises to when facing a blocking bet. When is this assumption inappropriate, and, in this case, how does it affect our decision-making process?

Note that the comparison between the BB's EV when he block-calls and when he bet-folds given in the previous equation applies for the strongest of the holdings marked in Figure 7.23. Slightly different trade-offs can apply to different holdings – the examples considered in this section are not comprehensive. For example, if the BB holds the middle of the three hands marked in Figure 7.23, then there is an additional contribution to $(\mathrm{EV_{BB}(block\text{-}call)} - \mathrm{EV_{BB}(bet\text{-}fold)})$ of $(B-L)$ times the frequency with which the SB holds a better hand than the BB and flat-calls L but would have flat-called B.

Finally, how about nut hands and pure air? When might you block-bet with these? As mentioned earlier, whether or not to block-bet bet with the nuts at equilibrium depends on the decision tree itself – the stack sizes and the strategic options Villain is capable of utilizing. Complete bluffs, however, should absolutely be worked into Hero's block-bet leading range against most players. All the other hands we have considered block-betting are actually ahead of the majority of the SB's range. If these were our only block-bets, we should expect him to fold to them quite frequently. This gives us the opportunity to mix in some bluffs as well. Since pure air hands never win at showdown, it is very easy compare the options here. We have, for pure air hands:

$$EV_{BB}(\text{block-fold}) - EV_{BB}(\text{check-fold})$$
$$= (+P)(\text{chance Villain folds}) + (-L)(\text{chance Villain does not fold})$$

This is one of those times that opponents' inexperience in dealing with the blocking bets can lead to big wins. Since you risk a small amount to win a relatively large pot, Villain does not need to fold very often to make this a profitable bluff with our pure air. If Villain just gives up with various non-paired hands with an appreciable frequency, that can be enough to make the blocking bet profitable in many spots. This is a common mistake among no-limit players who have little experience dealing with bets which are very small compared to the size of the pot.

Bluff-raising too often is another common tendency among aggressive players who will read the blocking-sized bet as weak. However, it is fair to say that most of them usually tone down this frequency after they get called a few times, especially if they are shown strong hands.

 When is bluffing B with air better than bluffing L?

Now, this has all been a bit abstract, and students of HUNL still often have problems working the blocking bet into their game effectively. We suggest a several-step approach to learning about this move and working it into your game. First, really be aware of your distribution on the river, that is, of your range and how it stacks up versus Villain's. Can you hold the nuts, or is your range capped? Do you have any pure air in your range or do all of your weak hands have a decent bit of equity? In the examples at the end of the chapter, we will see a few situations in which the BB uses his block-betting option with a significant fraction of his river starting range at the equilibrium. Studying those examples and asking these questions will help you to identify good spots.

Once you can spot river situations where the block-bet sizing is likely to be used with almost all of the BB's betting range at equilibrium, begin by incorporating the play into your strategy there. The fact that it is used so frequently in these spots in GTO play will let you use it very often without worrying too much about balance. In other words, it is likely easier to just identify river spots to use the blocking-bet with your whole betting range, than to try to recognize spots where you should block with some small fraction of your range and then to keep that rare event well-balanced.

There are a couple of things to be said about balance with respect to block-betting. By balance in this context, we are mostly referring to the inclusion of some bluffs and slow-plays into our blocking range in addition to the normal weak value stuff. First, balance is important here. When you start using this move, most of your opponents will see it as an interesting and notable action, distinct from your other river bets. They will immediately start categorizing your use of the move, and will likely see it as something to try to attack and probe for weakness. Thus, it is nice to be able to show up with a strong hand occasionally. However, even if your opponent is not thinking very hard, it is still the case that folding and bluff-raising too frequently are common inclinations in HUNL players, and so you should design your default strategy to earn money against those tendencies. Of course, the bluffs do well against players who fold too much, and the slow-plays do well against players who raise too often. On the other hand, you do not want to block with too many bluffs or nut hands, because it will cost you money versus opponents who respond loose-passively. So, an unexploitable or well-balanced approach is a good place to start.

The other thing about balancing your block-betting range is that you can probably do it without worrying too much, at least initially, about how it affects the ranges with which you take other lines. That is, if you feel that your use of block-betting, whether through your attempts to balance or play exploitatively, is unbalancing your checking or normal-sized-betting ranges, that is probably fine. Through force of habit, most opponents will continue to view your other lines as your standard moves, and will continue to respond to them as if they still contain all the sorts of hands they are used to seeing there. It will take many players a long time to adjust, allowing you to focus on composing your block-betting distribution without worrying too much about how it affects your other ranges. (Of course, if you are playing 100k-HUNL against Phil Galfond, you may have to be a little more careful here, but you probably know that already.)

Once you have gained a bit more experience, you can begin to focus on using the move exploitatively. Every time we encounter use of the blocking-bet at equilibrium in the example hands, it indicates a spot where the move is pretty good, and we have an opportunity to think about how Villain could respond to make it even better. A little practice evaluating the tradeoffs we outlined above in the context of specific examples will help you find plenty of spots to use the move exploitatively in your games.

Comparing two strategic options by breaking down the trade-offs based on Villain's possible holdings is a very powerful technique and important skill for developing exploitative strategies. In cases with arbitrary river starting distributions or where Villain has exploitable tendencies, players' ranges may even be entirely devoid of or dominated by one type of hand. For example, we saw earlier that the only reason that bet-folding could be better than block-calling a certain hand was that the blocking bet could miss value when the SB just calls but has a hand with which he would have called a larger bet. In what situations might the SB not actually have any such hands in his range, and what should you do in this case? We will see more examples of this sort of reasoning when we discuss some real hands.

 In deriving the above formulas, we assumed that the SB is folding more hands versus the blocking bet than he is bluffing versus a check. Indeed, this is the case at equilibrium with symmetric distributions and the bet sizings given above. However, certainly there are river situations against some opponents where the opposite will be true. Can you think of when this might be? How does this change the criterion we derived describing the relative values of block-betting?

7.4 Examples, Continued

With the benefit of all we have learned, we will now go back and analyze the hand examples we set up at the beginning of the chapter. We will essentially assume that the players get to the river with the ranges given earlier, and then take a look at the equilibrium play from that point on, just as we did in Section 2.2.3. The unexploitable strategies will give us a good baseline from which to discuss exploitative adjustments.

Our discussion will have several goals. As mentioned previously, each action region in the solution represents a spot where playing some hands a certain way is better than the others. Each one presents an opportunity to understand why the action is the best choice at the equilibrium and then to find the conditions (as far as Villain tendencies) under which another choice might be better. It is important to understand any counter-exploitative measures which Villain could try. In addition to discussion of the decision tree itself, these will be the main thrusts of our analysis of each example.

We will leverage the analytical solutions and try to build intuition for applying them, but we will primarily reference the exact computationally-generated equilibria to describe unexploitable river play in each example. This will let us see the effects of asymmetric starting distributions as well as card removal effects. We will want to pay special attention to how the ranges are broken up at equilibrium in cases where these play a big role.

Before reading the solution to each of the examples, review the context from the discussion surrounding each hand at the beginning of the chapter. Then, try to estimate or describe the players' equilibrium strategies.

7.4.1 Example 1

In this spot, the BB's range is narrowly defined as king-high except for the occasional slow-played three-of-a-kind. The SB can have many better and worse hands. Given that the BB's range is so bluff-catcher-heavy, we do not expect him to ever lead the river. There is only about one pot-sized bet behind on the river, and the SB's range is quite polar, so he might do well to use all-in as his only bet sizing.

Thus, we have exactly the SB bet-or-check game from Section 7.3.2, and we can find the SB's unexploitable betting and checking frequencies by plugging into and solving the equations therein. Since the equity distribution itself is a bit messy, it is best that we use a computer algebra program to actually solve the equations. Again, please check out the supplemental resources on this book's website to see how this is done and try it for yourself!

So, with $P=16$, $S=B=17$, and the equity distribution from Figure 7.2, we find a SB bluff frequency of about 24%, a value-bet frequency of about 48%, so that he is shoving with nearly 3/4 of his range in total. These numbers agree with the exact equilibrium to within a percent. In particular, the SB value-bets all of his sixes, but checks back with pocket fives.

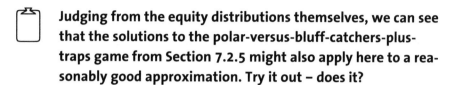 **Judging from the equity distributions themselves, we can see that the solutions to the polar-versus-bluff-catchers-plus-traps game from Section 7.2.5 might also apply here to a reasonably good approximation. Try it out – does it?**

At the equilibrium, the BB calls all-in around 48% of the time. Remember that his calling frequency in this game is just the amount needed to keep the SB's bluffs (which never win at showdown) indifferent to showing down, i.e. $P/(P+B)$. However, in the real game, this is only approximate. Few of the SB's bluffing hands are truly indifferent because of card removal effects which, as we will see, can be quite significant.

As a simple example, consider bluffing on the river as the SB here with Q♥-3♥ and with Q♠-3♠. Neither hand can ever win at showdown. At the equilibrium, it turns out that the hand with spades is indifferent between bluffing and showing down: both actions have an EV of 17 BB. With hearts, however, bluffing is quite a bit better! The reason is simply that Q♠-10♠ is in the one of the approximately 45 hands in the BB's check-folding range. The rest of his check-folding range consists of various K-high hands. But when our SB bluffs with Q♠-3♠, the BB can not have Q♠-10♠. In other words, there is actually one less hand he can have that will fold to the bluff than there are if the SB is bluffing with Q♥-3♥.

In more detail, we have assumed that the BB gets to the river with 86 hand combinations total. The Q♥-3♥ blocks the BB's K♥-3♥ hand which is check-folding, but the Q♠-3♠ blocks two of the BB's check-folding hands: K♠-3♠ and Q♠-10♠. Thus, when the SB holds spades, the BB calls a shove with about 40.7 hands and folds with about 43.3, and the SB's bluff-shove has an EV of about $(33) \times 43.3/(43.3+40.7) \approx 17$ BB. When the SB holds hearts, however, the BB check-calls with about 40.7 holdings and check-folds 44.3 of them for a SB EV of $(33) \times 44.3/(44.3+40.7) \approx 17.19$ BB. Bluffing with the hearts does better by almost 19 BB per 100 hands!

This sort of effect will often show up when a draw misses or it is otherwise possible that a player can get to the river with particularly weak hands. If you are choosing a bluffing range from a variety of your own 0-equity holdings, it is best to choose those hands that make it as likely as possible for your opponent to have one of his check-folding hands. This usually means that you have cards that do not conflict with hands that had draws on the early streets. This effect is often significant, and paying attention to these issues when choosing your bluffing hands can make a big difference to your bottom line over the long term.

Now, with the decision tree as described, the BB's exploitative adjustments come directly from our discussion of the SB bet-or-check game. So, too, are those with the SB's bluffs: if the BB is not calling quite enough, the SB should jam with all of his air. However, there is a remaining issue with the SB's deuces and small pocket pair hands. These all have upwards of 70% equity versus the BB's river starting range but are checked back since that is not quite good enough to make the value shove. This situation indicates that perhaps a smaller sized river bet would be a valuable strategic option for the SB. Indeed, if given the choice to bet 12 BB as well as to shove, he does prefer to go smaller with many of his value hands at the equilibrium. Interestingly, he does not bother including any nutted hands in his bet-smaller range. The very short remaining stacks and lack of strong hands in the BB's range make the threat of a check-raise unimportant. Making the 12 BB betting option available to the SB does not, however, make an especially large difference in the value of the game – about half a BB per 100 hands..

Notice finally that, had the third spade come on the river, the possible flush would have made a very significant difference in the hand. In this case, the BB gets to the river with 10 hand combinations which are suited in spades, so they make up nearly 12% of his range. Players have a tendency to disregard runner-runner draws in the BB's range since he check-called the flop, especially in short-stack spots such as this one. However, the BB can fold a lot on the turn in this hand, but he is never doing so (presumably) if he turned a flush draw to go along with his high-card value. So after getting to the river this way, spades are a non-negligible component of his range.

7.4.2 Example 2

We get to the river here with a pot of 20 BB and remaining stacks of 40 BB. The SB's river starting distribution is fairly polar (see Figure 7.2b), and the BB does not make use of options to lead the river. When we looked at the solutions to the symmetric distributions case of the complex river game (Section 7.3.3), we noted that the BB was checking the river with the majority of his distribution, even though it contained plenty of strong hands. The issue was that removing too many strong hands from his betting range leads to difficulties after he checks. The SB does not have the same problems playing troublesome mediocre hands – he can just show them down and then bet a polar range like he wants to. Anyway, this is something we will continue to notice in these examples: the BB does need to have a moderately polar river starting distribution to lead the river very often.

So, at equilibrium in this spot, the BB checks, and the SB can bet or check. Suppose we allow him to choose between a variety of different bet sizes: 40%, 60%, 80%, etc. up to 200% of pot which is all-in, and we allow the BB to call, fold, or raise all-in when facing a bet. Then, it turns out that the SB uses two sizes with non-negligible frequencies: 60% of pot and all-in.

Both of the SB's betting ranges are polar, but his all-in range is more-so. That is, he tends to value-bet larger with stronger hands. This should remind you of our discussion of bet sizing in the SB bet-or-check game towards the end of Section 7.3.2. Here, however, the BB can check-raise. Thus, the SB can not always bet larger with stronger hands – he includes some nuts in his 60% betting range for balance.

In particular, the SB bets with around three quarters of his hands, and around two fifths of his bets use the all-in sizing. The weakest value hands in this range are Q-J combos which have about 93% equity versus the BB's checking range, and he bets all-in with most hands stronger.

The value portion of his small betting range is primarily composed of weaker queens. However, many of these are quite close to checking. For example, his Q-2o, Q-3o, and Q-4o bet when the kicker is a 2, 3, or 4 of clubs or diamonds but check when it is of spades. Why might this be? The

SB also makes a small bet with all of his Q-Q hands (i.e. top full house). In fact, the small bet does better than a jam by about 60 BB/100 for this hand. We noted that this sort of play might be necessary for balance, but why is Q-Q a particularly good hand to use for the purpose?

The SB has few hands with 0 equity here, and he has enough value bets that he has to start drawing bluffs from holdings with a decent bit of showdown value. His weakest bluff is J-high, which would win around 15% of the time were it to simply check down.

Versus the smaller bet, the BB folds 49% of the time, calls 36%, and raises the rest. The bottom of his re-raising range is Q-10. In fact, his Q-10 combos are indifferent to calling. He flat-calls with weaker queens, and happily raises with hands like Q-9, 9-9, and K-6, the only sixes he gets to the river with this way. Notice that the BB did get to this river spot with a variety of hands he could raise for value. If he had not, then he may not have been able to raise enough to incentivize the SB to small-bet with any of his strong hands. In that case, the SB's small betting range would have been capped.

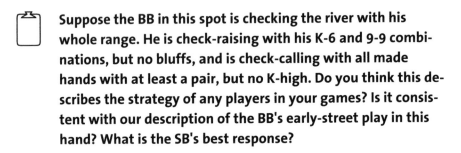 **Suppose the BB in this spot is checking the river with his whole range. He is check-raising with his K-6 and 9-9 combinations, but no bluffs, and is check-calling with all made hands with at least a pair, but no K-high. Do you think this describes the strategy of any players in your games? Is it consistent with our description of the BB's early-street play in this hand? What is the SB's best response?**

7.4.3 Example 3

In this hand, we saw a strong flop for the BB, and the SB continuation-bet but apparently gave up after he was called. We see from the BB's equity distribution in Figure 7.2c that the BB always has "something" when he gets to the river this way, given our assumptions about the river starting ranges. In particular, even his missed straight draws such as J-9 have about 40 percent equity versus the SB's river starting range. The reason is that there are a lot of low-card hands that the SB can bet the flop and then give up with, and these are over-represented in his range since he is not often bluffing the turn with them on this board, but he is going to double-barrel with many of his "real" hands. We discussed earlier the possibility that this presents a good opportunity for the BB to get to the river with more air in his range. For this example, we will focus on the differences in the BB's GTO river play if he does happen to have some air in his range here.

Two BB equity distributions on K♣Q♠8♡5♡5♣

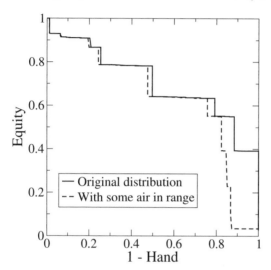

Figure 7.24: Example 3 BB river starting distribution originally and modified to include more air.

First, consider the original situation where the BB's distribution is bounded below at around 40 percent equity. How will he play? We can gain intuition from some of the earliest river situations we studied. Recall that in the extreme case that the BB always has the best hand, a variety of strategies achieved the equilibrium value: anything is fine as long as he does not fold since he always wins at showdown and the SB will never put any money in the pot. When the BB just *almost* always had the best hand, he could do best by making a fairly small bet. In this case, all of his range is fairly strong. However, it is essentially capped high since the SB can have a five. The BB can have K-5 suited in diamonds and spades exactly, but this is not a large part of his range. Thus, he uses a blocking-sized bet for his whole betting range.

In particular, if we give him the option to lead 3 BB on the river, he uses it with a bit over a third of his hands. These are his kings and queens (for value), and some missed straight draws (as bluffs). The rest of the time, the BB checks. He does this with some kings and queens as well as all of his A-high and eights.

Versus the blocking bet, the SB can raise all-in, and does so with almost all his nut-type hands (his fives) and some bluffs to balance. He also value-raises a more standard size with some weaker value hands, and balances with bluffs and a small number of his nut holdings. He has too much air to bluff with all of it, so he folds some, and calls with many other hands that have the equity he needs, 15 percent. The SB's play facing a check is rather similar to other hands we have seen except that he does have to check back and give up with much of his air.

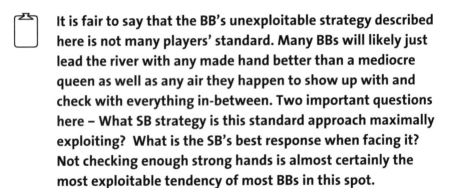 **It is fair to say that the BB's unexploitable strategy described here is not many players' standard. Many BBs will likely just lead the river with any made hand better than a mediocre queen as well as any air they happen to show up with and check with everything in-between. Two important questions here – What SB strategy is this standard approach maximally exploiting? What is the SB's best response when facing it? Not checking enough strong hands is almost certainly the most exploitable tendency of most BBs in this spot.**

Now, how does the BB's strategy change if he has some air in his range? In particular, suppose we have the same spot except that his equity distribution is as shown in Figure 7.24. We have essentially just replaced his missed draws with weak showdown value with some very-low-equity holdings. It is not that we think he is especially likely to get to the river with this new distribution in this particular hand, but the changes to his equilibrium strategy are instructive. So, what happens?

The BB still usually has the best hand, but now he has some pure air as well. So, he now has more of a reason to bet: to not have to show down his air. Just as importantly, whereas before even his bluffing hands were ahead of almost half of his opponent's range, he can now tempt many of the SB's weaker hands to call a bet, and thus he has more reason to bet with his real hands too. So, before, the BB blocked with 35 percent of his range and checked the rest. Now, if we let the BB have the option to make 12 BB bets as well (an option he did not use previously), his equilibrium strategy involves block-betting 60 percent of the time and splitting the rest of his range almost evenly between his checking and his near-pot-sized bet options. That is, adding some air to his range increased his river-leading frequency from about a third to over 80%!

In this case, his 12 BB leading range is Q-8 and better for value and some pure air as bluffs. This is sufficient to turn a large portion of the SB's range into bluff-catchers that he will have a hard time playing profitably. The BB blocks with some kings as well as value hands as weak as mediocre eights, and he again uses the opportunity to bet some bluffs. Since his river starting range still contains mostly value hands, he can actually bluff with all of his air and does not have to give up and show any of them down. This is despite the fact that most of his bets are quite small and must thus be used with mostly value and relatively few bluffs. In fact, if he had more air in his range, he might very well decide to make the larger bet size with more of his range. Thus, you can think of his strategizing here as beginning with his bluffing hands. He bets all his bluffs and then adds in enough value hands to balance, while checking with the rest. In fact, his distribution after he checks looks much like it did before we changed part of the starting distribution to air, and his range plays just fine after a check.

This example goes to show that it is absolutely necessary to be aware of one's whole range to strategize properly. We can not just consider play with individual hands. Many players fail to take these issues into account in spots like this one, and their strategies are quite exploitable.

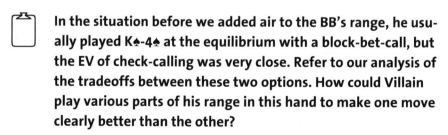

In the situation before we added air to the BB's range, he usually played K♠-4♠ at the equilibrium with a block-bet-call, but the EV of check-calling was very close. Refer to our analysis of the tradeoffs between these two options. How could Villain play various parts of his range in this hand to make one move clearly better than the other?

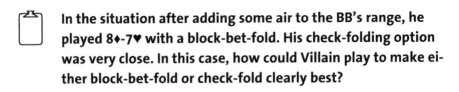

In the situation after adding some air to the BB's range, he
played 8♦-7♥ with a block-bet-fold. His check-folding option
was very close. In this case, how could Villain play to make either block-bet-fold or check-fold clearly best?

7.4.4 Example 4

This hand example comes from a minraised pot 50 BB deep in which the
flop and turn checked through. We assumed that the SB took this line exclusively with weak showdown value hands. Thus, we have a simple distri-
butional structure. About 6% of the SB's range is the nuts, and the rest is
more-or-less bluff-catchers with between 35 and 55 percent equity. Thus,
inverting, we find that the BB's distribution is about 100−55=45 percent
hands with 100−6=94 percent equity and about 35 percent air. The remaining 20 percent of his hands are somewhere in between. With quite a
variety of hand strengths, the BB has a lot of reason to lead the river. However, despite having a lot of strong hands, he has very few near nuts – his
range is nearly capped at 94 percent equity. So, he may not be able to get
away with large over-bets.

Where does the number 94% come from? We assumed that the SB gets to
the river this way with 48 hand combinations, 3 of which are pocket treys
which were lucky enough to river three-of-a-kind, and 3 is approximately 6
percent of 48. Since we assumed that the BB's preflop play eliminates 54
and pairs 66+ from his range, the SB's pocket treys are effectively the rivered
nuts. There is a tendency on the part of players in the BB's place to think of a
rivered three-of-a-kind hand as unlikely to the point of being insignificant in
a spot like this. However, many SBs will check down postflop with quite a
narrow range but will play 22-55 this way all the time, making the possibility of having rivered three-of-a-kind non-negligible as we will now see.

To set up and solve the decision tree, we give the BB the options to lead
river (1/4)P or (3/4)P – he did not use several over-bet options. We find that
he leads with the larger sizing with 253 of the 447 hand combinations with
which he gets to river. These are bluffs as well as hands for value as weak
as 55 which has about 91% equity versus his opponent's river starting

range. Admittedly, a hand like 5-5 could be significantly weaker versus a SB who protected his checking back range with more slow-plays, but it is true that plenty of otherwise good, aggressive players just never do that. He uses his smaller sizing with only about 33 combinations: his 2-2, 4-4, A-3,and Q-3, and a bit of strong value and pure bluffs for balance. He checks the rest of his hands. His checking range is even weaker showdown value such as A-high, some slow-plays, and some air that has to check and give up since he did not have enough value hands to allow him to bluff with all of them.

Now, let us take a look at the SB's re-raising strategy versus the BB's 3 BB lead, the BB's most common bet sizing by far. The thing to notice about this spot is that the SB has a fairly small and very well-defined set of value re-raising hands: rivered three-of-a-kind. These are the effective nuts, but he has no other strong value hands in his range. This situation has two important consequences. First, the SB's total re-raising frequency versus the 3 BB lead is fairly small. He does not have enough strong hands to do it any more often. This lets the BB lead 3 BB with a very wide range of hands – over half his range as we have seen.

Secondly, the SB has no hands which are value-raising but have to be worried about the possibility of running into better hands. His only raising hands are pure nuts and pure bluffs. So, there is no reason for him to raise smaller than all-in. With the all-in bet, he can bluff as often as possible and thus maximize his profit at the equilibrium. This should resonate strongly with our earlier discussion of river play with a polar distribution. So, the SB's GTO re-raising strategy versus a bet is easy to approximate. He raises with his nut hands and bluff-jams enough to keep the majority of the BB's hands indifferent to calling, i.e to give them an equity of 0.45. Some of the BB's hands, it turns out however, are very clear calls. For example his J♦-3♦ has almost 60 percent equity versus the SB's jamming range since holding the 3 cuts down the number of SB's nut holdings by a factor of 3. Of course, it also blocks some of the SB's bluffing hands since A-3s is the primary hand he uses to bluff.

When setting up this example, we noted that this is a spot where different players can get to the river with very different ranges of hands. So too will you see quite a variety of tendencies once you have gotten to the river this way. However, you may have noticed that this spot is essentially a polar-versus-bluff-catchers-plus-traps situation of the sort we discussed in Section 7.2.5, and you can catch all the theory behind the exploitative adjustments therein.

You may also recall that one of the primary results from our discussion of that game was the polar player's optimal bet sizing. We found that it was still all-in in some cases, but that it became smaller as stacks got deeper and if the SB had a significant number of trapping hands. Using the notation of that discussion, we have here the SB's trapping frequency $T=0.06$ and the stack size $S=12P$. Plugging into Equation 7.2 we estimate that the BB's optimal bet sizing here is about 134% of the pot or 5.37 BB. Indeed, if we change the SB's 3 BB bet sizing option to 5.37 BB and re-solve for the equilibrium, the value of the game for the BB increases by about 4 BB per 100 hands.

7.4.5 Example 5

This example comes from a minraised pot moderately deep. The BB check-raised a flop with a flush draw, the SB called, and the flush came on the turn. The SB called another bet on the turn. At the beginning of the river play in this hand, there are 48 BB in the pot and 136 BB behind. The players' starting distributions are shown in Figure 7.3a, and it is helpful to focus on the BB's distribution since he is going do the most betting here. Much of his range is quite strong or at least strong enough to want to get to showdown, but about a quarter of it is pure air. Thus, many of the SB's hands will have right around 25 percent equity, and the BB will probably want to have a considerable betting frequency versus this chunk of bluff-catchers. Given this, a decision tree like the one we considered in Figure 7.15 with initial bet sizing $B=(5/6)P$ and re-raise sizing all-in, with the added BB block-betting subtree that we discussed is more or less appropriate, and we will also give the players options to over-bet. What do we find?

Firstly, the BB does continue betting on the river with almost all of his range. The only hands he always checks on the river are K♥-10♥, K♠-10♠, and K♣-10♣, and those make up half of his river checking range. He also checks K-J and A-10 sometimes as well as the equivalent of about 1 combination worth of slow-played flushes. We could probably predict the BB's general approach by looking at his equity distribution – he has strong enough holdings in his distribution that he never has to give up and check the river with any of his pure air.

His block-betting range is mostly A-10. It is about a fifth nut hands to play versus a raise as well as enough bluffs to make the SB's weak tens hands indifferent between calling and folding. This is a good example of the construction of an unexploitable block-betting range. Intuitively, the BB starts out with A-10 since that is the only hand he really wants to play that way. Then he adds in some bluffs, because he can, and some slow-plays for balance reasons. If he did not include some strong hands in his blocking range, he would be vulnerable to frequent, large river raises. Of course, once Villain started to make such raises, the BB would be strongly incentivized to start block-betting with his strong hands.

The BB makes his standardly-sized river bet with a range that contains a bit over half of the hands with which he gets to the river. It is fairly polar, with value hands as weak as all his sets and some A-10. Finally, he very rarely uses the option to over-bet jam the river, but an 80 BB over-bet sees action with about a fifth of the BB's range. He uses that action with flushes and enough bluffs to balance.

What we mean by "enough bluffs to balance" should be clear, but it might help to be a little more specific for practice. What we mean is that the SB's hands that lose to the value over-bets but beat the bluffs (more than 85% of the SB's range in this case) are all indifferent between calling and folding. (At least, except for card removal effects. The SB's Q♦-10♥ actually has about 6% more equity versus this polarized over-betting range than Q♥-10♥. In fact, Q♦-10♥ has more equity than 5♦-2♦!) Anyhow, they all lose to all the value hands and beat all the bluffs, and they are indifferent between calling and folding when the BB bets the value hands mentioned and then adds in enough bluffs so that these SB bluff-catchers have equity equal to the odds they are getting on a call: $80/(2 \cdot 80+48) \approx 0.385$. If the BB bets fewer bluffs than this, then the SB can fold all of these bluff-catchers, and this would incentivize the BB to start bluffing more. If the BB bets more bluffs than this, then the SB can call with all of his bluff-catchers, thus incentivizing the BB to bluff less.

Finally, in the hand on which this example is based, the BB held 6♦-3♦. If he leads the river 40 BB and gets shoved on, it is an almost exactly a break-even call at the equilibrium given our assumptions about the river starting distributions and decision tree. That said, in order to call, the SB does have to be bluff-shoving here some amount. Now, the SB certainly gets to the river with some nut hands he can represent as well as plenty of hands that could be turned into bluffs since they do not really have enough value to call. So, it is a fine spot for the SB to bluff raise some, in theory.

However, for him to be bluffing, he does have to be turning a hand with *some* value into a bluff. Some players, with hands such as 10-7 in the SB's spot here, only think about whether they can call or have to fold. They do not consider turning made hands into bluffs. Since all of the SB's hands have some showdown value, such a tendency would severely reduce his bluffing frequency. Additionally and probably more significantly at a high level of play, for the SB to be bluffing, he does have to expect the BB to occasionally fold flushes. Certainly some players are wary that their opponents are too attached to absolute hand strength and will not make bluffs whose profitability requires their opponents to fold flushes on non-paired boards. Again, if the SB is not bluff-jamming here much, then low flushes quickly become bet-folding hands. On the other hand, if the BB sees mediocre flushes as easy bet-folds, then this could be quite a good spot to bluff. However, my experience here is that BBs do not fold flushes very often, and SBs do not frequently bluff.

7.4.6 Example 6

In this hand, a J♥-10♣-2♥ flop made many draws possible, but the top and second pairs are high enough that over-cards are not too big of a threat. The 8♣ turn improved some of the draws either to a pair or better, and then the river paired the second card on the board. The stacks are a bit awkward on this river. There are 14 BB in the pot and 23 BB behind. The BB gets to the river with just 32 hand combinations, and they break down into fairly well-defined groups. He holds a very small number of near-nuts – 10-8 with 98% equity and Q-9 with 88%. Then, he has a bunch of tens with around 75% equity and a number of weaker made hands such as some jacks with between 25 and 40 percent. Finally, he has several missed draws with little to no equity.

In this situation, the BB will both check the river and block-bet sometimes at the equilibrium. He does not lead larger with any hands. Facing the blocking bet (which we fix at 4 BB), the SB can fold, call, or raise. Facing the check, the SB can of course check or bet. If he bets, the BB can call, fold, or check-raise.

There is really no reason for either player's raise sizing on this river to be less than all-in. If the SB raises a blocking-bet, the hands with which he is doing it for value are just his near-nuts, as we might expect from his equity distribution in Figure 7.3b. His range has very few hands between 60 and 90 percent equity with which he might want to make a smaller bet, so he may as well go big and include as many bluffs as possible as well. There is not that much money left behind, anyhow. He does occasionally make non-all-in bets when facing a check if given the option, but we will focus on the decision tree where SB's only raise or bet sizing is all-in. This assumption simplifies our discussion and is not too severe an approximation.

Consider the BB's block-betting strategy. His primary holding is his approximately-75% equity stuff: his tens. We likely could have predicted this approach from looking at the BB's equity distribution itself. Unlike most of the river cards which could have come, the 10♦ improved much of the BB's bluff-catcher-heavy range into fairly strong hands. This gives him the opportunity to lead out some where he would have otherwise had to play check-and-guess. Our assumption that he slowplayed on the turn with some Q-9 and 10-8 does not hurt either – this allows him to protect somewhat his otherwise-capped ranges.

Additionally, although his equity distribution looks rather like the symmetric case overall, if you focus on the details of the weaker part of his distribution, he actually only has a few hands with very low equity which thus have strong incentive to bluff. After the bottom 12% or so of his range, all of his holdings have at least around 25% equity, i.e. a decent bit of showdown value. So, he does not have to lead too large or too often for value to allow himself to also bet with the hands he really wants to turn into bluffs.

In particular, the BB blocks with tens with low kickers and those with hearts. He prefers to check those without hearts since hearts block a lot of the hands the SB will use to bluff when facing a check. Additionally, the BB blocks with a fraction of his nut hands and some bluffs.

We can gain some insight into the effect of the blocking bet by examining the SB's distribution facing it. This is shown in Figure 7.25. Normal-sized bets must generally be made with a range such that the value portion is not going to run into too many better hands. When he blocks, however, the BB holds a range which contains many weaker value hands, and also he can only get away with relatively few bluffs. So, the SB's bluff-catchers, which make up about 2/3 of his range here, have only around 20% equity. However, almost a third of his hands are very strong, ahead of over 90% of the BB's block-betting range.

SB Distributions in Example 6 after each BB action

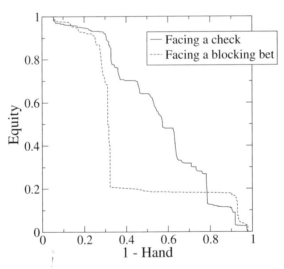

Figure 7.25: SB distributions in Example 6 facing a blocking bet and a check.

Take a look at the SB's equity distribution. What is his GTO strategy facing a blocking bet? You should be able to describe it with moderate accuracy.

The structure of his strategy facing the block, then, is about what you would probably expect. He shoves a bit under half the time. He does this with his clearly-defined set of high-equity holdings and he turns enough of his bluff-catchers into bluffs to balance. About a third of the time he calls, and he folds his weakest hands. His threshold between folding and calling is in the middle of the long stretch of bluff-catchers. That is, he is very nearly indifferent between the two actions with all of them.

The need to make his opponent indifferent to bluffing gives his bulk not-folding frequency, and card removal effects are the decisive factor in any particular case. Since the BB's bet-sizing is so small, the SB does need to continue most of the time.

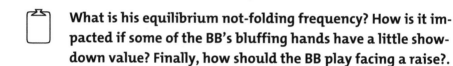 **What is his equilibrium not-folding frequency? How is it impacted if some of the BB's bluffing hands have a little showdown value? Finally, how should the BB play facing a raise?.**

Now, what is the situation after the BB checks? Both players still hold a wide variety of types of hands, although the top part of the SB's distribution is relatively strong – this is shown in Figure 7.25. After checking, the BB holds some nuts, some stronger tens, all his jacks, and his A-high missed flush draws. The SB's play here of course is to bet with some of his best and worst hands and to check back those in between. His weakest value-shoving hand is Q-10, and he also bets bluffs to balance. The SB's bluff-shoving range is made up of his air hands which have a nine or queen to block the straight. Facing the shove, all tens are clear calls for the BB, and all his jacks are clear folds. Standard stuff.

Now, how would things have been different if the BB did not use any block-betting in his strategy? First of all, we can see that it is an important strategic option for the BB. At the equilibrium, the value of the game improves by about about 6 BB per 100 hands for the BB if we give him the blocking option. However, the SB's strategy in response, it turns out, does not change too much. The set of hands he jams for value when facing a check is actually the same whether or not we give the BB his blocking option. Again, this is because his strategy is somewhat constrained by his equity distribution. His lack of holdings in the 60- to 90-percent equity range makes it hard for him to expand or contract the number of hands he value-bets. This inflexibility gives the BB the ability to take certain lines with less fear of being exploited.

Still, it is a bit tricky to see why the block-betting option is beneficial for the BB. At the equilibrium, all of the hands with which he is block-betting are nearly indifferent between blocking and checking. That is, he is just about as happy checking as blocking – but if he never blocks, he loses value. So it is not that the blocking bet option is significantly better with any of his hands, but it allows him to play more profitably. What's going on?

One way to look at it is basically as follows. Consider the case that the BB is not block-betting. He always checks the river to the SB who over-bet shoves about 45% of the time at equilibrium. Despite the fact that this is a high frequency, he has a strong enough range that the BB's weaker tens are in-different between calling and folding. That is, the equity he needs to call is more or less the same as the equity that various tens have facing the jam. The BB's equity distribution at the beginning of river play is shown in Fig-ure 7.3b. The segment of hands with around 75% equity consists of his tens, and you can see that they make up a large fraction of his range. All of these hands are put in a tough spot by not being able to find an edge in their call-or-fold decisions.

So, what the BB can do is to open up a block-betting range whose primary contents are these tens. He also blocks with a fraction of his nut hands as well as some bluffs. In particular, he has just a couple of pure air hands in his range at the beginning of river play, and he takes the opportunity to play most of these with the small bluff lead. Leading with his pure air sig-nificantly changes the equity of some of the SB's weak showdown-value hands such as A-high. When the BB was always checking the river, these could go to showdown and win at least occasionally versus missed draws. Now, however, in the decision facing those hands between bluffing and checking down, checking down is less attractive. In the final analysis, sev-eral of the SB's air hands bluff whereas they checked down before. Since the SB is bluffing more now (while his value-betting range, as we noted, is essentially fixed), all of the BB's tens can happily call a shove and his aver-age profit is improved.

This analysis may seem to rest on the minute details of the distributions in this case, but there is an important big-picture idea here. In order to play profitably, the BB wants to organize things so that when he is facing the call-or-fold decision, he has an easy, clear-cut decision with as many of his hands as possible. Graphically, this means that the equity he needs to make the call falls in a part of his distribution where there are few hands, i.e. where there is a vertical line in his equity distribution graph. If this is the case, then all of his holdings are clearly stronger or clearly weaker than the cutoff holding which would be a break-even call. Thus, he can play all of his hands profitably.

Indeed, his river-leading strategy in this hand is designed to make it so that the equity he needs to call falls clearly in-between the tens he check-calls and the jacks he check-folds. It does this by moving many of those borderline hands (the weak tens) to his block-betting range as well as by inducing a change in the SB's strategy to change slightly the equity he needs to call.

This is, of course, undesirable for the SB. The SB wants to make it so that a large portion of the BB's range is actually indifferent between his options. By doing this, he maximizes his EV at the equilibrium. We saw this over and over again in the simpler river situations. The math here is that, if we are indifferent between calling and folding with a group of hands, our total EV is essentially as if we just folded all of them. We end up, on average, with whatever money we have behind at that point – call it S. However, suppose we slightly prefer calling with some of them and slightly prefer folding with others. That is, the first group of hands is stronger (relative to Villain's range) than it was before, and the second group is relatively weaker, but we have the same equity versus his range on average. In this case, we can go ahead and happily call with the first group, thus winning some amount greater than S on average. But, we do not have to make that up in losses with the second group – we can just fold those and still end up with S. By playing so that one of his choices is clearly best with each of his particular holdings, that is, so that he holds as few true bluff-catchers as possible when facing a bet, the BB can improve his expectation.

There is an old-fashioned poker principle lurking here which is sometimes misunderstood or misapplied, but makes perfect sense given this discussion: try not to put yourself in hard spots. That is essentially what the BB is doing by opening up a gap in his checking distribution right at the equity corresponding to the odds he will need to call a shove. He is making it so that he has a clear decision with each of his holdings.

The corollary to this point is clear. You can profit by putting your opponent in hard spots. (This is not meant as a general principle but should be understood in the context of this example's discussion.) In particular, if you can choose your betting range and sizing so that it makes many of Villain's hands indifferent to calling or folding, then you can profit. Because those hands are indifferent to folding, you essentially win the whole pot, on average, when you bet and Villain holds a bluff-catcher. This is nothing new – this is what any polarized betting range does. However, it is particularly useful to think in these terms in situations like this one where the BB has so many hands which are essentially equivalent. We pointed out earlier that the BB's tens form a long flat region in his equity distribution (see Figure 7.3b). To the degree that a long, flat region is a dominant feature of the player's distribution, his opponent's equilibrium strategy will favor bet sizings and ranges which target those hands. This should be reminiscent of the results we found at the very beginning of the chapter in the case where all his range is bluff-catchers and yours is relatively polar. But even if all his hands do not have the same equity, we can think of targeting any large groups of his hands that do.

7.4.7 Example 7

This was a limped pot. The SB bet 1 BB on the flop, the BB called, and then the turn checked through. The BB's perceived range is quite strong since he called a bet on the flop, and the board ran out well for both flopped pairs and flopped draws. The players' river starting distributions are shown in Figure 7.3c. Over half of the SB's range has little to no equity. The rest of his hands have a variety of strengths, although he does have an extended region of equivalent hands with around 45% equity (various sixes) and no hands from there up to about 75% equity.

Inverting the SB's distribution, we find the BB's. Nearly all of his hands have upwards of 55 percent equity. Other than that, however, he holds hands with a variety of different strengths, so we do expect the BB to frequently lead the river with a bet. In fact, the BB's distribution in this hand looks a lot like that from Example 3 (see Figure 7.2c), but there is an important difference between the two spots. In the prior hand, the BB's range was mostly capped at around 94% equity whereas here he holds a significant number of pure nuts and near-nut hands. This will give him the opportunity to mix in some larger bet-sizings.

The stack-to-pot ratio at the start of river play is 6. At the top of the decision tree we use to study this situation, we give the BB the options to check or to lead with sizings $(1/4)P$, $(3/4)P$, or $2P$. He does not utilize an all-in leading option. If he checks, the SB can bet all-in or a more standard $(5/8)P$. After the smaller of these, the BB has the option to raise all-in or to 12 BB, or to call or fold. Similarly, if the BB leads 1 BB, the SB can raise small or all-in, and if small, the BB can call, fold, check-raise all-in or check-raise smaller. After the BB leads 3 or 8 BB, the SB can jam or raise smaller, and after the latter, the BB's only check-raise sizing is all-in.

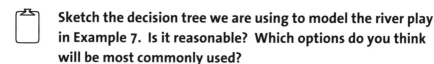 **Sketch the decision tree we are using to model the river play in Example 7. Is it reasonable? Which options do you think will be most commonly used?**

Ok, great. So first of all, let us take a look at the BB's river strategy at his first decision point. He checks or block-bets most of his hands – he takes these actions with a bit more than two-fifths of his starting range each. He bets $(3/4)P$ 6% of the time, and over-bets $2P$ 9% at equilibrium.

The distributions with which the BB takes each of his actions on the river, relative to the SB's starting range, are shown in Figure 7.26. A few things are noteworthy. His betting ranges are appropriately polar as usual. The larger the bet sizing, the stronger the value portions of his betting ranges become on average. However, all of his betting ranges include some strong and nut hands for balance. Also, the larger the bet sizing, the more bluffs are included.

BB distributions (Example 7)

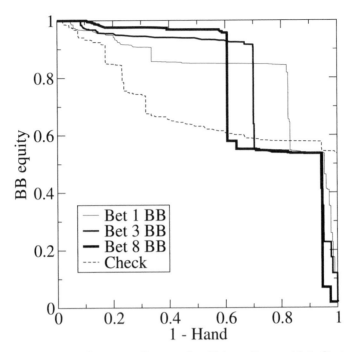

Figure 7.26: BB distribution after each of his actions at his first decision point.

The BB's cut-off hand for value-betting with his smallest sizing is around A-6 which may come as a surprise. A-6 is quite a strong hand for the BB here since we assumed the SB would have bet any 9 on the turn. The BB's tight betting criteria are the result of an effect we have seen previously which has to do with his entire distribution. Since his range is generally quite strong, the SB's calling criteria will tighten up, and thus the BB can not value-bet hands as weak as he might otherwise. This sort of spot is frequently an opportunity for exploitative play when facing an opponent who is not accurately estimating your distribution. If the SB does not recognize your range is strong and is thus calling more than he should, you can keep value-betting a wider range. In fact, most BBs will value-bet an exploitatively wide range here. On the other hand, perhaps it is the case that they float the flop more, too, and thus get here with more weak hands.

Now, we can see in the figure that the BB's checking range has to contain many strong hands, too, since he has so many holdings with around 60% equity that he wants to check down and needs to protect. Having 60% equity means, of course, that they are beaten by about 40% of the SB's hands. So, they have a lot of value if they can get to showdown, but if that were his strongest river checking hand, he would be very vulnerable to an exploitative SB betting strategy, especially since stacks are quite deep. Notice also that the BB's checking range is bounded below fairly high. He has enough value bets that he can turn all of his low-equity holdings into bluffs.

Now, let us focus on the SB's situation after the BB leads. The overall structure of the SB's response in each case should be clear by now. He raises his strongest holdings, folds his worst, calls most hands in the middle except for a few holdings between the bottom of his calling range and the top of his folding range which he uses to bluff-raise. The particular locations of the cutoff hands are not so clear cut due to blocker effects. For example, facing the 3 BB bet, the SB prefers to hold certain deuces to A♠-6♠.

However, we can again gain some insight into the SB's response and how it changes depending on the size of the bet he faces by looking at how he splits his ranges at the equilibrium. His distribution facing each BB bet sizing is shown in Figure 7.27. In each case, his range breaks down fairly cleanly into three regions. He has some high-equity holdings which are actually ahead of some of the BB's value range. There are more of these when he faces the smaller bets since these are made with weaker holdings. Then, he holds a region of bluff-catchers. These have higher equity for the larger bet sizings since the BB's larger betting ranges include more bluffs. Of course, the SB needs more equity to call a larger bet, and all the hands in this region are all more or less indifferent between calling and folding. Lastly, we can see that about 55% of the SB's holdings lose to even most of the BB's bluffs. This is to be expected since we assumed the BB does not get to the river with much air.

SB distributions when facing a bet (Example 7)

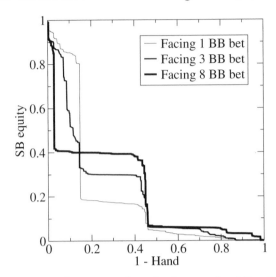

Figure 7.27: SB distributions when facing each of the BB's first decision point actions.

How, then, does the SB play each of his distributions? His cutoff for raising falls right around the 85% equity mark in each case. His weakest calling hand falls somewhere within the stretch of bluff-catchers and is chosen so that his total not-folding frequency makes the BB indifferent to bluffing and checking with his strongest bluffing hands. The BB's EV of checking, however, is quite high with those, since his strongest bluffing hand started the street with around 55% equity and gets to realize its value at show-down frequently after checking. So, it only takes relatively little bluff-catching on the SB's part to keep the BB indifferent to trying to show down this hand. Indeed, the SB is folding enough so that the little pure air with which the BB does get to the river does much, much better by bluffing than by checking.

Finally, the SB's bluff-raising hands are drawn from all over his low-equity holdings and do not form a coherent group. These are holdings with good card removal properties like 7-6 or 6-4 with a single diamond.

What actual holdings correspond to the SB's weakest raising hand facing each bet size?

7.4.8 Example 8

In this hand, the SB bet the flop and turn, and the BB check-called twice. Many draws came in on the river. The players' river starting distributions are shown in Figure 7.3d. Some of the BB's weaker made hands were absolutely devastated by this river. For example, J♣-9♥ has a mere 5% equity versus the SB's range (it beats only Q-J). This is largely because we assumed that the SB was not semi-bluffing the turn with many particularly speculative hands since the 9♠ is not generally seen as a good card to bluff. That said, it is not too hard to have a "legitimate" hand or draw on 10♠-7♣-2♥-9♠ – the double-barreling range we gave the SB here is about 23% of all hands.

So, there are a bit more than two pot-sized bets in the remaining stacks, and the distributions are moderately close to the symmetric case, although the BB's range is a bit stronger than his opponent's. We expect the BB to use a lot of his options here. We will study this spot with a decision tree that is similar to our most complex [0,1] game except that we allow several different bet-sizings, including blocking bets and over-bets, in many spots.

Our discussion will revolve around the BB's play at his first decision point. Here, his bet sizings are $(2/3)P$ and $(1/6)P$. It turns out that he does not make much use of any over-bets. With this decision tree, we find that he block-bets about a quarter of his range, bets $(2/3)P$ with about a third of it, and checks the rest of the time at equilibrium.

He leads the larger sizing with a polar range. The weakest value hand is 9-8 for the straight. He uses all his J-9 combinations with the J♠ and some of those without it to bluff. The spade blocker makes those hands better for the purpose. This betting strategy makes all of the SB's hands better than J-9 but worse than a straight indifferent between calling and folding at the equilibrium up to card removal effects. These effects, however, can be significant. For example, calling the bet with the 1-pair hand Q♥-10♥ earns the SB over 3 BB more than calling with the two-pair hand 10♥-9♥ since the 9 blocks J-9, the BB's only bluffing hand, and makes it significantly less likely that the BB is bluffing.

Now, the BB's block-betting range consists of various 2-pair, straights, and the occasional flush or bluff for balance. The SB's most frequent raise size versus the blocking bet is all-in. He does so for value with flushes, the J-8 straight, and some bare one-card straight hands which contain a spade for the blocking effect. He bluff-shoves with his Q-J which is pure air, but that is not enough bluffing combinations, so he also uses a few hands which have some showdown value, most notably A-A and K-K.

An additional interesting effect here can be seen by comparing the BB's play with 9-8 and 10-8. The hands are the same in absolute strength – they have the same straight. However, it is significantly better for the BB to lead with the blocking bet with 10-8 and with the larger bet with 9-8. About 55% of the hand combinations in the SB's range contain a ten, and so the BB's holding one of them significantly impacts the SB's range – it makes it less likely that the SB holds a ten. As mentioned earlier, the larger bet makes the SB's 1-pair tens mostly indifferent between calling and folding. That is, intuitively, these are put in a hard spot by the larger bet and are actually played less profitably at the equilibrium. So, the BB uses his 9-8 to make the larger bet and the 10-8 combinations to have some straights in his block-betting and checking ranges.

Now, all that is well and good, but did you catch what is especially note-worthy about this hand? The BB check-called on the flop and turn but then led the river with most of his range! What happened here? First of all, the bottom line is that strategic river play really just depends on the starting distributions and the pot and stack sizes (or, more specifically, just the ra-tio of the effective stack size to the pot size). (Technical exceptions to this point do exist, and we will consider them when we look at earlier-street play, but it is not clear that they are of too much practical significance.) Nothing we have discussed all chapter about river strategizing has needed to take any details of the early-street play into account beyond their effect on those things. It just so happens that most players tend to check-call early streets with distributions that do lend themselves to river leads.

So, it is mostly just important to identify the situations in which the BB might want to lead the river, regardless of the earlier-street play. We have seen a number of specific examples so far where the BB does and does not have a river leading range at the equilibrium. In general, though, we have seen that having a distribution which contains sufficiently strong hands is an obvious prerequisite for betting, but it is not enough. He also needs to hold weaker hands as well so that he has incentive to bluff. Additionally, for the BB to lead with a bet, it is important that he not have too many weak showdown value hands. If he does, he will be incentivized to check with his strong holdings to protect his weak hands that want to go to showdown. In an analogous spot, the SB does not have to worry about facing a bet after checking, nor is it a factor for the BB if he checks and faces a bet.

For some more river-leading examples in the context of this particular hand, consider Figure 7.28 which shows the BB's distribution at the end of turn play and at the beginning of river play on the 6♠ river which we have considered so far as well as a few alternate river cards, the 3♥ and the Q♠. We can see that, on the turn, the BB's whole range is solidly mediocre. Of course, equity distributions do not show the whole picture on early streets since they do not incorporate notions of draws, but still it is clear that we gave the BB almost all hands that did not want to raise nor to fold.

BB starting distributions on alternate rivers in Example 8

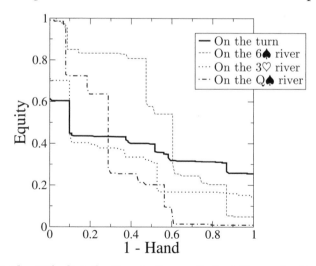

Figure 7.28: The BB's distribution in Example 8 at the end of turn play and at the beginning of river play for the 6♠, 3♥, and Q♠ rivers.

On many rivers that do not really connect with the board, the BB's river starting distribution will look a lot like that on the 3♥. That is to say that it is about the same as on the turn except that some of his holdings got a bit stronger since draws missed and most of it got somewhat weaker for the same reason. His situation on this river is pretty dire. He is definitely not going to be leading any. He check-raises 9-7o, the one fairly strong hand we assumed he slow-plays, and a few associated bluffs, but that is about it. This is almost purely a check-and-guess situation, and one which he is not going to get the best of. One easy thing he really should do is to get to the river this way with some hands such as J-8s. We assumed that he either check-raised the flop with the draw or else check-raised the turn with the straight. However, given his weak, bluff-catcher-heavy distribution, he should probably just go ahead and slow-play with turned nuts for more or less the same reasons he does not lead himself in river situations where he holds mostly bluff-catchers and a few traps.

Finally, consider the BB's situation if the Q♠ had come on the river. This case is a bit different, as the Q♠ does greatly improve some of the BB's range and devalue other parts. However, it does not give him nearly as many very strong, value-betting hands as does the 6♠. In particular, he has about the same amount of flushes but holds no straights. The 2-pair hands he rivers (e.g. Q-10) have about 10% less equity than do his straights on the 6♠ river. He has to check with a lot of these weaker hands, and as a consequence, mostly wants to check with his nuts as well for balance-related reasons. It turns out that, on the Q♠ river, he block-bets a small chunk of hands 2-pair and better for value and some bluffs, but he mostly checks. However, he can certainly raise a lot more facing a bet than he could after checking the 3♥ river, and he does a lot better on average here for having the stronger range.

The bottom line is that things like the betting initiative are illusory but have a legitimate basis in standard play insofar as the bettor's range is relatively polar. However, even if you are in the BB with a range which is very bluff-catcher-heavy on an early street, sometimes a card can come that mixes up hand values a lot, and then you may want to be leading some. And sometimes you may just want to slow-play earlier streets, especially if you think you will get to the river with a lot of hands that need to bluff as well. But these are really considerations for a discussion of earlier-street play, and we are getting ahead of ourselves.

River check-raises are usually some of the biggest bets in the game. Thus, these situations often present the opportunity to find a large edge on an opponent, especially since players tend to play these spots especially poorly. In particular, in many player pools, most big blinds do not bluff frequently enough, especially if the check-raise is all-in or for a lot of money. Besides the number of chips involved, many players tend to just lead the river with any hands they want to use to bluff – this is especially true if the turn check-ed through or the the BB actually started the river with the betting initiative. Of course, we have seen that check-raise bluffs are usually best drawn from the set of hands that just barely can not call a bet but are happy enough to go to show-down if the SB checks behind. With these holdings, many players tend to focus on evaluating their calling and folding options but do not con-sider turning their hand into a bluff. For these reasons, some strong SB play-ers default to playing exploitably tight facing the river check-raise.

 Now, go back over each of the river examples. In which cases did the BB have a check-raising range? In those in which he did not – why not? In those in which he did – what was the weakest hand he check-raised for value? Which hands did he use as a bluff? How did the SB respond at equilibrium? Is the SB's equilibrium play close to your default? If not – what population tendencies are you adjusting to? What details of a new opponent's play might tip you off that this default ad-justment is not good versus him?

7.5 You Should Now...

♠ Understand how community cards and players' early-street actions can lead to various types of river starting distributions

♠ Be able to play unexploitably or exploitatively in any sort of river polar-versus-bluff-catchers situation

♠ Understand how a few slow-plays in the bluff-catching player's range can be very valuable in themselves and and also improve the value of the bluff-catchers

♠ Be able to solve [0,1] games with asymmetric distributions using the Indifference Principle

♠ Understand the structure of a player's strategy on the river when facing a bet and when facing a check when in the SB

♠ Understand the structure of the BB's strategy from the beginning of river play in the case of symmetric distributions

♠ Be able to evaluate the trade-offs facing thin value bets from each position

♠ Understand the issues surrounding effective bluff-catching on the river

♠ Use blocking bets as part of GTO and exploitative BB river strategies

♠ Know how value-betting and bluffing frequencies are connected and understand the effect that a properly-constructed polarized betting range has on an opponent's distribution

♠ Understand how asymmetric starting distributions affect equilibrium river play

Chapter 8

Epilogue to Volume I

The smarter you play, the luckier you'll be. – Mark Pilarski

8.1 Range Splitting in Practice

We have seen that as you play a hand, you should always keep in mind an estimate of both your own range as well as your opponent's and constantly update those estimates whenever you get new information. When you get to one of your decision points, you should strategize by thinking of how best to split your range into your different options. We saw that the structure of such partitions was pretty simple in a lot of river spots in that most hands are best played exactly one way. This will not necessarily be the case on earlier streets where balance-related issues frequently lead to mixed strategies with many hands.

In Chapter 7 we broke down the structure of the equilibrium strategies in various archetypal river situations. In particular, in Section 7.3.3, we looked at the game shown in Figure 7.15 which models river play including bet-raising and check-raising. In the solution to this game, the BB split his range at his first decision point, and the SB split his in two ways depending on whether he was facing a bet or a check.

As a review, recall that the BB's range was divided into seven regions. From strongest to weakest these were:

1. Check-raise for value

2. Bet-call for value

3. Bet-fold for value

4. Check-call

5. Check-fold

6. Check-raise as a bluff

7. Bet-fold as a bluff

Similarly, when SB was facing a lead, he responded by splitting his range into four regions, which are, from strongest to weakest:

1. Raise for value

2. Call

3. Raise as a bluff

4. Fold

And when the SB was facing a check, his regions from strongest to weakest were:

1. Value-bet with the intention of calling a raise

2. Value-bet with the intention of folding to a raise

3. Check back and show down

4. Bet-fold as a bluff

These structures will almost always describe the SB's strategy at equilibrium. Intuitively, he can simply choose to put a bet in with a polar range while going to showdown with any problematic intermediate holdings. The BB does not have that luxury, and his river strategy is the result of more balance-related considerations.

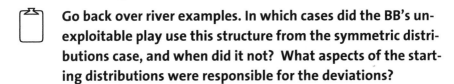 **Go back over river examples. In which cases did the BB's unexploitable play use this structure from the symmetric distributions case, and when did it not? What aspects of the starting distributions were responsible for the deviations?**

This decision tree can model a wide variety of river spots as long as the stack-to-pot ratio is not too large, and it is very helpful to have these structures internalized. To this end, study the symmetric distribution solutions for various stack sizes (see Figure 7.17) as well as the solutions to the river examples in Section 7.4. Only by being familiar with these solutions can you start to modify them in response to asymmetric distributions or exploitable opponent tendencies.

One particularly important feature of these structures which we talked about a lot and is easy to keep in mind at the table is that every group of betting or raising hands has a corresponding region of bluffs. Thus, if it is too difficult to imagine splitting your entire range at any decision point, you can at least think, whenever you find yourself value-betting, about the hands you are bluffing with in the same spot, and vice versa. If you find that you are only value-betting in a spot, then perhaps you should be turning some of your weaker made hands into bluffs.

Using this decision tree generally assumes that any re-raise is all-in, but the model could be made more complex by including 3- and 4- bets, etc. In this case, the solutions would include regions for each option. The enterprising student in need of a weekend project could consider solving a river game with another round of betting. He could then think about equilibrium frequencies, exploitative adjustments, and counter-adjustments for each region of hands. One issue which does arise, however, has to do with the fact that after putting in multiple raises, ranges become pretty tight. In these cases, card removal effects can play a big role in choosing the particular hands used for certain plays. However, the [0,1] approximation will still give a good estimate of the overall frequencies with which the players take their various actions.

Now, these range-splitting ideas are easy to say (kind of), but players sometimes have a hard time working them into their play. Let us take an example of a simple situation for concreteness. Recall river Example 1. Many players get to a spot like this in the SB where their opponent's range is well-defined and they are relatively polar. They know they should play jam-or-check at the equilibrium, but they bet smaller instead. Perhaps with value hands, they do not want to shove since they worry about getting a fold, and they want to bet smaller and try to get paid. Perhaps with bluffs, they worry that they do not represent too many hands and an over-bet could look bluffy and get called. Not this time, they say.

The first thing to keep in mind with value hands is that getting called more often does not necessarily mean making more money. For example, suppose you are in this situation with a value hand 4 times, and you make 3/4-pot sized value bets and get called and win all 4 times. Suppose, on the other hand, that you over-bet three times the pot each time and he folds thrice and only calls once. On average, you made the same amount of money in both scenarios. However, most people generally feel better about the smaller bet that that always got paid off. This is one of the many spots where peoples' minds play tricks on them. You get positive emotional reinforcement for getting paid off and negative reinforcement when your opponent folds in amounts which are not exactly consistent with your real profit. With your bluffs, the thing to keep in mind is that you have chosen your frequencies so that you break even (as compared to checking back) with these hands in the long run at the equilibrium. And if it does turn out, unbeknownst to you, that Villain is calling too much, it does not really matter since you will just make more money when you have a value hand.

Following up on this last point, the bottom line is to trust the math. If you know the equilibrium play, making excuses to not follow through is just costing yourself money. If you do not worry about first-time effects, then they will not be a big deal. In other words, if you avoid making a move for the first time with a bluff for certain reasons and avoid making it the first time for value for other reasons, you will simply never make the move. If you just focus on playing unexploitably in individual spots and over-bet-shove whenever the spot comes up, regardless of which part of your range you happen to have, you need not worry about being exploitable. As we have seen in several examples, the value lost at equilibrium by using non-optimal bet sizings can be quite large. Thus, improper adjustments can be quite costly. Do not avoid using "non-standard" bet sizings if you think they are optimal. The fact of the matter is that most players are not very experienced in dealing with over-bets or blocking-sized bets, so your opponents will probably respond more poorly than you might imagine.

Of course, it is also important to not lose sight of what is important here – making as much money as possible! Although in a situation such as the one above, betting all-in with your entire betting range may be the GTO strategy, it might not be the most profitable against a particular player. If you know your opponent will fold all of his bluff-catchers to a jam but call some smaller bets, then by all means, jam with your bluffs and bet smaller for value. However, do not be too quick to make such an adjustment. Although this set of exploitable tendencies might seem reasonable, many players act in just the opposite fashion. Perhaps they know their range looks weak and are suspicious of large bets which "look like they don't want a call" while giving smaller bets more credit for being for value. These players can actually be more likely to call the larger bet! You really need to have a solid reason to make an assumption either way. If you see your opponent fold once to an over-bet shove with a hand you think was a bluff-catcher, that does not constitute a read for which you should adjust your play to value-bet smaller next time. For one thing, he is probably more likely to call next time. Remember that he does not need to call the over-bet nearly as often to make the larger bet more profitable. Making non-equilibrium plays as a standard without a good, player-specific reason, is not playing exploitatively – it is just weak, lazy poker.

This brings us to the problem of actually choosing hands on the fly for each strategic region when attempting to play unexploitably. It is one thing to be able to solve for the frequencies, but how do you actually know if some value hand is in the top X percent of your range? Even trickier can be your bluffing hands. Players tend to have a good sense for whether or not their value hand is strong enough to bet, but choosing bluffing hands is harder. In spots where your range contains mostly strong hands, you may be able to bluff every time you happen to get there with air. However, in spots where your range contains a lot of potential bluffs, you have to have a smaller total bluff frequency which means an even smaller frequency of betting any particular time you are in that spot with air. So, how do you proceed?

Know thyself. The fact is that you need to know your play well enough to know what your ranges look like in a spot. You should get plenty of practice if you are conscientious while playing, and it is important to get in the habit of working out your strategy away from the tables after encountering an unusual situation. It will make you a much more knowledgeable player in general. And like many things in this game, it will become second nature with practice.

However, there are a few rules of thumb for filling out your bluffing ranges, many of which we encountered over the course of the river examples. First, if you are deciding between bluffing and showing down, you should tend to bluff with hands that will never win at showdown while checking hands that might. Since neither will ever win if they bet and are called, there is no reason to bluff with a hand that has some chance of winning at showdown while showing down a hand that does not. Thus, if you find yourself on the river about to check down one of the very worst hands you can have, it should probably be in your bluffing range instead. If you find yourself in a river spot where you hold many missed draws, perhaps you should show down the ones that happen to have a decent high card and bluff with the ones that do not. Similarly, if you are facing a bet and deciding between bluff-raising and folding, there is no reason to fold a better hand and raise with a worse one. Who knows – maybe your opponent will make a bad call. These considerations are built-in to the solution structures we listed above.

The second rule of thumb for choosing bluffs has to do with card removal effects. For example, suppose you are on the river and the board contains three clubs. Then, having a single club in your hand reduces the chance Villain has a flush – not a lot, but HUNL is a game of small edges. Thus, bluffing ranges on this board will often be composed entirely of 1-club hands. There is no reason to ever bluff with a non-club-containing hand if you can instead use another hand which is equivalent except that it contains a club.

Now, although these guidelines are good to keep in mind, you can not just bluff whenever you have no showdown value or you have blockers. With that plan, you would certainly be bluffing too much in some situations and not nearly enough in others. We have seen spots where your overall range is strong enough that you should just bet all of it, even essentially turning weaker hands such as one or two pair into bluffs. We have seen other situations where we just have to give up with almost of our air. So, it is necessary to first figure out your own range, decide how much you should be bluffing in total, and then use these rules to decide which of your possible bluffing hands would be best used to add up to the frequency you need. Again, spending some time away from the tables breaking down your range in spots and grouping hands into regions will pay off greatly.

Of course, the same sort of range-partitioning ideas are useful as the player facing a bet. We can often proceed by finding the frequency with which we need to take an action and then choosing our holdings to meet that quota. Consider the following hand.

Effective stacks: 43 BB
Hero (SB): J♣-9♥
Preflop:
Hero raises to 2 BB, Villain raises to 6 BB, Hero calls
Flop: K♥ J♦ 2♠ (12 BB)
Villain checks, Hero checks
Turn: 7♦ (12 BB)
Villain bets 6 BB, Hero calls
River: 3♠ (24 BB)
Villain bets 31 BB and is all-in

We are in the SB facing an over-bet on the river with J♣-9♥. Villain is something of a weak player with uncommon tendencies. In particular, he rarely flat-calls open-raises preflop, preferring to 3-bet with most of his playable hands. He c-bets his air with an unusually low frequency, but he can decide to start bluffing on later streets. We have also seen him play top-pair hands unusually passively on early streets in what could be an attempt to balance.

In this hand, his bet sizing is interesting. He went somewhat small on the turn and then over-bet-jammed on the river. This is odd since he could have easily bet a bit bigger on the turn to set up stacks better for his river shove. So, his line and sizing tell at least two different stories. Perhaps he has a weak hand that did not want to put too much money in on the turn but then shoved the river in desperation to try to win the pot. Or, perhaps he has a strong hand that he decided to slow-play on the flop, made the small turn bet for value as sort of an extension of his slow-play, but then decided to shove on the river to try to get maximum value. Unfortunately, the plays suggested by these two possibilities are in conflict, so that line of reasoning does not help us much. It is a good thing we know some theory.

We know the structure of our strategy in this spot will involve a single cut-off hand. We will call with all better hands and fold all worse. We know that at the equilibrium, our cutoff hand will likely be the one such that we are calling enough so that the BB's strongest bluffing hand is indifferent between betting and checking. Also, we can assume for simplicity that the BB's strongest bluffing hand is weak enough that it will always lose the pot if it does not bluff. This is probably true since it is likely an unpaired low-card hand which the SB always has beat after calling the turn bet. So, how much do we have to call to keep the BB indifferent to checking and losing the pot? We solve the following indifference equation.

$$\mathrm{EV_{BB}(bluff) = EV_{BB}(check)}$$

$$(55 \text{ BB})(\text{Hero's folding frequency}) + (0\text{BB})(\text{Hero's calling frequency}) = 31 \text{ BB}$$

We find that Hero's folding frequency equals about 56 percent. Thus, Hero can simply figure out his own range in this spot (what is your range in this spot?) and then call with the best 44% of it.

If we call any less than this, Villain can profitably shove all his air. (Of course, this does not mean he shoves his whole range at equilibrium. He still might find it best to check some holdings that have showdown value.) Now, it could be the case that Villain gets to the river with a range strong enough that he indeed can just shove all of his bluffs and we still can not call with our 56th-percentile hand. Perhaps this would be the case if Villain had a tight 3-betting range and was particularly prone to slow-playing when he hit the flop but c-betting his air. As mentioned, however, the BB in this hand 3-bets a lot and gets to the river this way with plenty of air, so we should certainly expect the above indifference to be satisfied at the equilibrium in this case.

8.2 Deliberate Play

Our last recommendation may sound like generic soft advice that you can skim, but this is probably one of the most important points in the book. Taking this advice to heart will likely win you more money in the long run than any betting or strategic concepts, and, indeed, is absolutely necessary for bringing everything together and correctly applying those concepts.

Play deliberately. Deliberate about every decision you make. Take a solid 5 seconds with even the "super standard" ones. Especially those. Do you have K-Jo in the SB preflop? Would you never do anything ever with it except make a standard open-raise? It does not matter – take at least 5 seconds and maybe more. This might not seem like much time, but it forces a significantly slower pace than that of most online matches. (Live players might already be used to a slower-paced game.)

Now, it is true that many players give away information with the timing of their actions, and it is certainly important that you avoid doing that. More importantly, however, we are trying to cultivate a calm, contemplative state of mind. If you do not actually need to think about the decision at hand, then give some thought to how you will react to a raise. Give some mental attention to the characterization of your opponent's overall play style and to nailing down your overall game plan. Think about how you play your whole range in a spot. Clearly you are opening K-Jo, but are you playing ATC versus this opponent? The idea is that mulling over every situation will let you make much better decisions narrowly tailored to exploit your specific opponent. By playing a slow, methodical game, and clearly identifying both players' ranges in every spot, you will also learn a ton and will regularly identify spots to make profitable exploitative plays that you had not thought of before.

So there – take the time to ponder and philosophize over every decision, and if a particular decision truly needs no thought, use the time to consider future decision you might face or to meditate on Villain's tendencies and your overall plan to take advantage of them. Some players get bored with this approach, but the fact is that if 5 seconds seems too long to spend on every decision, you are not thinking enough. In fact, forcing yourself to take a few extra seconds before each action is a good way to practice self-control, a virtue that is not very well fostered by poker itself. If you have a hard time waiting a few seconds to make a move and focusing your thought processes in the meantime, it is probably time to take a break.

I hope it does not distract from the main point, however, to mention that the nonstandard decisions deserve a lot of thought too! In particular, whenever you face an all-in decision (and you hold a hand other than the nuts), take some extra time to think about it. All-in decisions are some of the most important ones to get right simply because they are the biggest pots and so therein lies the chance to win or lose the most money, so give them some extra attention. If you ever snap-call a shove without the nuts, you played it wrong, regardless of the results.

There are a couple of psychological benefits (or, at least, effects that can be benefits if leveraged correctly) to playing with a methodical pace that should be mentioned as well. When you act with slow, controlled actions, your opponent will get the impression that you are in control of your play and the situation. In my experience, this leads them to play somewhat more timidly and to give you more credit in general. They are less likely to make bluffs because they know that you are thinking hard and feel that you are likely to catch them. Also, a few moments can feel like a long time to sit wondering if one's bluff is going to get called! It is psychologically painful, and opponents are unconsciously conditioned to avoid these spots.

This same psychological trick can be used in reverse. Suppose it is early in a match – the players know little-to-nothing about each other – and Hero flops a strong hand. In this spot, it can be good for Hero to bet big, instantly, on all 3 streets. In my experience, Hero will often get called down very lightly. The reason is that betting quickly, seemingly without giving your decision any thought at all, gives the impression that you are just spewing chips without any regard for the money. Opponents will generally perceive such play as much more loose and aggressive than that of someone who takes the same actions but does so in a more methodical pace. That said, do not get in the habit of playing this way! Play deliberately!

8.3 Looking Ahead

In the next volume, we will have a bit more opportunity to focus on the exploitative side of things – not only in the psychological and opponent-modeling sections, but also in the early street chapters. There are a couple of reasons for this. Remember that we need to know what GTO play looks like in order to identify how Villain is deviating and thus to exploit him. We now have a better idea about the general form that optimal HUNL play takes, and so we can move on from there. More importantly, however, it is much easier to get an accurate picture of how an opponent plays on earlier streets since we play more early street hands and early street situations are more similar to one another.

So, in the next volume, we will continue studying game-theory-optimal and exploitative heads-up no-limit play in ever-widening circumstances. We will start off by considering turn play. We will leverage what we have learned about the value of having various holdings on the river to evaluate turn decisions and will focus especially on correctly handling situations involving volatile hand strengths. We will also discuss by way of examples how to build a mental model of an opponent's strategy and to think outside the box to exploit him. Our discussion of preflop and flop play will emphasize getting to later streets with unexploitable distributions as well as manipulating our distributions to take advantage of opponents' mistakes. Our approach will be a lot more equilibration exercise and somewhat less Indifference Principle. We will also discuss the psychological errors people make when estimating frequencies from noisy data, how to exploit these tendencies in opponents, recursive games and waiting for better spots, and many other topics!